Legalines

Editorial Advisors:
Gloria A. Aluise
  Attorney at Law
David H. Barber
  Attorney at Law
Robert A. Wyler
  Attorney at Law

Authors:
Gloria A. Aluise
  Attorney at Law
David H. Barber
  Attorney at Law
Daniel O. Bernstine
  Professor of Law
D. Steven Brewster
  C.P.A.
Roy L. Brooks
  Professor of Law
Frank L. Bruno
  Attorney at Law
Scott M. Burbank
  C.P.A.
Jonathan C. Carlson
  Professor of Law
Charles N. Carnes
  Professor of Law
Paul S. Dempsey
  Professor of Law
Jerome A. Hoffman
  Professor of Law
Mark R. Lee
  Professor of Law
Jonathan Neville
  Attorney at Law
Laurence C. Nolan
  Professor of Law
Arpiar Saunders
  Professor of Law
Robert A. Wyler
  Attorney at Law

W9-CGL-214

PROPERTY

Adaptable to Fourth Edition of Dukeminier Casebook

By Gloria A. Aluise
Attorney at Law

HARCOURT BRACE LEGAL AND PROFESSIONAL PUBLICATIONS, INC.
EDITORIAL OFFICES: 111 W. Jackson Blvd., 7th Floor, Chicago, IL 60604

Legalines

REGIONAL OFFICES: Chicago, Dallas, Los Angeles, New York, Washington, D.C
Distributed by: **Harcourt Brace & Company** 6277 Sea Harbor Drive, Orlando, FL 32887 (800)787-8717

SERIES EDITOR
Roger W. Meslar, B.A., J.D.
Attorney at Law

PRODUCTION COORDINATOR
Sanetta Hister

THIRD PRINTING—2001

Legalines™

Features Detailed Briefs of Every Major Case, Plus Summaries of the Black Letter Law.

Titles Available

Administrative Law .... Keyed to Breyer	Decedents' Estates & Trusts .. Keyed to Ritchie
Administrative Law .... Keyed to Gellhorn	Domestic Relations .... Keyed to Clark
Administrative Law .... Keyed to Schwartz	Domestic Relations .... Keyed to Wadlington
Antitrust .... Keyed to Areeda	Estate & Gift Tax .... Keyed to Surrey
Antitrust .... Keyed to Handler	Evidence .... Keyed to Sutton
Civil Procedure .... Keyed to Cound	Evidence .... Keyed to Waltz
Civil Procedure .... Keyed to Field	Evidence .... Keyed to Weinstein
Civil Procedure .... Keyed to Hazard	Family Law .... Keyed to Areen
Civil Procedure .... Keyed to Rosenberg	Federal Courts .... Keyed to McCormick
Civil Procedure .... Keyed to Yeazell	Income Tax .... Keyed to Freeland
Commercial Law .... Keyed to Farnsworth	Income Tax .... Keyed to Klein
Conflict of Laws .... Keyed to Cramton	Labor Law .... Keyed to Cox
Conflict of Laws .... Keyed to Reese	Labor Law .... Keyed to Merrifield
Constitutional Law .... Keyed to Brest	Partnership & Corporate Tax .. Keyed to Surrey
Constitutional Law .... Keyed to Cohen	Property .... Keyed to Browder
Constitutional Law .... Keyed to Gunther	Property .... Keyed to Casner
Constitutional Law .... Keyed to Lockhart	Property .... Keyed to Cribbet
Constitutional Law .... Keyed to Rotunda	Property .... Keyed to Dukeminier
Constitutional Law .... Keyed to Stone	Real Property .... Keyed to Rabin
Contracts .... Keyed to Calamari	Remedies .... Keyed to Re
Contracts .... Keyed to Dawson	Remedies .... Keyed to York
Contracts .... Keyed to Farnsworth	Sales & Secured Transactions .. Keyed to Speidel
Contracts .... Keyed to Fuller	Securities Regulation .... Keyed to Jennings
Contracts .... Keyed to Kessler	Torts .... Keyed to Epstein
Contracts .... Keyed to Murphy	Torts .... Keyed to Franklin
Corporations .... Keyed to Cary	Torts .... Keyed to Henderson
Corporations .... Keyed to Choper	Torts .... Keyed to Keeton
Corporations .... Keyed to Hamilton	Torts .... Keyed to Prosser
Corporations .... Keyed to Vagts	Wills, Trusts & Estates .... Keyed to Dukeminier
Criminal Law .... Keyed to Boyce	
Criminal Law .... Keyed to Dix	
Criminal Law .... Keyed to Johnson	**Other Titles Available:**
Criminal Law .... Keyed to Kadish	Criminal Law Questions & Answers
Criminal Law .... Keyed to LaFave	Excelling on Exams/How to Study
Criminal Procedure .... Keyed to Kamisar	Torts Questions & Answers

All Titles Available at Your Law School Bookstore, or Call to Order: 1-800-787-8717

Harcourt Brace Legal and Professional Publications, Inc.
111 West Jackson Boulevard, Seventh Floor
Chicago, IL 60604

1 Get you through **LAW SCHOOL**

2 Get you through the **BAR EXAM**

O.K. we'll throw in a highlighter*

*Available at your local BAR/BRI office.

 gilbert LAW SUMMARIES

Over 4 Million Copies Sold!

- Gilbert Law Summaries
- Legalines
- Law School Legends Audio Tapes
- Employment Guides
- Casebriefs Interactive Software

 barbri BAR REVIEW

Relied On By Over 600,000 Students!

- Lectures, Outlines & Mini Review
- Innovative Computer Software
- Multistate, Essay & Performance Workshops
- Complete MPRE Preparation
- First Year Review Program

 THE barbri GROUP

Our <u>Only</u> Mission Is Test Preparation

BAR/BRI Bar Review 1-888-3BARBRI
GILBERT LAW SUMMARIES 1-800-787-8717

SHORT SUMMARY OF CONTENTS

                                                                      Page

I.   ACQUISITION OF PROPERTY   1

     A.   Introduction   1
     B.   First in Time   2
     C.   Finding   9
     D.   Adverse Possession 12
     E.   Gifts 18

II. ESTATE SYSTEM 22

     A.   Possessory Estates 22
     B.   Future Interests 31
     C.   Co-Ownership 40

III. LANDLORDS AND TENANTS 56

     A.   Leasehold Estates 56
     B.   Landlord's Duties 68
     C.   Tenant's Duties and Obligations 73
     D.   Government Intervention 75

IV. VOLUNTARY TRANSFERS OF PROPERTY 79

     A.   Sales and Gifts 79
     B.   Deeds 88
     C.   Real Estate Finance 96
     D.   The Recording System 99
     E.   Chain of Title Problems 103

V.   NUISANCE 115

     A.   Introduction 115
     B.   Remedies 117

VI. EASEMENTS, SERVITUDES, AND THE LIKE 120

     A.   Easements 120
     B.   Real Covenants 131
     C.   Servitudes in Gross 134
     D.   Termination of Servitudes 139
     E.   Homeowners' Associations 141

VII. ZONING 143

     A.   Introduction 143
     B.   Administration of Zoning Ordinances 144
     C.   Nontraditional Zoning Objectives 151

VIII.   **EMINENT DOMAIN** 160

    A.   **Introduction** 160
    B.   **Public Use** 160
    C.   **Types of Taking** 161

TABLE OF CASES 173

TABLE OF CONTENTS AND SHORT REVIEW OUTLINE

			Page
I.	**ACQUISITION OF PROPERTY**		**1**
	A. INTRODUCTION		**1**
		1. Acquisition	1
		2. Possession	1
		a. Legal fact vs. legal conclusion	1
		b. Ownership is not necessarily possession	1
		c. The legal fiction of constructive possession	1
	B. FIRST IN TIME		**2**
		1. Conquest	2
		a. Native American Indian rights to property	2
		2. Capture	3
		a. Hunting wild animals	3
		b. No appropriation by chance finder of dead whale	3
		c. Luring wild animals to one's property	4
		3. Creation	5
		a. Creation and ownership	5
		b. No protection against imitation	5
		c. Physical personal property	6
		d. Private property	8
	C. FINDING		**9**
		1. Introduction	9
		a. Prior possessors	9
		b. Finder's interest	9
		c. The two elements of possession	9
		2. Finder vs. "Unconscious" Possessor	9
		a. Servants and employees	10
		b. Trespassers	10
		c. Buried property	10
		d. Absentee owner	10
		e. Public part/private part distinction	11
		1) Lost vs. mislaid	11
		2) Application	11
		3. Abandoned Property	12

4. Statutes 12

D. ADVERSE POSSESSION **12**

1. Introduction 12
2. Elements of Adverse Possession 12
3. Actual Entry and Possession 13
4. Open and Notorious Possession 13

    a. Statutory requirements 13
    b. Claim of title 13
    c. Mistaken claim of ownership 14

5. Adverse 15

    a. Majority view 15
    b. Minority view 15
    c. Color of title 15
    d. Boundary disputes 15

6. Continuous Possession 15

    a. Tacking 15
    b. Parol transfers 15

7. Chattels and Adverse Possession 16

    a. Special rule 16
    b. Application 17
    c. Possible exemption 18

E. GIFTS **18**

1. Introduction 18

    a. Gifts inter vivos 18
    b. Gifts causa mortis 19
    c. Revocable gifts 19
    d. No symbolic delivery 19
    e. Retention of chattel by donor 20

II. ESTATE SYSTEM **22**

A. POSSESSORY ESTATES **22**

1. Historical Background 22

    a. The feudal system 22
    b. Statute Quia Emportes 22
    c. Death of feudalism 22
    d. Estates in land 22

        1) History 22
        2) The three freehold tenancies 22

		a)	Fee simple	22
		b)	Fee tail	22
		c)	Life estate	23

| | | 3) | Seisin | 23 |

| | e. | How estates are created | 23 |
| | f. | Present and future estates | 23 |

		1)	Present estates	23
		2)	Future estates	23
		3)	Examples	23

| | g. | Miscellaneous matters | 23 |

| 2. | Fee Simple | 23 |

| | a. | Example | 24 |
| | b. | Defeasible estates | 24 |

| 3. | Fee Tail Estate | 24 |

	a.	Introduction	24
	b.	Disentailing	24
	c.	Modern results of conveying a fee tail	24

| 4. | Life Estates | 24 |

| | a. | Introduction | 24 |

| | | 1) | Life of grantee as measuring life | 25 |
| | | 2) | Pur autre vie | 25 |

	b.	Defeasible life estates	25
	c.	Transferability	25
	d.	Preference for largest estate in constructing wills	25
	e.	Limitations on life tenants	26
	f.	Equitable intervention	26

| | | 1) | Application | 26 |

| | g. | Statutes | 27 |

| 5. | Defeasible Estates | 27 |

	a.	Fee simple determinable	27
	b.	Fee simple subject to a condition subsequent	27
	c.	Difference between fee simple subject to a condition subsequent and fee simple determinable	28
	d.	Fee simple subject to an executory limitation	28
	e.	Distinctions between a fee simple subject to a condition subsequent and a fee simple determinable	28
	f.	Restraints on alienation	29

  g. Determinable fee and right of partial entry 30

B. **FUTURE INTERESTS** **31**

 1. Introduction 31

  a. Definition 31
  b. Limited forms of future interest 31
  c. Future interest is fixed when created 32
  d. Alienability of future interest 32
  e. Statutory termination of future interest 32

 2. Future Interests in Grantors 32

  a. Reversion 32
  b. Possibility of reverter 32
  c. Right of entry 32

 3. Future Interests in Grantee 32

  a. Remainders 32

   1) Vested remainders 33
   2) Contingent remainders 33
   3) Three subcategories of vested contingent remainders 33

    a) Indefeasibly vested 33
    b) Vested remainder subject to open 33

     (1) Closing the class 33

    c) Vested remainder subject to complete defeasance 33

   4) Examples of contingent remainders 33
   5) Separating conditions subsequent from conditions
    precedent 34
   6) Alienability 34

  b. Executory interests 34

   1) Shifting executory interest 34
   2) Springing executory interest 34

 4. Trusts 34

  a. Resulting trusts 34
  b. Constructive trusts 34
  c. Requirements for an express trust 35
  d. Judicial modification of trusts 35
  e. Spendthrift trusts 35

 5. Destruction of Contingent Remainders 36

  a. Rule in Shelley's Case 36

| | | b. | Doctrine of merger | 36 |
| | | c. | Doctrine of worthier title | 36 |

| | 6. | The Rule Against Perpetuities | | 36 |

		a.	Introduction	36
		b.	Purpose of the Rule	37
		c.	Corporations	37
		d.	Gestation	37
		e.	Invalid devise passes under residuary clause	37
		f.	Repurchase option void	38
		g.	Vesting	38

			1) Special rule	39
			2) Fertile octogenarian	39
			3) Unborn widows	39

| | | h. | Blue penciling | 39 |
| | | i. | Reforming the Rule Against Perpetuities | 40 |

			1) The wait and see doctrine	40
			2) Cy pres	40
			3) Reformation	40

| **C.** | **CO-OWNERSHIP** | | | **40** |

| | 1. | Common Law Concurrent Tenancies | | 40 |

| | | a. | Tenancies in common | 40 |

| | | | 1) Presumption | 41 |
| | | | 2) Partitioning | 41 |

| | | b. | Joint tenancies | 41 |

| | | | 1) Special requirements in creating a joint tenancy | 41 |

			a) Unity of title	41
			b) Unity of time	41
			c) Unity of interest	41
			d) Unity of possession	41

			2) Split conveyance	42
			3) Grantor's intent	42
			4) Bank accounts	42

| | 2. | Severance | | 42 |

| | | a. | Elimination of common law fictions | 42 |
| | | b. | Effect of a mortgage on a joint tenancy | 43 |

	3.	Partition		44
	4.	Rights and Duties of Co-ownership		44
	5.	Leasing the Property		45

		a.	Application	45
		b.	Expenses	46
		c.	Ouster by exclusive possession	46
	6.	Marital Interests—The Common Law System		46
		a.	Marital estates	46
			1) Dower	47
			2) Jure uxoris	47
			3) Curtesy	47
			4) Rationale for common law marital estates	47
			5) Remarriage	47
			6) Curtesy and dower abolished	47
		b.	Tenancy by the entirety	47
			1) Common law	47
			2) Modern law	47
			3) Application	48
			4) Civil forfeiture by innocent spouse	49
		c.	Dissolution	50
			1) Common law approach	50
			2) Modern approach	50
			3) Determining what property is subject to division	51
			4) Celebrity status or property	52
			5) Professional goodwill	53
	7.	Community Property		53
		a.	Distinguishing separate property from community property	53
		b.	Effect of commingling separate and community property	53
		c.	Rights at divorce	53
		d.	Characterizing property when the couple moves	53
	8.	Unmarried Cohabitation		53
		a.	Express contracts between unmarried cohabitants	53
	9.	Same Sex Couples		54
III.	LANDLORDS AND TENANTS			56
A.	LEASEHOLD ESTATES			56
	1.	Introduction		56
	2.	The Types of Tenancies		56
		a.	Tenancy for years	56
		b.	Periodic tenancy	56
		c.	Tenancy at will	56

		d.	Tenancy at sufferance	56
		e.	Construing lease terms	56
		f.	Holdover tenants	57
			1) Rent increases	57
			2) Landlord's election	57
	3.		The Lease	58
		a.	Conveyance	58
		b.	Contract	58
	4.		Selection of Tenants—Discrimination	59
		a.	Familial status	59
		b.	No reasonable accommodation for house pet	60
	5.		Landlord's Duty to Deliver Possession	61
		a.	Majority rule	62
		b.	Minority view ("American rule")	62
		c.	Application	62
	6.		Assignment and Subleasing	62
		a.	Assignments	62
		b.	Subleases	63
			1) The effect of a reversion	63
			2) The effect of retaining a right of entry	63
			3) Modern trend	63
		c.	Construing terms of a sublease	63
		d.	Commercial lessor's duty to act in good faith	64
		e.	Landlord's remedies for defaulting tenants	65
			1) Eviction	65
			a) By judicial process	66
			b) Self-help	66
			c) Application	66
			d) Self-help authorized by lease	67
	7.		Abandonment	67
		a.	Landlord's options	67
		b.	Application	67
B.			**LANDLORD'S DUTIES**	**68**
	1.		Habitability of the Premises	68
		a.	Quiet enjoyment and constructive eviction	69

	1)	Quiet enjoyment	69
	2)	Actual eviction	69
	3)	Constructive eviction	69
		a) Substantial interference	69
		b) Notice to the landlord	69
		c) Tenant must vacate	69
		d) Fault	69
	4)	Damages	69
	5)	Measuring substantial interference	69
	6)	Partial constructive eviction	70
b.		Illegal lease agreements	70
	1)	Generally	70
	2)	Limitations	70
c.		Implied warranty of habitability	71
	1)	Traditional approach	71
	2)	Implied warranty of habitability	71
		a) Commercial leases	71
		b) Standards applied	71
		c) Waiver	71
	3)	Tenant need not abandon premises	71
d.		Tort liability	72
	1)	Conditions existing at time of lease	72
		a) Modern rule	73
		b) Publicly used portions of the premises	73
	2)	Conditions arising after execution of the lease	73
		a) Liability for voluntary repairs	73
		b) Contractually obligated repairs	73
	3)	Common areas	73
	4)	Legal duty to repair	73

C. TENANT'S DUTIES AND OBLIGATIONS **73**

1.	Tenant's Affirmative Duties	73
a.	Duty to repair	74
b.	Duty not to commit waste	74
	1) Ameliorating waste	74
	2) Damaging waste	74
	3) Involuntary waste	74

   c. Duty to pay rent 74
   d. Modern approach 74

  D. **GOVERNMENT INTERVENTION** **75**

   1. Selection of Tenants 75

    a. Civil Rights Act of 1866 75
    b. Fair Housing Act of 1968 75

     1) Exceptions 76
     2) Remedies 76
     3) Prima facie case and burden of proof 76

   2. Rent Control 76
   3. The Chicago Ordinance 76
   4. Government Subsidized Housing 77

    a. Legislation 77
    b. Regulations 77
    c. Local approval 77
    d. Admission to public housing 77
    e. Rent increases in public housing 77
    f. Eviction 78

IV. **VOLUNTARY TRANSFERS OF PROPERTY** **79**

 A. **SALES AND GIFTS** **79**

   1. Contracts of Sale 79

    a. Statute of Frauds 79
    b. Essential terms 79
    c. Specific performance 79
    d. Oral revocation 79
    e. Time of performance 79
    f. Who prepares the contract? 79
    g. Specific performance 80

   2. Marketable Title 81

    a. Good record title 81
    b. Defects in title 81
    c. Curing title defects 81
    d. Violations of building codes and zoning restrictions 82
    e. Violation of public and private restrictions 82
    f. Adverse possession and its impact on the marketability
     of title 83

   3. Risk of Loss 84

    a. Equitable conversion 84
    b. Alternative approaches 84

	4.	Duty to Disclose Defects	84
	5.	Material Defect Known to Seller	86
	6.	Warranties from the Seller	87
		a. Implied warranty of workmanlike quality	87

B. **DEEDS** **88**

	1.	Requirements	88
		a. Consideration	88
		b. Failures in the description of the property	88
		c. Example	88
		d. Modern trend	88
	2.	Warranties of Title	89
		a. Introduction	89
		b. Types of deeds warranting title	89
		1) Warranty deed	89
		2) Special warranty deed	89
		3) Quitclaim deed	89
		c. The usual covenants	89
		1) Present covenants	89
		a) Covenant of seisin	89
		b) Covenant of right to convey	89
		c) Covenant against encumbrances	89
		2) Future covenants	89
		a) Covenant of quiet enjoyment	89
		b) Covenant of warranty	89
		c) Covenant of further assurances	90
		3) Merger	90
	3.	Breach of Covenants	90
		a. Present versus future covenants	90
		b. Latent land use violation	91
		c. Remote grantees	92
	4.	Delivery	93
		a. Delivery defined	93
		1) Evidence of intent	93
		2) Delivery cannot be cancelled	93
		3) Estoppel	93

     b.   Types of delivery 93

         1)   Grantor-grantee delivery 93
         2)   Delivery subject to a condition 94

     c.   Unsuccessful conditional delivery 94
     d.   No intent to part with the power to retake 95
     e.   Delivery to third parties (escrow) 95

         1)   Escrow 95
         2)   Reservation of the power to revoke 96

     f.   Estoppel of grantor 96
     g.   Estoppel by deed 96

C.   **REAL ESTATE FINANCE** **96**

   1.   Introduction 96
   2.   Mortgages and Foreclosure 96
   3.   Mortgagee's Duty Upon Foreclosure 97
   4.   Deeds of Trust 98
   5.   Installment Contracts 98
   6.   Defaulting Vendee 98

D.   **THE RECORDING SYSTEM** **99**

   1.   Introduction 99
   2.   Method of Recording 99

     a.   Grantor-grantee index 99
     b.   Tract index 99

   3.   Effect of Failure to Describe the Property with Specificity 99
   4.   Misspelled Name 101
   5.   Types of Recording Acts 101

     a.   Race statutes 101
     b.   Notice statutes 101
     c.   Race-notice statutes 102
     d.   Example 102
     e.   Application 102

   6.   Effect of Recording 103

     a.   Effect of not recording 103
     b.   What is a BFP? 103

E.   **CHAIN OF TITLE PROBLEMS** **103**

   1.   Introduction 103

     a.   Prior unrecorded deeds in chain 103
     b.   Deeds recorded before grantor obtains title 104
     c.   Subdivision restrictions 104

| | 1) | Application | 104 |

	d.	Recorded instrument that refers to unrecorded instrument	105
	e.	Recorded instrument that is defective	105
	f.	Knowledge	105

| 2. | Protected Persons | | 106 |

	a.	Equitable conversion theory waived	106
	b.	Lis pendens recorded but not indexed	107
	c.	Purchase not completed	107

| 3. | "Inquiry Notice" | | 108 |

	a.	Duty to inquire	108
	b.	Inquiry from the subdivision	109
	c.	Inquiry from possession	109
	d.	Possession of condominium	109

| 4. | Improving the Recording System | | 110 |

| | a. | Marketable title acts | 110 |
| | b. | Independent chain of title | 110 |

| 5. | Title Registration | | 112 |

| | a. | Introduction | 112 |
| | b. | Exception | 112 |

| 6. | Title Insurance | | 112 |

	a.	Introduction	112
	b.	Title policy or title search	112
	c.	Hazardous substances	114

V. NUISANCE 115

A. INTRODUCTION 115

| 1. | Private Nuisances | | 115 |

	a.	Weighing the harm	115
	b.	Nuisances at law	115
	c.	Nuisances in fact	115

2.	Public Nuisance	115
3.	Unintentional Act	115
4.	Compared to Trespass	115
5.	Negligence Is Not Element If Act Is Intentional	116

B. REMEDIES 117

| 1. | Weighing the Value of the Offending Conduct | 117 |
| 2. | Rule of Necessity | 117 |

3. Economic Considerations 118
4. Preexisting Lawful Industries 119

VI. **EASEMENTS, SERVITUDES, AND THE LIKE** **120**

A. **EASEMENTS** **120**

1. Introduction 120

   a. Easements, profits, and licenses 120

2. Various Types of Easements 120

   a. Affirmative easement 120
   b. Negative easement 120

3. Easements Appurtenant 120
4. Easements in Gross 120
5. Creation of Easements 120

   a. Reservation of an easement 121
   b. Reservations in favor of third parties 121
   c. Licenses 122

      1) Licensee's reliance 122

6. Creation by Implication 123

   a. The two types of implied easements 123

      1) Easements by necessity 123
      2) Intended easement based on quasi-easement 123

   b. Prescription 123
   c. Equity 123
   d. Easement of necessity 124

7. Easements by Prescription 125

   a. Introduction 125
   b. Public trust doctrine 126

8. Assignability of an Easement in Gross 127
9. Scope of Easements 127

   a. Introduction 127

      1) Express easements 128
      2) Easements by necessity 128
      3) Other implied easements 128
      4) Prescriptive easements 128

   b. Attempt to expand scope of use of easement to nondominant
      tenement 128

      c.   Negative easements 129

   10. Termination of Easements 129

      a.   Introduction 129
      b.   From commercial to recreational use 129

B.   REAL COVENANTS **131**

   1. Introduction 131

      a.   Benefits and burdens 131
      b.   Writing required 131
      c.   Enforceability 131
      d.   Determining whether burdens run with the land 131
      e.   Privity 132
      f.   Determining whether benefit runs with the land 132

   2. Equitable Servitudes 132

      a.   Writing 132
      b.   Reciprocal negative or restrictive equitable servitudes 132
      c.   Equitable servitudes may be enforced by third parties 132
      d.   The running of benefits to prior buyers 132

   3. Enforceability By and Against Subsequent Assignees 132
   4. Inquiry Notice 133
   5. Affirmative Covenant 133

C.   SERVITUDES IN GROSS **134**

   1. Introduction 134

      a.   English rule 134
      b.   American rule 134

   2. Restatement View 134
   3. Personal Covenants Do Not Run with the Land 135
   4. Restrictive Covenant in Violation of FHA 136
   5. Judicial Enforcement of Discriminatory Private Agreement 138

D.   TERMINATION OF SERVITUDES **139**

   1. Introduction 139
   2. Merger 139
   3. Test for Determining If the Covenant Fulfills Its
      Original Purpose 139
   4. Change of Conditions 140
   5. Attempted Abandonment of Fee Simple 141

E.   HOMEOWNERS' ASSOCIATIONS **141**

   1. Introduction 141

			a.	Condominiums	141
			b.	Cooperatives	142
		2.		No Cats Allowed	142

| **VII.** | **ZONING** | | | | **143** |

| | **A.** | **INTRODUCTION** | | | **143** |

		1.	Zoning Power	143
		2.	Goals of Zoning	143
		3.	How Zoning Works	143
		4.	Constitutional Considerations	143

| | | | a. | Taking | 143 |
| | | | b. | Leading case | 143 |

| | **B.** | **ADMINISTRATION OF ZONING ORDINANCES** | | | **144** |

		1.	Introduction	144
		2.	Comprehensive Plans	144
		3.	Nonconforming Use	145
		4.	Variances	145

			a.	Special exceptions	146
			b.	Justification for refusing variance request	146
			c.	Excessive discretion granted to local zoning board	147

| | | 5. | Amending Zoning Ordinances | 148 |

			a.	Spot zoning	148
			b.	Application	148
			c.	Modification by voter initiative	149

| | | 6. | Contract and Conditional Rezoning | 150 |

| | | | a. | Introduction | 150 |
| | | | b. | Condition that owner create restrictive covenant | 150 |

| | | 7. | Discretionary Zoning (Non-Euclidean Zoning) | 151 |

			a.	Cluster zoning	151
			b.	Floating zoning	151
			c.	Planned unit development	151

| | **C.** | **NONTRADITIONAL ZONING OBJECTIVES** | | | **151** |

| | | 1. | Aesthetic Legislation | 151 |

			a.	Architectural style	152
			b.	Aesthetic compatibility and harmony	152
			c.	Limitation on residential signage	153

| | | 2. | Household Composition | 155 |

		a.	Introduction	. . . .	155
		b.	Exclusion of nonfamilies	. . . .	155
		c.	Family composition rule	. . . .	156
	3.	Exclusionary Zoning	. . . .	157
		a.	Exclusionary goal	. . . .	157
		b.	Modern trend—the fair share test	. . . .	157
		c.	Application	. . . .	157
		d.	Mount Laurel II	. . . .	158
	4.	Regulating Growth	. . . .	159

VIII. EMINENT DOMAIN **160**

A. INTRODUCTION **160**

| 1. | Defined | . . . . | 160 |
| 2. | Government "Taking" | . . . . | 160 |

B. PUBLIC USE **160**

1.	Introduction	. . . .	160
2.	Public Use that Benefits Individual Homeowners	. . . .	160
3.	Commercial and Industrial Development	. . . .	161

C. TYPES OF TAKING **161**

1.	Physical Invasion	. . . .	161
2.	Permanent Physical Occupation a Taking	. . . .	162
3.	Taking by Regulating	. . . .	162
	a. Harm	. . . .	162
	b. Loss of economic value	. . . .	163
4.	The Harm Test	. . . .	163
5.	Total Restriction of Use of Land	. . . .	164
6.	Historical Landmarks	. . . .	165
7.	Remedies	. . . .	166
8.	Access to Public Property	. . . .	168
9.	Rough Proportionality Standard	. . . .	168
10.	Property Value Extinguished	. . . .	170

TABLE OF CASES **173**

I. ACQUISITION OF PROPERTY

A. INTRODUCTION

1. **Acquisition.** Property may be acquired in numerous ways, but the most common method is some form of voluntary transfer, such as a gift, a bequest, or a purchase. While each of these is an important subject and is examined in depth at appropriate places later on, the very concept of ownership may be illustrated by the means of acquiring property other than by voluntary transfer. In many cases, ownership is acquired by acquiring possession. The old axiom that possession is nine-tenths of the law has some legal basis. The law protects possessors. Rationales for this include preservation of law and order, rewarding those who possess and maintain property, etc. However, it is important to realize first that possession and ownership are not the same thing.

2. **Possession.** The legal concept of possession includes not only physical custody of something, for example, holding a pencil in one's hand, but also possession of things not in one's immediate physical custody. An example of this would be a lakeside lot in the mountains that is used by the owner as a weekend retreat. Indeed, people may be in possession of something and not know it, such as a cache of money hidden for years in the walls of a recently purchased old house.

   a. **Legal fact vs. legal conclusion.** "Possession" is often used in one of two contexts. It may refer to a legal fact, such as who was in possession of the automobile at the time of the accident. Or "possession" may refer to a legal conclusion of the court (or other legal body authorized to make legal conclusions), such as whether the owner of Blackacre lost title of the land due to Interloper's adverse possession of the land for seven years. In this last example, if Interloper has not acquired title to the land by adverse possession, Owner is still in possession even though he has not seen the land in 50 years.

   b. **Ownership is not necessarily possession.** For instance, once a tenant leases an apartment, absent contractual provisions to the contrary, her landlord may not come on the premises without the lessee's permission. Since the lessee has legal possession of the apartment, she could even have her landlord arrested for trespass if the landlord did not leave when asked to do so.

   c. **The legal fiction of constructive possession.** A person who is not in actual possession of property is in "constructive possession" of property if the law treats him the same as an actual possessor. This is a legal fiction that allows courts to achieve equitable results. For example, if a grantor gives a deed to a third party with instructions not to deliver the deed to the grantee until the grantor's death, depending on the facts (such as whether the third party was in the grantor's control or whether the third party was a neutral party), courts may find that the grantor was still in constructive possession of the deed.

B. FIRST IN TIME

1. **Conquest.** Property rights exist because they are recognized by the government under whose dominion the rights are asserted. The source of this dominion is frequently overlooked. Ultimately, a property owner's chain of title reaches back to the sovereign. In the United States, dominion is often based on the concept of discovery. In reality, conquest is probably a more realistic concept to explain the basis for property rights.

Johnson v. M'Intosh

a. **Native American Indian rights to property--Johnson v. M'Intosh, 21 U.S. (8 Wheat.) 543 (1823).**

   1) **Facts.** M'Intosh (D) owned land in Illinois that he acquired under a grant from the United States. Johnson (P) had purchased the same land from the Piankeshaw Indians. P brought an ejectment action. The district court granted judgment for D and P appeals.

   2) **Issue.** May the courts of the United States recognize a title to real property obtained under a grant made by an Indian tribe?

   3) **Held** (Marshall, C.J.). No. Judgment affirmed.

      a) When the American continent was discovered by the European nations, each of those nations made claims to the land discovered. The nations agreed that discovery would give title to the discovering nation. The discovering nation also acquired the exclusive rights to regulate its relationship with the Native American Indians. Thus, the Europeans claimed exclusive title, subject only to the right of occupancy in the Indians.

      b) After the revolution, the United States obtained by treaty all the rights to realty that Great Britain previously had. The United States also acquired land from Spain. In these cases, the United States followed the practice of the European nations and claimed the right by discovery.

      c) Discovery gives an exclusive right to extinguish the Indians' right of occupancy either by purchase or by conquest. Normally, title by conquest is limited by humanitarian considerations, so that the conquered people are assimilated into the society of the victorious nation. Because they are fierce savages, the Indians are not susceptible to becoming part of society. The only alternatives are to abandon the land or enforce the claims of the United States by force.

      d) Consequently, the Indians are merely occupants. Their possession may be protected in peace, but they cannot transfer absolute title to others. The courts of the United States cannot recognize title based on a grant by the Indians.

2. **Capture.** At common law, in an age when many people had to hunt to survive (either needing the animals for food or protecting themselves or their crops from the animals), a fairly involved set of rules evolved in determining who had possession of the wild animal. Basically, wild animals (animals ferae naturae) were possessed (the old term was "occupied") only when actually captured. For instance, if a trap was involved, the trap door had to be actually shut before the trapper possessed the animal. A similar approach was applied to natural resources.

a. **Hunting wild animals--Pierson v. Post,** 2 Am. Dec. 264 (N.Y. 1805).

Pierson v. Post

1) **Facts.** Post (P) and his hounds found a fox on a wild, uninhabited stretch of land. As P was hunting and chasing the fox, Pierson (D), knowing that P was pursuing the fox, killed it and carried it off. P brought a suit of trespass on the case against D for taking the fox. P won. D appeals.

2) **Issue.** Does the pursuer of a wild animal acquire a right to the animal?

3) **Held.** No. Judgment reversed.

a) A fox is an animal ferae naturae and a property right in such an animal is acquired by "occupancy" only.

b) Authorities agree that mere pursuit of a wild animal does not vest any rights to the animal, even if the animal is wounded by the pursuer (in other words, "occupancy" equals actual corporal possession).

c) The best approach is to treat pursuit alone as insufficient to constitute occupancy. However, the mortal wounding of a beast, or the trapping of a beast, does give possession to the person who so apprehends the beast.

d) To allow possession based upon the mere sight or pursuit of wild animals would produce numerous arguments and litigation.

4) **Dissent** (Livingston, J.). The death of foxes is in the public interest. This court's decision should be made with a view to the greatest encouragement of the destruction of these animals. I favor the rationale that wild animals may be acquired without having to touch them, provided the pursuer is within reach, or has a reasonable prospect of taking (such as in this case). Thus, the trial court should be affirmed.

b. **No appropriation by chance finder of dead whale--Ghen v. Rich,** 8 F. 159 (Mass. 1881).

Ghen v. Rich

1) **Facts.** Libellant in Provincetown shot and killed a fin-back whale which immediately sank and was carried away by the tide. Ellis found the whale 17 miles from where it was killed and instead of sending word to Provincetown, as was the custom or usage in the trade, he advertised for the whale sale and sold it to respondent.

Respondent sold the blubber and tried the oil. Libellant heard that the whale had been found and sent a boat to claim it. Neither Ellis nor respondent knew the whale had been killed by libellant, but if they had wished, they might have known it had been killed by a bomb-lance, each of which has an identifying mark.

2) Issue. In whom is title to a killed whale invested?

3) Held. The property in the whale was in libellant.

    a) The usage on Cape Cod for many years has been that a whale killed and anchored and left with marks of appropriation under the circumstances described above becomes the property of its captors.

    b) Other cases have held that a whale is *ferae naturae* and firm and complete possession by the taker must be established before it becomes property.

    c) The custom in the Arctic that "the iron holds the whale" was held to be valid. It has also been held that "usage for the first iron, whether attached to the boat or not, to hold the whale was fully established," and although local usages should not set aside general maritime law, this objection does not apply to a custom which embraces an industry.

4) Comment. In admiralty law, a libel is the counterpart to a lawsuit and the libellant the counterpart to a plaintiff.

Keeble v. Hickeringill

c. Luring wild animals to one's property--Keeble v. Hickeringill, 103 Eng. Rep. 1127 (Q.B. 1707).

1) Facts. Keeble (P) owned land that included a pond. P prepared and installed decoys, nets, and other equipment that he used to lure and catch wildfowl. Hickeringill (D) on three occasions went to P's pond and discharged guns to scare away the wildfowl. D succeeded and P sued for damages. D appeals from a verdict for P.

2) Issue. Does a landowner have a right to attract wildfowl to his property unimpeded by the direct interference of another aimed solely at keeping the wildfowl away?

3) Held. Yes. Judgment affirmed.

    a) P's conduct was lawful. As the landowner, he may use the pond for his trade of attracting, catching, and using the wildfowl. One who hinders another in his trade in a violent or malicious manner is liable for damages.

    b) This case is not one where D was setting up a competing pond, in which case P would have no action.

    c) Public policy favors protection of those who use their skill and industry to promote trade.

4) **Comment.** The court discussed a similar case in which a schoolmaster set up a new school, attracting students from an older school. The master of the older school had no action. However, if D in this case had used his guns to intimidate the students and keep them from going to school, the schoolmaster would have had a cause of action.

3. Creation.

a. **Creation and ownership.** The notion that the person who creates property also owns it may seem elementary, but the scope of such ownership is not always clear. Apart from statutes that specifically protect creators' rights, such as copyright, trademark, and patent statutes, a creator's ownership rights may be uncertain. For example, an artist's painting or a secret food formula is susceptible to being copied, diminishing the value of the original.

b. **No protection against imitation--Cheney Bros. v. Doris Silk Corp.,** 35 F.2d 279 (2d Cir. 1929), *cert. denied*, 281 U.S. 728 (1930).

Cheney Bros. v. Doris Silk Corp.

1) **Facts.** Doris Silk Corp. (P) manufactures and designs silk patterns for the fashion industry. The designs have no such originality as would support a patent and they are impossible to copyright under the Copyright Act. Cheney Brothers (D) copied one of P's popular designs at the beginning of the 1928 season and undercut P's prices. D denied that it knew the design was P's. The parties wish a decision upon the equity of the bill.

2) **Issue.** May P's designs be protected only during the first season in which they are introduced?

3) **Held** (Hand, J.). No. Order affirmed; bill may be dismissed.

a) P seeks protection for only the first season, but "the reasoning which would justify any interposition at all demands that it cover the whole extent of the injury." A person who deals with designs that develop popularity in two or five years has prima facie as good a right to protection as P.

b) A man's property is limited to the chattels which embody his invention. Others may imitate these at their pleasure.

4) **Comment.** The United States Supreme Court in *International News Service v. Associated Press*, 248 U.S. 215 (1918), protected AP from other news organizations who wished to copy news gathered by AP. The Court found that AP had a "quasi-property" interest in the news it had gathered and could prevent competitors from using it "until its commercial value as news had passed away." A branch of property interest known as "misappropriation" was created. In *Smith v. Chanel, Inc.*, 402 F.2d 562 (9th Cir. 1968), a case that involved a perfume company's right to claim in advertisements that its product was "the equivalent of the more expensive Chanel No. 5," the Court upheld the perfume company's right to copy the unpatented Chanel No. 5. In rejecting the district court's reasoning that the values in the Chanel trademark required great expenditures of money, effort and ability, the Court found Chanel was not entitled to a monopoly even though it created the product. The "copyist," the Court stated, "serves an important public interest by offering comparable goods at lower prices."

Moore v. Regents of the University of California

c. Physical personal property--Moore v. Regents of the University of California, 793 P.2d 479 (Cal. 1990), *cert. denied,* 499 U.S. 936 (1991).

1) Facts. In 1976 Moore (P) sought treatment for hairy-cell leukemia at the Medical Center of U.C.L.A., owned by the Regents (Ds). Ds confirmed the diagnosis after conducting tests and told P his condition was life-threatening and that his spleen should be removed. P was not told that his cells were unique and had scientific and commercial value. After P's splenectomy, Ds retained his spleen for research purposes, and during seven years of follow-up tests, samples of P's blood, tissue, and other fluids were taken and used for research without his consent. Ds established a cell line from P's cells, obtained a patent for it, and entered into commercial agreements that earned Ds hundreds of thousands of dollars by the mid-1980s. The potential commercial value is estimated in the billions. P sued for wrongful conversion, alleging his blood and bodily substances were his "tangible personal property." The trial court sustained Ds' demurrers for this claim and held that because it was incorporated into other causes of action, all claims were defective. The court of appeal reversed, finding that absent P's consent to Ds' disposition of the tissues, or lawful justification, such as abandonment, the complaint adequately pleads all the elements of a cause of action for conversion. Ds petitioned for certiorari.

2) Issues.

a) Has P stated a cause of action for breach of fiduciary duty or lack of informed consent?

b) Has P stated a cause of action for conversion?

3) Held. (a) Yes. (b) No.

a) By failing to disclose the extent of the research and commercial interests in P's cells before obtaining P's consent to the procedures by which P's cells were extracted, Ds invaded a legally protected patient interest.

b) The tort of conversion does not give P a cause of action under existing law and this court is not willing to extend the theory of conversion to include P's claim.

(1) Under existing law, to establish a conversion, P must establish an actual interference with his ownership or right of possession. Where P neither has title to the property, nor possession thereof, he cannot maintain an action for conversion.

(2) P did not expect to retain possession of his cells after their removal and he did not retain an ownership interest in them because: (i) no reported judicial decision supports the claim;

(ii) state law drastically limits a patient's continuing interest in excised cells; and (iii) Ds' patented materials—the cell line and derivative products—cannot be P's property.

(3) The nature of genetic materials and research in this case, if properly understood, prevents any analogy to wrongful publicity cases; courts that have addressed the issue of a person's proprietary interest in his likeness have failed to resolve the debate over the proper characterization of this proprietary interest. It is redressible as a tort. The characterization of the right at issue is a necessity as only property can be converted.

(4) The goal and result of Ds' work is the manufacture of lymphokines; they and the genetic material that produces them have the same molecular structure in every human being; they are not unique to P. The court of appeal erred in forcing the concepts of privacy and dignity into the concept of conversion of personal property. This was not necessary; fiduciary duty and informed consent theories directly protect privacy and dignity by requiring full disclosure.

(5) California law, in an effort to ensure safe handling of potentially hazardous biological waste materials, severely limits a patient's control over excised cells, restricts their use and requires their eventual destruction, thus limiting many rights ordinarily attached to property. A patient who does not approve of the ultimate use of his excised tissue may withhold consent to treatment by a physician. This right is one protected by the fiduciary duty and informed consent theories.

(6) P's contention that he owns the patented cell line and its resulting products is not consistent with the patent, which is "an authoritative determination that the cell line is the product of invention."

(7) It is inappropriate to impose liability for conversion here because: (i) a balancing of the relevant policy considerations, *i.e.*, protection of a patient's right to make autonomous medical decisions, and the protection of innocent parties, such as persons engaged in research, from disabling civil liability, counsels against such an extension of the tort; (ii) resolution of these types of problems is best left to the legislature; and (iii) the tort is not necessary to protect patients' rights.

4) Concurrence. Whether P's cells should be treated as property is properly determined in the legislature.

5) Concurrence and dissent. A consideration of the Uniform Anatomical Gift Act reveals that the pertinent inquiry is not whether a patient retains an ownership interest in a body part after it has been removed, but whether prior to removal the patient has the right to determine the use to which the part will be put after removal. Under common law principles, the right to control future use is protected by the law of conversion.

6) Dissent. P's complaint does state a cause of action for conversion. At the time of removal of P's tissue, P at least had the right to do with it whatever Ds did;

thus, P could have contracted with Ds to develop its vast commercial potential. The nondisclosure cause of action is illusory: (i) it fails to protect a patient's right to grant consent to commercial use of her tissues; (ii) it fails to reach those potential defendants who are removed from the direct physician-patient relationship; and (iii) proving a causal connection between a patient's injury and a physician's failure to inform, and further proving that had she been fully informed, in the same circumstances *no reasonably prudent person* would have given such consent, are barriers to recovery.

7) **Comment.** Although this case deals with a problem that has grown out of sophisticated medical technology, it is laden with ghosts of such early legal concepts as trespass to chattels and the law of capture.

State v. Shack **d.** **Private property--State v. Shack,** 58 N.J. 297, 277 A.2d 369 (1971).

1) **Facts.** Shack is a legal services attorney; he and another field worker for a nonprofit corporation funded by the U.S. Office of Economic Opportunity (Ds) sought to enter Tedesco's land to provide health services, legal advice, and representation to migrant farm workers working for and housed on Tedesco's property. Ds refused to depart upon Tedesco's demand and were charged with and convicted of trespassing in the municipal court and again on appeal in a trial de novo in county court. The complaints in both courts were prosecuted by private counsel retained by Tedesco. Ds appeal. The county prosecutor does not seek to sustain these convictions and disclaims any position as to whether the trespass statute reached Ds' activity.

2) **Issue.** Are Tedesco's rights in his land absolute and do they include dominion over the destiny of persons the owner permits to come upon the premises?

3) **Held.** No. Judgments reversed with orders to enter judgments of acquittal.

a) Under state law, the ownership of real property does not include the right to bar access to governmental services available to migrant workers; there was no trespass within the meaning of the penal statute.

b) Here we are concerned with a highly disadvantaged segment of our society; the law will deny the occupants the power to contract away what is deemed essential to their health, welfare, or dignity.

c) It has long been the case that necessity, private or public, may justify entry upon the lands of another.

d) Tedesco may regulate access to his property as long as his purpose is not to gain a commercial advantage for himself or if the regulation does not deprive the migrant worker of practical access to things he needs.

C. FINDING

1. **Introduction.** When an owner loses property, in the eyes of the law she is still the owner. Her title to the lost property is superior to that of everyone else including the finder. The finder of the lost property, as a general rule, has title to the lost property superior to all but the true owner. This legal rule, as do most legal rules, has some notable exceptions.

   a. **Prior possessors.** The general rule applies to the case of the subsequent possessor. Suppose an owner (O) loses a ring and a finder (F) finds it, only to lose it himself. If someone else (G) later finds it, F has a title to the ring superior to G's. G would be obliged to give it back to F. If O came along, G would then be obliged to give it to O, rather than F, since the true owner's rights are superior to anyone else's. This rule applies even if F steals the ring from O.

   b. **Finder's interest--Armory v. Delamirie,** 1 Strange 505 (K.B. 1722).   Armory v.
                                                                                      Delamirie

      1) **Facts.** Armory (P), a chimney sweeper's boy, found a jewel and took it to Delamirie's (D's) goldsmith shop. Under the pretext of weighing it, D's apprentice removed the stones. D offered P three half pence for the jewelry, which P refused. When D refused to return the stones, P sued.

      2) **Issue.** Does the finder of lost property have title to the property superior to all the world except the true owner?

      3) **Held.** Yes. Judgment for P.

         a) The finder's interest is good as against all the world except the true owner.

         b) D, the master, is responsible for his apprentice's act of removing the stones.

         c) As to the amount of damages, unless D produces the stones, the jury could presume that the removed stones were of the finest quality.

      4) **Comment.** This case states the general rule that has been applied for over 200 years.

   c. **The two elements of possession.** The finder must both acquire actual (physical) possession of the lost property and intend to have dominion over it. Someone may have unconscious possession of lost property if he has possession of the premises where the article is. [*See, e.g.,* Hannah v. Peel, *infra*]

2. **Finder vs. "Unconscious" Possessor.** Often the finder of lost personal property does not own the land upon which the property is found. In these cases, for O (the landowner) to prevail, he must have actual or constructive possession of the object. Usually, if the property is found in a private residential home of O, O prevails. In other cases different sets of rules have evolved.

a. **Servants and employees.** Often, if the servant or employee finds the object while about his master/employer's business, the master/employer prevails.

b. **Trespassers.** Trespassers always lose.

c. **Buried property.** If it is buried property, it belongs to O.

Hannah
v. Peel

d. **Absentee owner--Hannah v. Peel,** [1945] K.B. 509.

1) **Facts.** Peel (D) bought a large house in 1938 but never moved in. In 1940 it was requisitioned by the military. While requisitioned, Hannah (P), a soldier, discovered a brooch in a room being used as a sick bay. The brooch was in an obscure place, covered with cobwebs and dirt. P gave it to the police. In 1942, the true owner never having been found, the police gave it to D, who sold it for £66. D never possessed the house himself nor did he have knowledge of the existence of the brooch prior to its discovery by P. P brought a writ seeking the recovery of the brooch or its money's worth.

2) **Issue.** Does the finder have a claim to the found property superior to that of the owner of the freehold upon which the property was found (if the freehold owner was never physically in possession of the freehold)?

3) **Held.** Yes. Judgment for P.

a) The law is very unclear as to whether an owner who has never occupied the freehold has a claim to lost property superior to that of the finder.

b) In *Bridges v. Hawkesworth*, a small parcel was found on the floor of a shop in that portion of the shop frequented by the public. The issue was whether the finder or the shop owner was entitled to the parcel (which contained bank notes). The court there held that the parcel was never in the custody of the shop owner, or within the protection of his house, and that the shop owner had no duty other than to notify the police. Thus, held that court, there were no circumstances warranting an exception to the rule that the finder has a superior claim over anyone but the true owner. There was some dispute among the judges as to whether the place where the parcel was found made any difference.

c) In *South Staffordshire Water Co. v. Sharman*, a worker, under the landowner's orders, was cleaning a pool of water when he discovered two rings. The issue was whether the finder had a claim to the rings superior to that of the landowner. That court held that if a servant or agent finds something, he finds it for his master. Thus, the finder, an employee, found the rings for the benefit of his employer, the landowner.

d) In *Elwes v. Brigg Gas Co.*, land was leased to a gas company for 99 years. A prehistoric boat was discovered buried on the leasehold. The court in that case held that the lessor owned the boat and that it made no difference that he did not know it existed prior to its discovery.

e)   It is clear from these authorities that: (i) a person possesses every-thing attached to or under his land, and (ii) a person does not nec-essarily possess everything that is unattached on the surface of his land.

f)   Here, it is clear the brooch was lost and that it was not attached to the land. D never physically possessed the premises; the brooch was never his. He had no knowledge of its existence prior to P's discov-ery of it. In these circumstances P prevails.

4)   Comment. The court noted that:

a)   If Lord Russell is correct in his analysis of *Bridges*, a landowner may possess everything on the land from which he intends to exclude others.

b)   If Sir Pollock is right (the English view), a landowner may possess those things over which he has de facto control.

e.   **Public part/private part distinction.** Some courts hold that if the object is found in the private part of a business, such as behind the counter or in the storeroom, then it belongs to the owner. If it is found in the public part of the business—the lobby, waiting room, public hallway—then it belongs to the find-er.

1)   Lost vs. mislaid. A distinction evolved at common law between property which was lost and property which was mislaid. Mislaid property was defined as property which the true owner placed somewhere and then forgot. Lost property belonged to the finder; mislaid property to the owner. It was felt that this facilitated the return of the property to the true owner. This required courts to guess whether the true owner had lost or mislaid the property. The lost-mislaid distinction has fallen into disrepute in recent years.

2)   Application--McAvoy v. Medina, 11 Allen 548 (Mass. 1866).

McAvoy v. Medina

a)   **Facts.** Tort action to recover money found. D owned a barbershop. A customer (P) found a pocketbook lying on a table in the shop. P told D to keep the money found in the pocketbook until the true owner came for it, otherwise to advertise that the money had been found. Subsequently, since the true owner was never found, P demanded the money and D refused to give it to him. P sued. The judge held that P could not maintain an action. P appeals.

b)   **Issue.** Does property which was voluntarily placed in a shop by its owner, who then neglects to remove it, belong to the finder?

c)   **Held.** No. Judgment affirmed.

(1)   The finder of lost property has a valid claim to the property against all the world except the true owner, and generally the place in which the property is found makes no difference.

(2) Here, the property was voluntarily placed in the shop by its owner. By merely finding it P did not acquire the right to take it from the shop; rather, it was his duty to use reasonable care for the safekeeping of the property until the true owner claimed it.

(3) *Bridges* (discussed in *Hannah v. Peel, supra*) is distinguishable since the parcel was not voluntarily placed there. There is a distinction between property placed by its owner, who neglects to remove it, and property that is lost.

(4) Here, P acquired no original right to the property and D's acts in receiving and holding the property do not create any rights in P. Thus, D gets the property. The lower court is affirmed.

    d) **Comment.** This case follows the general rule regarding lost and mislaid property.

3. Abandoned Property. Abandoned property belongs to the finder.

4. Statutes. Some legislatures have modified the common law rules on finders. Some have abolished the lost-mislaid distinction, others the distinction between finding property in public vs. private places.

D. ADVERSE POSSESSION

1. Introduction. The theory of adverse possession is fairly simple. If a person who does not own land possesses it for the period of time specified in the applicable statute of limitations, she acquires title to the land. The prior owner loses her right to the land. Depending on the state, the time period for acquiring title by adverse possession is five to 21 years. Furthermore, the general rule of possessors applies to the adverse possessor before the statute of limitations has run. Thus, if, in a jurisdiction having a seven-year statute of limitations, a third party interferes with the would-be adverse possessor's use and enjoyment of the land, the would-be adverse possessor can go to court and enforce her right to possession. However, until the statutory period has lapsed, she has no rights as against the landowner.

2. Elements of Adverse Possession.

a. Actual entry onto and possession of the land.

b. The possession must be open and notorious.

c. The possession must be continuous for the statutory period.

d. The possession must be adverse.

3. **Actual Entry and Possession.** The possession must be exclusive and of such a nature that the community would think of the adverse possessor as the true owner.

4. **Open and Notorious Possession.** This is not very different from the preceding requirement. Constructive possession is never sufficient to satisfy the possessory requirements of adverse possession. Just what is open and notorious depends upon the land, its size, condition, and locality. For instance, farming on farmland is clearly "open and notorious."

   a. **Statutory requirements.** Some states have codified the requirements of adverse possession. These statutes typically require specific kinds of acts. The next case is a good example of a court applying an adverse possession statute.

   b. **Claim of title--Van Valkenburg v. Lutz,** 106 N.E.2d 28 (N.Y. 1952).

      1) **Facts.** Lutz (D) purchased lots 14 and 15 of a subdivision in 1912. In 1937 Van Valkenburg (P) purchased lots 31 and 32. Between P's and D's property was an unsold, irregularly shaped parcel of land composed of lots 19-22. At first D used lots 19-22 only for access to his property. Later D built a shed and a chicken coop on these lots. He also gardened on these lots, selling his produce in the neighborhood. In 1947 P purchased lots 19-22 at a tax sale. P erected thereon a fence across the access way that led to lots 14 and 15 (D's purchased property). D sued P, admitting P owned lots 19-22 but claiming a right of access across them. D won both at trial and on appeal. P then sued D to have him removed from lots 19-22. D hired a new attorney and asserted that he had acquired, by adverse possession, title to lots 19-22 previous to P buying the lots at the tax sale. The trial court found for D. The intermediate appellate court reversed, finding that D had not acquired title by adverse possession. D appeals to the court of appeals.

      2) **Issue.** Must a party occupy another's land "under a claim of title" in order to acquire title by adverse possession?

      3) **Held.** Yes. Judgment affirmed.

         a) Under the statute, to by acquire by adverse possession one must clearly and convincingly show that for at least 15 years there has been "actual" occupation of the land (enclosing the land or cultivating or improving) under a claim of title.

         b) Here, since there was no enclosure, D must show the land was cultivated or improved sufficiently to satisfy the statute.

            (1) D's garden was not shown to be substantial.

            (2) D's shed was not much of an improvement.

            (3) D's garage encroached on the parcel of land in question only a few inches. This is insubstantial occupation of the land.

(4) D's putting junk (car parts, building materials, etc.) on the land was not a substantial improvement of the property.

c) D, in a prior lawsuit, voluntarily admitted P owned the land. Thus, D's occupation of the land was not "under a claim of title."

4) Dissent (Feld, J.). There was substantial evidence to indicate that D had a substantial truck farm, cultivating most of the land in question. It is obvious D intended to acquire and use the property as his own. That should be enough to satisfy the statute.

Mannillo
v. Gorski

c. Mistaken claim of ownership--Mannillo v. Gorski, 54 N.J. 378, 255 A.2d 258 (1969)

1) Facts. In 1946, Gorski (D) entered land under a contract to purchase. The land was conveyed to D and her husband in 1952. In 1946 D's son made some improvements to D's home, including building concrete steps to replace existing wooden steps. D's steps encroach upon the Mannillos' (Ps') adjacent lot by 15 inches. Ps filed a complaint seeking an injunction against D's alleged trespass. D counterclaimed, seeking a declaratory judgment to determine D had gained title to the disputed premises by adverse possession. The trial court found for Ps. D appealed. Before argument at the appeals court, the supreme court granted D's motion for certification.

2) Issue. Does an entry and continuance of possession under the mistaken belief that the possessor has title to the land involved exhibit the hostile possession required to obtain title by adverse possession?

3) Held. Yes. Remanded for further factual determination.

a) There are two opposing views on this question. The Maine doctrine, which has been highly criticized, would reward the possessor who entered another's land with a premeditated and predesigned "hostility." The Connecticut doctrine makes no inquiry into the recesses of the adverse claimant's mind. "The very nature of the act (entry and possession) is an assertion of his own title, and denial of the title of all others." We favor the latter view.

b) Whether or not the adverse possessor is mistaken, the result is the same—the owner is ousted from possession. If he fails to attempt to recover possession within the requisite time, it is probably the result of lack of knowledge that he is being deprived of lands to which he has title.

c) Thus, any entry and possession for the required time, which is exclusive, continuous, uninterrupted, visible and notorious, even though under a mistaken claim of title, is sufficient to support a claim of title by adverse possession.

d) However, the element of "open and notorious" possession may not be met where the encroachment is of a small area or where the intrusion requires an on-site survey.

e)   "[N]o presumption of knowledge arises from a minor encroach-ment along a common boundary....[O]nly where the true owner has actual knowledge thereof may it be said that the possession is open and notorious."

4)   Comment. The case was remanded to determine whether the true owner had actual knowledge of the intrusion; and, if there was no knowledge, to determine whether Ps should be obliged to convey the land in dispute to D; and if so, what consideration should be paid.

5.   **Adverse.** To satisfy this requirement the adverse possessor must have a claim to the land adverse to the owner. Thus, if the possessor has the owner's permission, she is not there adversely. Adverse has nothing to do with personal animosity or malice.

a.   **Majority view.** What is "adverse" depends upon the actions of the possessor, not her subjective intent. The possessor's acts must look like claims of ownership.

b.   **Minority view.** In these jurisdictions the possessor must have a good faith belief that she has title to the property.

c.   **Color of title.** A minority of jurisdictions also require that the possessor claim title via a written instrument. The written instrument can be some-thing like a forged deed, a deed from a grantor who did not own the land, etc.

d.   **Boundary disputes.** In the case of boundary disputes most courts will apply the objective test to determine if one of the parties has acquired title to the disputed strip of land by adverse possession. Thus, by putting up a fence and using the land for the necessary number of years, the one party can acquire title to the land.

6.   **Continuous Possession.** This requirement is met when the possessor maintains possession for the statutorily required period of time. The key here is that the property be used in a customary manner. Thus, if a farmer farms someone else's field for enough years, he may obtain title to the land by adverse posses-sion even though he never lives on the land. The same applies to summer cabins.

a.   **Tacking.** Some, but not all, courts will allow an adverse possessor to tack the time he is in possession onto that of his predecessor in interest's period of adverse possession. In order to tack there must be privity of estate between the two adverse possessors. This usually requires more than mere transfer of physical possession. In most instances this would require a document that gives the successor not only physical possession but also the right to physical possession. Nevertheless, some courts will permit parol transfers (transfers where all that the succeeding adverse possessor gets is physical possession).

b.   **Parol transfers--Howard v. Kunto,** 477 P.2d 210 (Wash. 1970).

1)   **Facts.** The Howards (Ps) and the Kuntos (Ds) are property holders in a summer resort area where the houses are used primarily for

Howard
v. Kunto

summer occupancy. Ps owned the land that was one lot away from that of Ds. When Ps tried to convey their holdings to a third party, it was found that the title they held was to the lot adjacent to that which they had occupied. In fact, most of the property owners occupied land different from what their deed gave records to. Ps then conveyed their deed to the occupant of the adjacent lot in exchange for his deed, which was for the lot occupied by Ds. Ps next brought action to have title quieted in them to the lot occupied by Ds. The trial court held that since Ds had owned the land for less than a year, and the principle of tacking was not established, the title was quieted in Ps. Ds appeal.

2)　**Issue.** May a person who receives record title to tract #1 under the mistaken belief that he has title to tract #2, and who subsequently occupies that tract, use the period of possession of tract #2 by his immediate predecessors (who also held record title to the other tract) for the purpose of establishing title to tract #2 by adverse possession?

3)　**Held.** Yes. Judgment reversed.

　　a)　The fact that this land was used only in the summer months makes no difference in establishing adverse possession.

　　b)　This case is unique in its claim for adverse possession. Usually the claimant is claiming more than his record title allows for. However, in this case Ds are asking for an area that is different from what they own. Therefore, the lower court held that because the deed did not describe any of the land that was occupied, the actual transfer of possession did not establish privity (which was needed to tack the estates in order to create the statutorily required time period).

　　c)　This court has held that the privity requirement is no more than a judicial recognition of the need for some reasonable connection between successive occupants of real property so as to raise their claim of right above the status of the wrongdoer or the trespasser. In this case, there was sufficient connection between estates. Thus, the prior estates could be tacked onto the present defendants' time period to meet the statutorily required time period.

4)　**Comment.** This was a parol transfer since Ps took physical possession of tract #2. The deed to tract #1 was inapplicable to tract #2, and hence Ps' possession of tract #2 was based on the prior owner telling Ps, in effect, "Here are the keys to the house I built. You now own it."

7.　**Chattels and Adverse Possession.** The doctrine of adverse possession also applies to chattels.

　　a.　**Special rule.** One of the requirements of adverse possession is "open and notorious possession." The old rule applied this requirement strictly to chattels. The modern trend, exemplified in the case that follows, applies the "discovery rule" to adverse possession.

b. Application--O'Keeffe v. Snyder, 416 A.2d 862 (N.J. 1980).

1) **Facts.** O'Keeffe (P) brought a replevin action to recover three of her paintings that were allegedly stolen from an art gallery in 1946. In 1976, P sued Snyder (D), owner of an art gallery, to recover these paintings. (P did not claim that D had actual knowledge of the alleged thefts.) D had received the paintings from Ulrich Frank. Frank claimed his father had had the paintings as early as 1943. D argued that: (i) he was a purchaser for value; (ii) he had title to the pictures by adverse possession; and (iii) the replevin action was barred by a six-year statute of limitations. The trial court granted D summary judgment. The appellate division reversed on the grounds that the pictures were stolen and that the defense of the statute of limitations and title by adverse possession were identical and D had not proved the elements of adverse possession. D appeals.

2) **Issue.** Does the "discovery rule" apply to stolen artworks to toll the statute of limitations?

3) **Held.** Yes. Judgment reversed and case remanded.

a) Whether the paintings were stolen or not is a fact issue for the trial court. The granting of the summary judgment while there was a fact question was, therefore, in error. Thus, the case must be remanded.

b) A thief acquires no title and cannot transfer good title to others regardless of their good faith or ignorance of the theft. Hence, if the pictures were stolen, D has no title to them.

c) It is possible that either Ulrich Frank or his father, who is alleged to have had the paintings as early as 1943, acquired a voidable title to the paintings (*see* UCC 2-403(1)) and that a subsequent good faith purchaser, such as D alleges he is, obtained good title. This can be determined on remand.

d) The key issue remaining, then, is when the six-year statute of limitations began to run.

(1) The "discovery rule" holds that a statute of limitations does not begin to run until the injured party discovers (or by reasonable diligence could have discovered) the facts which form the basis of the cause of action. The purpose of this equitable principle is to mitigate harsh results of the statute of limitations. We hold this rule applicable to replevin actions brought to recover paintings.

(2) At trial the court should consider what reasonable steps P could have taken after the alleged theft to recover the paintings.

e) To acquire title to chattels by adverse possession, the possession must be hostile, actual, visible, exclusive, and continuous. It is difficult to apply this doctrine to such things as paintings and jewelry.

f) The discovery rule is a much fairer way of handling the problem of stolen artworks than is the doctrine of adverse possession. The "due diligence" required under the discovery rule will vary with the nature, value, and use of the personal property involved.

g) This holding does not change the doctrine of adverse possession as applied to real estate.

h) The expiration of the six-year replevin period should vest in the possessor title to the property as effectively under the discovery rule as under the doctrine of adverse possession.

i) Transfer of the property to others neither tolls nor recommences the statute of limitations. The right of replevin tacks.

j) On the limited record, any question of copyright infringement cannot be evaluated.

4) Comment. Prior to retrial, the parties settled. O'Keeffe took "Seaweed," Snyder took another painting, and to pay the expenses of the litigation, a third was sold at auction at Sotheby's.

c. **Possible exemption.** Congress enacted legislation in 1990 requiring museums to inventory and return, upon request, sacred objects and other cultural artifacts to Native Americans. In order to retain the object, a museum must prove that its possession was obtained with the voluntary consent of one who had authority of disposition over it.

E. GIFTS

1. **Introduction.** A gift is defined as a voluntary conveyance to another. No consideration is involved. As in the case of deeds, the gift must be intended (sometimes referred to as donative intent) and there must be delivery. An additional requirement is that the grantee (also called the "donee") must accept the gift. Delivery means that there must be a change of possession from the grantor ("donor") to the grantee. Manual delivery is not required if it is impractical. Instead the grantor can effect constructive delivery (*e.g.*, handing over the means of acquiring possession, such as the car keys). Some courts will permit the gift to be made by a written instrument if manual delivery is impractical (either due to the size of the object or due to the circumstances the parties are in). This form of delivery is called "symbolic" delivery. In addition to delivery, the intent to transfer must be a present intent. "I will give you my car next week," for example, does not evidence present intent. Finally, as with deeds, an escrow agent can be used in conveyance.

a. **Gifts inter vivos.** These are gifts made during the grantor's life when his or her death is not imminent. Once made, an inter vivos gift is irrevocable.

b. **Gifts causa mortis.** These are gifts made in contemplation of imminent death (this includes surgery that the grantor may not survive). This permits death bed conveyances outside of a will. If the would-be donor survives, the gift is automatically revoked.

c. **Revocable gifts.** If the grantor reserves the right to revoke the gift, the general rule is that there is *no* gift at all.

d. **No symbolic delivery--Newman v. Bost,** 29 S.E. 848 (N.C. 1898).

1) **Facts.** The intestate, a widower without issue, was stricken ill and, due to paralysis, was confined to his bed. In the presence of a witness (Enos Houston) the intestate gave to Julia Newman (P), a woman of 28 who had been the intestate's live-in housekeeper since she was 18, everything he owned. The intestate, who had previously announced his intention to marry P, gave her several keys and announced that he was giving her everything in the house, then pointed out specific pieces of furniture, including a bureau, and repeated that everything in the house was hers. A few days later he died. P sued Bost (D), the intestate's administrator, for $3,000 (the amount of an insurance policy on the intestate which was kept in a locked drawer in the bureau to which only P had the key); $300, the value of an insurance policy on a piano upon which D had collected; $200.94, the value of the household property sold by D; and $45, the amount D collected on the sale of property from P's bedroom. P claimed the $3,000 and $200.94 as gifts causa mortis and the $45 and $300 as gifts inter vivos. The trial court found for P, and D appealed.

2) **Issue.** Is constructive delivery of a gift sufficient if actual delivery is not possible?

3) **Held.** Yes. Judgment reversed.

   a) It is unclear whether the intestate meant to give to P merely the bureau the intestate pointed to, or the bureau along with the insurance policy and everything else in the bureau. If the latter had been his intent, he could have had Houston, who was present, get the policy out of the bureau and then have delivered it to P. Since actual delivery was possible, constructive delivery of the insurance policy was insufficient and thus the insurance proceeds belong to the estate and not to P.

   b) As to the furniture to which P had the keys given her (the bureau, etc.), constructive delivery of these items was sufficient since, due to their size and weight, manual delivery was impossible. Delivery of the keys was sufficient.

   c) As to the other articles of household furnishings, except the furniture in P's bedroom, title did not pass to P since they were not constructively or actually delivered to her.

   d) As to the furniture in P's bedroom, there was sufficient evidence to support the jury's finding that that furniture was given to P as a gift inter vivos.

e) As to the piano, it was bought by the intestate, placed in the parlor, and called "Miss Julia's piano." But when the piano burned, the intestate used the insurance money as his own, and although he said he would, he never did buy P another piano; thus P cannot recover the piano insurance money since there never was delivery.

Gruen v.
Gruen

e. Retention of chattel by donor--Gruen v. Gruen, 505 N.Y.S.2d 849, 496 N.E.2d 869 (1986).

1) Facts. When Gruen (P) was a college student, his father wrote him a letter telling him he was giving him a Klimt painting for his birthday. P's father stated he would retain possession for his lifetime, however. For tax reasons, P's father later sent another letter describing the gift without referring to the life estate. P's father also asked that P destroy the first letter, which P did. When P's father died 17 years later, the painting was still in the possession of Gruen (D), P's stepmother. P had never had physical possession of the painting. D refused P's request for possession of the painting and P sued. The trial court found that the elements of an inter vivos gift were not satisfied and that a donor cannot retain a possessory life estate after purportedly giving personal property to another. The appellate court reversed, and on remand the trial court awarded P $2,500,000, which was the value of the painting. D appeals.

2) Issue. May a donor make a valid inter vivos gift of a chattel if the donor retains a life estate in the chattel and never surrenders possession to the donee before the donor's death?

3) Held. Yes. Judgment affirmed.

a) To be valid, an inter vivos gift must have three elements: (i) an intent by the donor to make a present transfer; (ii) actual or constructive delivery of the gift to the donee; and (iii) acceptance by the donee. Thus an inter vivos gift differs from a testamentary disposition, which is an intent to make a transfer only upon the donor's death. The critical test is whether the donor intended the gift to transfer a present interest or intended the gift to have no effect until after the donor died. Once an inter vivos gift is made, it is irrevocable and title vests immediately in the donee.

b) In this case, the evidence clearly shows that P's father intended to give the painting to P while retaining a life estate. D claims that reservation of the life estate defeated the gift. However, there is a difference between ownership and possession, which is recognized in real property law and also applies to personal property.

c) The element of delivery may be satisfied by constructive delivery, depending on the circumstances. While physical delivery is usually the best form of delivery, it is not always practical. In this case, for example, it would have been impractical and useless for P to have gone to his father's residence to receive the painting and then redeliver it to his father. The delivery of the letters satisfies the delivery requirement in this case.

d) The acceptance element may be satisfied by the presumption that a recipient accepts a gift of value. In addition, P here showed that he had told others about the gift and he kept the second letter for over 17 years to verify the gift.

II. ESTATE SYSTEM

A. POSSESSORY ESTATES

1. **Historical Background.** The law pertaining to freehold estates has its roots in the feudal ages. An understanding of these feudal roots is necessary to make sense of modern real property law.

   a. **The feudal system.** Starting with William the Conqueror, England developed a feudal ladder. William claimed the whole of England as his own property. In return for certain services (providing yearly a given quantity of food, a certain sum of money, and/or a number of knights and soldiers), William gave vast tracts of land to his tenants-in-chief. These tenants-in-chief, in order to fulfill their obligations to the king, subdivided, so to speak, their vast landholdings to subtenants who provided a given quantity of services. The subtenants would subdivide their land and obligations in turn. In time, a feudal ladder was built with, on the bottom rung, the man in possession who actually grew the wheat, plucked the goose, etc. Since the services were fixed and the value of the land increased, landlords were anxious for their tenants to either die without heirs (in which case the land returned to the landlord) or to breach their obligations (in which case the landlord retook the land).

   b. **Statute Quia Emportes.** Some 200 years after William conquered, the lords who were high on this feudal ladder had the Statute Quia Emportes enacted. This statute prohibited further subdividing of the land and services. In return for this concession, the lords had to give the tenants the right to alienate their land without the lord's consent. The principle that the land should be freely alienable was thus established. This principle of free alienability is the keystone of English and American freehold law.

   c. **Death of feudalism.** The Statute Quia Emportes marked the beginning of the decline of feudalism. In a few centuries the land was once again owned and controlled by the king.

   d. **Estates in land.**

      1) **History.** From the feudal ages evolved a system of estates in land. The system gradually simplified until *all* estates had to be one of six types (three freehold and three leasehold). The leasehold estates (tenancies at will, periodic tenancies, and tenancies for a fixed term) are discussed *infra*.

      2) **The three freehold tenancies.**

         a) **Fee simple.** A fee simple estate has the potential to endure forever. The various types of fee simple estates are discussed hereafter. The granting language was often "to B and his heirs."

         b) **Fee tail.** A fee tail estate has the potential of lasting forever, but will cease whenever the tenant does not have a lineal descendant to succeed him. This was important in feudal times as it was a common mechanism to keep land in the family of the wealthy nobles. This type of estate is recognized in only a handful of American jurisdictions. The granting language was "to B and the heirs of his body."

    c) **Life estate.** This is an estate which will end at the death of some person. The granting language could be "to B, so long as he lives" or "to B for his life." At the death of the measuring life, the estate ends.

    3) Seisin. The concept of "seisin" was extremely important in feudal times and is often spoken of in modern real estate cases. Only the holder of a freehold estate could have seisin. One was "seised" of the land if he had a freehold estate and was in possession or a tenant was in possession from him. Using the example of a landlord/tenant situation, it is the landlord who has seisin. In ancient times, a grantor delivered seisin to a grantee. This was accomplished by actually going onto the land and the grantor's giving the grantee, in front of witnesses, a clod of dirt or twig from the freehold estate. In a time when few persons could read or write, this formal ceremony was important to protect from fraud, duress, etc. As England evolved and more and more business began to be conducted in London, this ceremony came to be abandoned.

    e. How estates are created. Estates are created by language in a deed or other instrument which describes the estate. For example, "I, John Doe, convey to John Brown and his heirs, the following real property . . ." would convey to Brown a fee simple estate.

    f. Present and future estates. This is where the system of estates begins to get complicated. All estates can be classified as one of two types, present (the word "possessory" is sometimes used) or future.

    1) Present estates. These are estates which give the grantee the immediate right of possession.

    2) Future estates. These are estates which do not give the grantee immediate possession. The grantee will (or "may" as will be seen hereafter) receive possession at a later date.

    3) Examples. Suppose G dies, leaving Blackacre "to A and his heirs," Whiteacre "to B for life, then to Z and his heirs," and Greenacre "to my nephew C, if he marries before he turns 25, else to T." A and B both have present estates. Z has a future estate which will vest in him or his successors. C and T both have future estates which may vest.

    g. Miscellaneous matters. Just as there are estates in real property, there may be estates in personal property. Finally, the only estates permitted are those which have been described. No new types of estates may be created.

2. Fee Simple. This is one of the simplest estates to understand. It is an absolute grant by the grantor to the grantee with no limitations as to its duration. The occurrence of no event can cut it short (hence, it is absolute). It has the potential of enduring forever (hence, it is simple). Typical language is "to A and his heirs." Anciently the phrase "and his heirs" was a requisite to creating a fee simple estate. The archaic practice is no longer required, but attorneys often use it when drafting instruments to be absolutely certain that there is no question that a fee simple estate is intended. Modern statutes often provide that it is rebuttably presumed that a grantor conveyed the largest estate that he could. As a practical matter, this usually means a fee simple.

a. **Example.** G conveys Blackacre "to A and his heirs." A receives a fee simple absolute from G. If A is alive, his heirs receive nothing, the words "and his heirs" being merely words which describe the type of estate conveyed to A. If A is dead, then Blackacre is parceled out as called for in A's will. If A has no will, then the state's intestate succession laws are applied to parcel out Blackacre.

b. **Defeasible estates.** A fee simple may be defeasible, as explained *infra*. The fee simple absolute is not defeasible.

3. **Fee Tail Estate.**

a. **Introduction.** If G conveys Blackacre "to A and the heirs of his body" then A has received a fee tail estate. The significance of this is that if A does not have lineal descendants, then the estate reverts back to the grantor. Since the grantor is usually dead, the land effectively passes to grantor's successor (typically his eldest son, if living, else to his eldest son's eldest son, etc.). This operates to keep land in the family. In essence then, a fee tail is a fee simple subject to the condition that the grantee always have descendants. This amounts to the grantee having only a life estate, since if he did not have issue, the estate goes back to the grantor. If the grantee has children, then it has to be passed on to them. This type of estate is recognized in only a few states.

b. **Disentailing.** In time, the fee tail fell into judicial disapproval. As a result, a lineal descendant could "cut off the tail" of the fee tail either by means of a specific lawsuit or by means of deeding a fee simple estate to a "straw man," who in turn reconveyed the estate to the lineal descendant.

c. **Modern results of conveying a fee tail.** Most states hold such a conveyance to be a fee simple absolute. A few others hold it to be a fee simple subject to the condition subsequent that the grantee have children. In these states, once the grantee has children, it becomes a fee simple absolute. In other words, the condition subsequent does not pass down from generation to generation as in the case of a true fee tail. The states that recognize fee tails also permit disentailing.

4. **Life Estates.**

a. **Introduction.** A life estate is one which lasts for the life of some person. There are two types, pur autre vie and for the life of the grantee. The corresponding future interest is called a reversion if the future interest is in the grantor, or remainder if it is in someone else.

1) **Life of grantee as measuring life.** This is the usual life estate. Typically, G will convey to A "for his life." When A dies, the life estate is terminated and, unless otherwise specified, the estate reverts to G. Of course, G could specify that the estate is to go to anyone else he chooses when A dies.

2) **Pur autre vie.** This French phrase means "for another's life." In this type of life estate, the measuring life is someone other than the grantee. Typical language is "to A for the life of X, then to his son B." Until X dies, the estate belongs to A. If A predeceases X, the estate devolves as A specified in his will, etc.

b. **Defeasible life estates.** Just as in the case of fee simple estates, life estates can be made defeasible or subject to a condition subsequent.

c. **Transferability.** The holder of a life estate, a life tenant, may lease the estate, convey it, encumber it, etc. However, the transferee gets nothing more than the life tenant has. Thus, if A has a life estate which he leases to X, once the life estate ends, X no longer has an interest. X's interest terminates simultaneously with A's.

d. **Preference for largest estate in construing wills--White v. Brown,** 559 S.W.2d 938 (Tenn. 1977).

White v.
Brown

1) **Facts.** Lide devised her home to White (P), "to live in and not to be sold." P contended that she received title to the home in fee simple. Brown (D) and the testator's other heirs at law claimed that the will conveyed only a life estate to P, leaving the remainder to pass to Ds by intestate succession. The Chancellor held for Ds and the court of appeals affirmed. P appeals.

2) **Issue.** Should the language of the will be construed to create in P a fee simple interest in the home?

3) **Held.** Yes. Judgment reversed and remanded for further proceedings.

a) When the intent of the testator is so ambiguous or obscure that it cannot be ascertained from the language of the instrument or the surrounding circumstances, rules of construction must be applied in interpreting the instrument.

b) This court will apply statutory rules of construction in effect in Tennessee. The statute provides that unless the "words and context" of the instrument clearly demonstrate an intention to convey a lesser estate or interest, the will should be construed as passing the testator's entire interest. This Tennessee statute is in contrast to the common law presumption that a life estate is intended unless the intent to pass a fee simple is clearly expressed in an instrument.

c) In the instant case, we find that the will failed to supply sufficient evidence of an intent to limit P's interest to a life estate. Accordingly, the home passed to P in fee simple.

d) We note that doubts should be resolved against limitation and in favor of the absolute estate. So interpreted, the caveat "not to be sold" expresses an attempt to impose a restraint on alienation of the fee, rather than an attempt to create a life estate. The attempted alienation, being inconsistent with the principle of free alienability of a fee estate, is void as contrary to public policy.

4) **Dissent.** The admonition that P was to have the house to live in and "not to be sold" clearly and unambiguously creates a life estate, precluding the need to resort to statutory rules of construction.

5) **Comment.** The majority resort to rules of construction is supported by the judicial preference for that construction which disposes of the whole estate, rather than one which results in partial intestacy.

e. **Limitations on life tenants.** Life tenants cannot do anything to the estate to detract from its value. They cannot commit waste; if they improve it, the party who receives it after the grantee's life estate is terminated is not liable to the life tenant for the value of the improvements. In other words, the life tenant makes improvements at his own financial risk. Furthermore, life tenants must maintain the estate in good order. Due to the limitations on life estates and their inflexibility, trusts are often a better way of providing someone with an estate for his lifetime. Finally, if the estate is damaged, the majority of jurisdictions hold that the life tenant can recover only for the damage to his life estate, not for the damage to the estate as a whole.

f. **Equitable intervention.** Equity may intervene and order sale of the life estate, if the sale is necessary for the best interest of all the parties. If the holders of the remainder are legally incapable of consenting to the sale (underage, insane, etc.), the court may consent for them. This is a flexible remedy, which equity exercises sparingly.

Baker v.
Weedon

1) **Application--Baker v. Weedon,** 262 So. 2d 641 (Miss. 1972).

a) **Facts.** Baker (P) sought an order permitting her to sell certain real property against the interests of Weedon's grandchildren (Ds). Weedon bequeathed by will certain property to his third wife, P. The will gave P a life estate with the remainder interest in P's children, if any. If P had no surviving issue, Ds were named as beneficiaries. The will expressly failed to provide for Weedon's children. P remarried after Weedon's death in 1932 and continued to live on the land bequeathed to her. In 1964, the Department of Highways sought a right-of-way through the land P was living on. Ds were, at that time, made aware of their remainder interests in the property. P and Ds made an agreement giving P part of the award from the sale to the government. P then sought a court order permitting her to sell the remainder of the land because she needed the money for living expenses. Ds opposed the sale. Although the land was of negligible agricultural value, it was of rapidly increasing commercial value. The chancellor in the lower court approved the sale, finding the property of negligible agricultural value. Ds appealed.

b) **Issue.** Can a court approve the sale of property where there are future interests in that property?

c) **Held.** Yes. The appellate court, however, reversed and remanded the case for a determination upon a motion by P to sell only enough of the land to adequately provide for P's reasonable needs.

(1) A court in equity has the power to order the sale of property, in which there are future interests, in order to preserve the estate from waste or deterioration.

(2) The court in this case followed not the test of waste or deterioration, but the test of whether a sale is necessary for the best interests of all the parties. The court determined that the best interests of all the parties would not be served by a judicial sale of *all* the property. The case was remanded for consideration of P's motion to sell only as much of the property as was sufficient for her needs.

d) **Comment.** As noted in the discussion of life estates, totally unproductive property can be put to more economically justifiable uses.

g. **Statutes.** In several states, statutes have been enacted authorizing the court to sell fee simple title to the estate if the life tenant petitions for it.

5. **Defeasible Estates.** Although any type of estate may be made defeasible, the fee simple defeasible is the most common example of a defeasible estate. There are two distinct types of fee simple defeasible estates; each one has a related future interest.

a. **Fee simple determinable.** This is a fee simple estate that will automatically end if some specified event occurs. This is a fee simple because it may last forever. It is "determinable" because at the occurrence of the specified event, it will automatically end. Typical language is "to A so long as . . .," "to A while . . . ," or "to A until . . . ." The grantor's future interest is "possibility of reverter."

1) **Example.** G conveys Blackacre "to School Board so long as Blackacre is used for an elementary school," or "to A until my son Paul returns from Rome," or "to City while Blackacre is used as a public park." In each of these cases, G has conveyed a fee simple determinable. In each case, if the specified event occurs (Blackacre is no longer used for elementary school, Paul returns from Rome, or City ceases to use the land for a park), then the estate automatically reverts to G. If G is dead, then it passes to his successors.

b. **Fee simple subject to a condition subsequent.** This is a fee simple estate (thus it may last forever) which will be cut short at the occurrence of some specified event. It does not automatically end, however. The grantor may end it, if he wishes, after the occurrence of the specified event. Typical language is "to A, but if A is ever adjudicated insane, then G has the right to reenter." The grantor's future interest is a "right to reenter."

1) **Example.** G conveys Blackacre "to A and his heirs, but if A does not live to be 18, then G has the right to reenter." If A does not live to be 18, then G may, if he chooses, retake Blackacre. If G does not retake Blackacre, then it goes to A's heirs in fee simple (or to whomever A specifies in his will). Once A reaches 18, the condition is satisfied and A has a "fee simple absolute" estate in Blackacre. G must affirmatively act to retake Blackacre in the event A does not live to be 18.

c. **Difference between fee simple subject to a condition subsequent and fee simple determinable.** The key difference is the word "automatically." Any fee simple determinable automatically ends at the occurrence of the specified event. Any fee simple subject to a condition subsequent may be ended by the grantor, if he so chooses, after the occurrence of the specified event. Of course, if the grantor is dead, then his successors are entitled to exercise the "right of entry." Note also the difference between the respective future interests. The grantor of a fee simple determinable has a "possibility of reverter" since it is possible that the land will revert back to him. In the case of a fee simple subject to a condition subsequent, the grantor has "a right to reenter" because at the occurrence of the specified event he has the right to reenter, but he does not have to do so. In case of ambiguity, the court will always declare the estate to be a fee simple subject to a condition subsequent. The reason for this is that courts disfavor the automatic divesting of estates.

d. **Fee simple subject to an executory limitation.** This is the same thing as a fee simple determinable except that it, by definition, divests in favor of a third person rather than the grantor. Typical language is "to A so long as he is sane, else to B." The respective future interests (the "springing executory interest" and the "shifting executory interest") are discussed later in this outline.

1) **Example.** G conveys Blackacre "to A unless B returns alive from the war, then to C." If B returns alive from the war then A's estate automatically terminates and C gets it.

e. **Distinctions between a fee simple subject to a condition subsequent and a fee simple determinable--Mahrenholz v. County Board of School Trustees,** 417 N.E. 2d 138 (Ill. 1981).

1) **Facts.** Action to quiet title to real property. On March 18, 1941, W.E. and Jennie Hutton deeded property to the Trustees of School District No. 1 and their successors in interest (D). The deed provided that the land "was to be used for school purposes only; otherwise to revert to Grantors herein." In July 1941, the Huttons conveyed to Earl and Madeline Jacqmain 390 acres surrounding the school property, specifically excluding the tract conveyed to D. W.E. and Jennie Hutton died, leaving Harry E. Hutton as their only legal heir. On October 9, 1959, the Jacqmains conveyed to Mahrenholz (P) the 390 acres, including a reversionary interest in the school grounds. D held classes on the property until May 30, 1973, at which time it was used for storage purposes only. On May 7, 1977, Harry Hutton conveyed to P all his interest in the school property. On September 6, 1977, Harry disclaimed his interest in the property in favor of D. Both conveyances were recorded. The trial court held for D. P appeals, contending that the deed of March 18, 1941, did not convey a fee simple subject to a condition subsequent, followed by a right of reentry for condition broken, but instead created a fee simple determinable followed by an automatic possibility of reverter.

2) **Issue.** Did the trial court correctly interpret the legal effect of the language of the deed so as to preclude P from acquiring any interest in the school property?

3) **Held.** No. The judgment is reversed and remanded.

   a) The trial court did correctly rule that P could not have acquired any interest in the property from the Jacqmains by the October 9, 1959, deed. Whether the future interest is characterized as a possibility of reverter or as a right of reentry for condition broken, Illinois statute forbids the transfer of either interest by will or inter vivos conveyance. The future interest remaining in the grantors could only be inherited by Harry Hutton.

   b) If the grantors retained a possibility of reverter, Harry became the owner of the school property by operation of law when the property ceased to be used for school purposes. If the grantors had retained a right of reentry, Harry becomes owner only after he acts to retake the property (which he did not do). Although the deed did not contain the classic language used to create a fee simple determinable ("for so long as," "while," or "until"), we find that the grantors intended to create such an estate followed by a possibility of reverter.

   c) The word "only" following the grant "for school purposes" constitutes a limitation within the granting clause. This suggests that a limited grant was intended, rather than a full grant subject to a condition.

   d) When read in conjunction with the phrase "otherwise to revert to grantors," the granting clause seems to trigger a mandatory return rather than a permissive return. There is no language, such as the words "may reenter," indicating that the grantor must act affirmatively to retake possession of the land.

4) **Comment.** The appellate court declined to decide whether the 1977 conveyance from Harry Hutton was legally sufficient to convey his interest in the property to P. It also refrained from determining the legal effect of Harry's disclaimer in favor of D, as well as the question of whether in fact D had ceased to use the property for school purposes.

f. **Restraints on alienation--Mountain Brow Lodge No. 82, Independent Order of Odd Fellows v. Toscano,** 257 Cal. App. 2d 22, 64 Cal. Rptr. 816 (1968).

Mountain Brow Lodge No. 82, Independent Order of Odd Fellows v. Toscano

   1) **Facts.** Action to quiet title to real property. James and Marie Toscano deeded a lot to Lodge (P). The deed contained a clause which provided that if (i) the land failed to be used by P or (ii) P sold or transferred the lot, then the lot reverted back to James and Marie, their successors, heirs, and assigns. James and Marie subsequently died. P sued Toscano heirs (D) to quiet title in itself. P lost and appealed. P contends the restriction was an absolute restraint on alienation and thus void. D contends the covenant created a fee simple subject to a condition subsequent.

   2) **Issue.** May a grantor restrict the use of the land?

3)   Held. Yes. The judgment, as modified, is affirmed.

a)   Conditions restraining the alienation of land are void. Clearly, forbidding P to sell the land is an invalid restraint on alienation. However, the clause limiting the property to P's use is not an invalid restraint on alienation.

b)   A grantor may restrict the *use* of land. Here, James was a member of P. It is obvious that the clause limits the land to P's use in order to ensure the land was used for P's purposes as a fraternal lodge.

c)   Thus, we conclude the clause created a fee subject to a condition subsequent with the title to the reverter in the grantors.

d)   Covenants such as this one, restricting land use and creating a defeasible estate, have long been recognized in this state.

e)   The trial court judgment is modified to conform to this holding.

4)   Dissent (Stone, J.). The entire clause is invalid as a restraint upon alienation. The clause the majority allows to stand has the same effect as the clause forbidding the sale of the land; it limits who can use the land without reverting to the grantors. This is impermissible.

5)   Comment. The dissent distinguished between restrictions that limit who can use the land and restrictions that limit to what use the land can be put.

Ink v. City of Canton

g.   Determinable fee and right of partial entry--Ink v. City of Canton, 212 N. E. 2d 574 (Ohio 1965).

1)   Facts. Suit for money on deposit. In his memory, descendants of Henry Ink gave 33 1/3 acres to City (D) for use as a park "and for no other use and purpose whatsoever." When this condition was not met, the land was to revert to the grantors. Also, the park had to be named after Henry Ink. The land was used for a park until 1961, when the state appropriated the bulk of the land for use as a roadway. The state deposited $130,000 in a fund. The sum represented the value of the taken land and the amount the remaining land declined in value. Ink (P), descendant of the grantors, sued D for the deposited money. D won and P appeals.

2)   Issue. Should the owner of the reverter be paid when, through no fault of the grantee, the land is no longer used for its conditionally granted purposes?

3)   Held. Yes. The trial court is reversed.

a)   Traditionally, in cases such as this, the grantee gets everything and the owner of the reverter gets nothing. This is unfair if the grantee has paid nothing for the land. It gives the grantee a windfall. He gets the value for the land as if he had put it to a more rewarding use than the restriction allows. On the other hand, the owner of the reverter would get a windfall if he was given the land or its value.

b) For these reasons, we hold that where the land is given to the grantee, the owner of the reverter is entitled to the following amount: The greater value of the land, less the value of the land with the restriction, which equals the amount due the owner of the reverter. The grantee gets that amount representing the value of the land with the restriction.

c) Some courts hold that where eminent domain is involved, the grantee is excused from the restrictive covenant, since the grantee has done nothing to violate the covenant. We reject this, since it still gives the grantee value for something he has not lost. We do not see any reason to distinguish eminent domain cases and the other cases.

d) D, by accepting the conveyance, undertook the fiduciary obligation to use the land as a park named after Henry Ink.

e) Thus, the money is to be divided as follows:

(1) D gets the value of the taken land insofar as this represents the value of the land as a park.

(2) P gets the excess value of the taken land.

(3) D gets the money for the decreased value of the remaining land, but only to the extent such money is, or reasonably can be, used for Ink Park purposes.

(4) D gets to keep the remaining land for as long as it uses it for Ink Park purposes.

(5) D gets the entire sum of money paid by the state for taking the structures D built in the park.

4) **Comment.** *Ink* also shows that the holder of a right of entry may exercise a partial right of entry.

B. FUTURE INTERESTS

1. **Introduction.** This is one of the most complex areas of real property law. Attention must be paid to details. The exact language used is important, as is the sequence of events.

   a. **Definition.** A future interest actually exists at the present time, but will or may become possessory only at some time in the future. For instance, if G deeds Blackacre to A, reserving a life estate for himself (G), A has a future interest in the property. At the end of G's life, A's interest in Blackacre will become possessory.

   b. **Limited forms of future interest.** There are a limited number of future interests. All future interests retained by the *transferor* fit into one of three categories: (i) reversion, (ii) possibility of reverter, and (iii) right of entry. A future interest created in a *transferee* may be:

(i) a vested remainder, (ii) a contingent remainder, or (iii) an executory interest. Remainders may be either vested or contingent.

   c. **Future interest is fixed when created.** The moment a future interest is created it is fixed. If it is subsequently transferred, that does not change its original character.

   d. **Alienability of future interest.** While it was not always the case at common law, all future interests are alienable with the exception of rights of entry. Many states apply the common law and do not allow a right of entry to be alienated. Some states do allow alienation.

   e. **Statutory termination of future interest.** The Rule Against Perpetuities, which is discussed hereafter, prevents executory interests from being handed down perpetually. However, the Rule does not apply to possibilities of reverter and rights of entry. Some states, by statute, have limited the duration of such interests, typically to 30 years.

2. **Future Interests in Grantors.** There are three possible types of future interests that a transferor may have, depending on the type of estate created: (i) a reversion, based on a life estate; (ii) a possibility of reverter, based on a fee simple determinable; and (iii) a right of entry, based on a fee simple with condition subsequent.

   a. **Reversion.** This is a future interest left in the grantor (or his heirs if the conveyance is by will) after he conveys a lesser estate than he holds. For example: Suppose G, who owns Blackacre in fee simple, conveys it "to A for life." A has a life estate and G has a reversion, since a life estate is less than a fee simple. The key word to understanding reversions is "lesser."

   b. **Possibility of reverter.** This is a future interest that arises when G conveys a determinable fee of the same quantum. It almost always follows a fee simple determinable. For example: If G conveys Blackacre "to A, so long as A remains unmarried," A has a fee simple determinable. G has a possibility of reverter, since Blackacre will automatically revest in G if A marries.

   c. **Right of entry.** This is the future interest that follows an estate subject to a condition subsequent. For example: If G conveys Blackacre "to A subject to the condition that he marry before he is 45, or G may reenter," G has a right of entry. Recall that a grantor only has the right of entry. The estate in A does not automatically terminate if A does not marry before he is 45.

3. **Future Interests in Grantee.** All future interests in grantees are one of two types.

   a. **Remainders.** This is a future interest in a grantee which can become possessory at the expiration of the prior estate. It cannot divest or cut short the prior estate. For example: G conveys Blackacre "to A for life, then to B and her heirs." B has a remainder which will become possessory at A's death. B's interest does not divest A of her life estate.

1) **Vested remainders.** All remainders are either vested or contingent. Vested remainders are both created in an ascertained person (*e.g.*, "Paul," "my children" (and G already has children), etc.) and are not subject to a condition precedent.

2) **Contingent remainders.** Contingent remainders are remainders that are either not created in an ascertained person, or are subject to a condition precedent.

3) **Three subcategories of vested contingent remainders.**

   a) **Indefeasibly vested.** This is a remainder which meets two tests. First, the holder of the remainder is certain to acquire a possessory estate. Second, once he receives the estate, he is entitled to retain it permanently. For example: G conveys Blackacre "to A for life, then to B and his heirs." B has an indefeasibly vested remainder. B is certain to acquire the estate when A dies, and once acquired, B is entitled to keep it permanently.

   b) **Vested remainder subject to open.** This is the same as an indefeasibly vested remainder with one exception. The "holder" of the remainder is a class of people which may expand; *e.g.*, G conveys Blackacre "to B for life, remainder to B's children." Suppose B has three children. The class of people entitled to the remainder is sufficiently clear ("B's children"). However, B may yet have other children, and if so, they would be entitled to their pro rata share of Blackacre.

      (1) **Closing the class.** If other people can conceivably join the class, it is open. When no other person can join the class, it is said to close. The "rule of convenience" dictates that the class close the moment the vested remainder subject to open becomes possessory. In the example above, this would be at B's death.

   c) **Vested remainder subject to complete defeasance.** If the vested remainder is subject to being divested by the occurrence of a condition subsequent or there is an inherent limitation of the remainder, it is a vested remainder subject to complete defeasance. For example: G conveys Blackacre "to A for life, then to B, but if B does not survive A, then to B's eldest surviving son." B has a remainder. However, if B does not survive A, then B will be divested of the remainder. This may not matter to B but it would to his children other than his eldest surviving son.

4) **Examples of contingent remainders.**

   a) "To A for life, then to A's children" (A has no children). Until A has a child, the remainder is contingent since there is no ascertainable person. Once A has a child it becomes a vested remainder subject to open.

   b) "To A for life, then to B's heirs" (B is alive). No one is an heir until B dies; thus there is no ascertainable person and the remainder is contingent.

   c) "To A for life, then to B if B returns from the war alive prior to A's death." This is a contingent remainder since there is a condition precedent to it vesting in B, to wit: he must return from the war alive. Conditions precedent must be stated in the conveying instrument. Further, the condition must be fulfilled prior to the interest vesting. It is perhaps easy to think of this as the "you will get it if . . ." remainder.

5) **Separating conditions subsequent from conditions precedent.** It becomes quite sticky trying to separate conditions subsequent from conditions precedent. It all depends on the language used. The intent of the grantor is irrelevant to the analysis. If the conditional language is incorporated in the description of the gift to the grantee of the remainder, it is a condition subsequent. On the other hand, if the conditional language follows words giving a vested remainder to the grantee, the remainder is vested subject to a condition precedent ("to A for life then to B's children who are then alive"). If the language is ambiguous, the law favors vesting the remainder.

6) **Alienability.** At common law, no contingent interest was alienable. Most jurisdictions allow alienation of inter vivos contingent interests. Most courts also allow alienation of them by will as long as survivorship is not a condition precedent.

b. **Executory interests.** This is a future interest in a grantee which either divests (cuts short) the prior estate or springs out of G at a later date.

1) **Shifting executory interest.** G conveys Blackacre "to A, but if B returns from the war alive, then to B." B has an executory interest that will divest A when B returns from the war alive. The estate will shift from A to B and hence is called a shifting executory interest.

2) **Springing executory interest.** G conveys Blackacre "to A, if A returns from the war alive." When A returns alive, A's future interest will spring from G (the grantor) to A. G's fee simple will then be divested. This is called a springing executory interest.

4. **Trusts.** A trust arises when a person, called a trustee, holds legal title to property (the "res") for the benefit of another person, the beneficiary. The person creating the trust is called the trustor or settlor. A common example of a trust is an attorney (settlor) setting aside a sum of money (the res) for the benefit of his children (the beneficiaries), the trust being managed by a bank (the trustee). An express trust is one expressly created by the settlor either inter vivos or by will. There are also two forms of implied trusts, resulting and constructive (technically, a constructive trust is not a trust at all, but an equitable remedy).

a. **Resulting trusts.** These trusts arise in two situations. In the first instance, a resulting trust will arise if an express trust fails. The second instance arises when someone gives an agent (using the term broadly) money to make a purchase. If the agent takes title, in his own name, to the property purchased with his master's money, he is said to hold the property in a resulting trust for the benefit of his master. The key with resulting trusts is that the person holding legal title did not furnish the consideration for the trust res.

b. **Constructive trusts.** This trust arises to prevent unjust enrichment. In such a case the person unjustly enriched is said to be trustee for the person who has been cheated; *e.g.*, A fraudulently induces G to convey Blackacre to A. Blackacre is said to be held in a constructive trust for G as beneficiary.

c. **Requirements for an express trust.** The trustor must manifest the intent that the res be held in trust by a trustee for the benefit of someone. Unlike gifts, there is no delivery requirement. Further, a settlor can make himself a trustee for someone else. In any case, the trustee has a high fiduciary duty to not use the res for his own benefit; he must also prudently invest or manage the res. A trustee may, however, charge for his services. If there is no res, or trustee, or beneficiary, there is no trust. However, a settlor can provide for a trust to arise in the event certain res does come into existence. A life insurance proceeds trust created by the settlor prior to his death is a common example.

d. **Judicial modification of trusts.** It is clear that a settlor cannot anticipate every possible future contingency when creating a trust. If there is a change of circumstances, the trustee or beneficiary can petition the court to modify the trust. Modification will not be allowed if the settlor anticipated the change in circumstances, or if compliance with the trust terms does not substantially impair the accomplishment of the trust's goal.

e. **Spendthrift trusts--Broadway National Bank v. Adams,** 133 Mass. 170 (1882).

Broadway
National Bank
v. Adams

1) **Facts.** Bill in equity by Bank (P) to reach Adams's (D's) interest in a trust. D's brother died. His will created a $75,000 trust, with the income to be paid semi-annually to D as long as D lived. The trust specifically provided that it was the testator's (D's brother's) intent that these semi-annual payments were not to be reachable by creditors. D owed money to P. P sued trying to attach the income from the trust fund in the same way future earnings could be attached.

2) **Issue.** May a creditor, contrary to the testator's intent, attach the debtor's interest in trust income?

3) **Held.** No. The bill is dismissed.

   a) At common law a person could not, to an otherwise apparently absolute transfer, attach the condition that the transferee could not alienate the transferred property. This rule does not make sense in situations involving trusts, since the beneficiary of the trust never has the right to alienate either the income or the principal.

   b) In England, the beneficiary's interest in a trust is liable for the beneficiary's debts.

   c) However, other American courts have rejected the English rule. They hold that trust income is not alienable by anticipation.

   d) Since a beneficiary for life has limited interest in trust income, we hold his interest cannot be alienated by anticipation.

   e) Creditors cannot complain that a person's receipt of income misleads them into relying on that income when they make him a loan. In this state, wills are part of the public record and potential creditors can go read the will to see if a debtor/beneficiary has the right to alienate his trust interest. For these reasons P's bill is dismissed.

    4)   **Comment.** The court here does not hold that income from a trust can never be attached; it holds that it cannot be attached in anticipation. Thus, once a debtor/beneficiary has received income, a creditor could take steps to levy on that income. This is an example of a spendthrift trust.

5.   **Destruction of Contingent Remainders.** The common law rule, still recognized in a minority of states, was that if the contingent interest did not vest at the termination of the prior freehold estate, the remainder was destroyed and never took effect; *e.g.*, G conveys Blackacre "to A for life, then to A's children who marry before 25." If when A dies none of his children have married before 25, then the remainder is destroyed and the estate returns to G, who is said to have the reversionary interest.

    a.   **Rule in Shelley's Case.** Also at common law (recognized in a few states) the Rule in Shelley's Case was applied. Under this rule if one instrument (i) creates a freehold estate in A and (ii) also creates a remainder in A's heirs, and (iii) both of the estates are either equitable or legal, then the remainder becomes a fee simple remainder in A. The doctrine of merger (discussed next) then steps in to merge the fee simple remainder and the life estate into a fee simple estate for A. This rule applied to fee tail estates as well; *e.g.*, if G conveys Blackacre "to A for life, then to her heirs," since one instrument has created a freehold estate (in this case a life estate) in A and a remainder in her heirs, under the Rule in Shelley's Case, A has a fee simple remainder. This remainder merges with the life estate and A winds up with fee simple title to Blackacre.

    b.   **Doctrine of merger.** Under this doctrine, if A has both a life estate and a remainder, unless there is some vested estate which intervenes between the life estate and the remainder (or one estate is subject to a condition precedent to which the other is not subject), then the life estate and remainder merge and A has fee simple title to Blackacre. If an intervening estate was only a contingent remainder, it would be destroyed when the two interests merged.

    c.   **Doctrine of worthier title.** Under this doctrine, if (i) an inter vivos conveyance (ii) creates a future interest in the heirs of the grantor, then the future interest is void and the grantor has a reversion. *Example*: G while alive conveys Blackacre "to A for life, remainder to my heirs." Since an inter vivos conveyance is involved which creates a future interest in G's heirs, G has a reversion. At common law this doctrine was a rule of law (and thus had to be applied in every case); most jurisdictions today recognize it as a rule of construction which can be rebutted. Note that the doctrine applies to any future interest in G's heirs. Today this rule applies to real and personal property.

6.   **The Rule Against Perpetuities.**

    a.   **Introduction.** This rule is the downfall of many unwary practitioners. Gray has stated the Rule as: No interest is good unless it must vest, if at all, not later than 21 years after some life in being at the time of the creation of the interest. The Rule applies to contingent remainders and executory interests. It does *not* apply to future interests in the grantor, nor to vested remainders.

b. **Purpose of the Rule.** The purpose of the Rule is to prevent the vesting of contingent future interests in the distant future. It is a rule of proof, not of construction. If there is any possibility, however remote, that the contingent future interest involved will vest outside of the "life in being plus 21 years," the future interest is void.

c. **Corporations.** Corporations have the potential of lasting for hundreds of years. Thus, for purposes of the Rule, a 21 year period is used.

d. **Gestation.** For purposes of the Rule, a life is in being from the time of conception, if the person is later born alive.

e. **Invalid devise passes under residuary clause--Brown v. Independent Baptist Church of Woburn,** 91 N.E.2d 922 (Mass. 1950).

1) **Facts.** Sarah Converse died on July 19, 1849. In her will she devised a parcel of land to the Independent Baptist Church of Woburn (D), for so long as it shall "continue a church" with its present religious beliefs. In the event of change in belief or dissolution, the land was devised in equal portions to 10 named legatees (Ps). The residue of the estate was to be distributed to the same 10 legatees. Sarah's husband retained a life estate in both the residue and the real estate. D ceased to "continue a church" on October 19, 1939. It is agreed that D enjoyed a determinable fee in the land, and that the attempted executory devise to Ps is void for remoteness (D's estate might not vest until long after lives in being plus 21 years). By "blue penciling" the invalid devise to Ps, D received a fee simple determinable with a possibility of reverter in the testator. A single justice ruled initially that the residuary clause was also void for remoteness. The present action is a review en banc.

2) **Issue.** May a possibility of reverter, resulting from the invalidation of a devise under the Rule Against Perpetuities, pass under the residuary clause of the same instrument?

3) **Held.** Yes. Affirmed.

   a) The possibility of reverter arose in the testator upon the failure of a devise to D. The Rule Against Perpetuities does not apply to reversionary interests, including possibilities of reverter. Like any possibility of reverter, the interest in the instant case is assignable inter vivos as well as devisable.

   b) There is no reason why a reversionary interest resulting from the invalidation of a devise should not be disposed of in the residuary clause of the same instrument. The very purpose of a residuary devise is to transfer any interest remaining in the testator and not otherwise disposed of.

f. **Repurchase option void--Central Delaware County Authority v. Greyhound Corp.,** 527 Pa. 47, 588 A.2d 485 (1991).

1) **Facts.** Greyhound Corp. (D) is a successor to Baldwin Locomotive, which conveyed to Central Delaware (P) in 1941 and 1950 two parcels of land. The deeds for both parcels conveyed a fee simple interest subject to a restrictive covenant expressed by the following language: ". . . [s]aid tract of land, while in the ownership and possession of [P] . . . , shall be kept available for and shall be used only for public purposes . . . ." In the event that either tract was no longer so used, D had a six-month right to retake upon the payment of a fixed amount. P maintained a sewage treatment plant on the land until 1980. In 1983, P brought an action to quiet title, alleging the deeds' public use restrictions are void as violative of the rule against perpetuities. The court held that the deed restrictions were options to purchase and they violated the rule; however, the court held that the restrictions were not invalid on public policy grounds, *i.e.*, were the court to find the rule applicable, they would be creating a climate where grantors would not freely give their properties for public use. P petitioned for appeal.

2) **Issue.**

(i) Are the restrictions options to purchase rather than interests subject to a condition subsequent?

(ii) Does the Rule Against Perpetuities invalidate the restrictive covenants?

3) **Held.** (i) Yes. (ii) Yes. Order reversed; title granted in P; option to repurchase void.

a) A fee simple subject to a condition subsequent arises when the provision is that upon the happening of a certain event, grantor has the right to terminate the conveyed estate. The power of termination is exempt from the Rule. An option is not a vested estate and is subject to the Rule.

b) We concur that the restriction is an option to repurchase. *4 Restatement of Property,* section 394; Comment c (1944) states that where language and circumstances of conveyance of a fee simple estate are susceptible of two constructions—under one creating a power of termination and under the other an option to repurchase—the latter is preferred.

c) The Rule Against Perpetuities is a "peremptory command of law" and not subject to negation by a countervailing consideration of public policy. The rule is to be "remorselessly applied." [Barton v. Thaw, 92 A. 312 (Pa. 1914)] Economic development and prosperity depend upon free alienability of land.

g. **Vesting.** The materials earlier in this outline on vesting vs. contingent become critical in applying the Rule. There is one exception to the previous discussion on vesting.

1) **Special rule.** Although for most purposes a grant to a class vests as soon as there is a member of the class, for purposes of the Rule, a grant to a class does not vest until the class closes and all conditions precedent are satisfied. The Rule applies if there is any possibility of vesting outside of the prescribed time period. The presumption is that so long as a person is alive, he or she may have children.

2) **"Fertile octogenarian" case--Jee v. Audely,** 1 Cox. 324, 29 Eng. Rep.   *Jee v. Audely* 1186 (1787).

   a) **Facts.** Suit to have money secured. Edward Audely bequeathed the interest on £1000 to his wife during her life. The principal was to be given to his niece Mary Hall and the issue of her body. In case of default, the money was to be given to the living daughters of his kinsmen, John and Elizabeth Jee. Edward died after his wife. At the time of his death, John Jee and his wife were 70 years old. Mary was 40 and unmarried. The daughters of John and Elizabeth (Ps) sued to have the money secured for their benefit, in the event Mary died without children. Ps claimed that John and Elizabeth were too old to have any more children and therefore the bequest did not violate the Rule Against Perpetuities. (An afterborn daughter would have raised the possibility of the interest vesting after the life in being plus 21 years allowed by the Rule.) D contended that the devise was void since technically it violated the Rule.

   b) **Issue.** Will the Rule Against Perpetuities apply even if it is physically impossible for it to be violated?

   c) **Held.** Yes. Judgment for D.

      (1) It would be dangerous to experiment and hold as a matter of law that John and Elizabeth are too old to have children. Perhaps a later case would arise where an old couple had a child.

      (2) The question is not whether the limitation is good as the events happened but whether the limitation was good in its creation.

      (3) This it was not, since the bequest was not limited to "daughters now living" or "daughters living at the time of my death." The bequest clearly transgresses the Rule and is void.

3) **Unborn widows.** Widows may yet be born. *Example*: G conveys Blackacre "to A for life, then to A's widow for life, then to their children." Even if A is now married, his wife could die and he could marry someone who was not yet born at the time of the conveyance. Thus, while the grant to A's widow is valid because it will vest immediately upon the death of A (a life in being), the grant to their children is void since their gift may not vest within 21 years after A's death. Thus, G has a reversion.

h. **Blue penciling.** When applying the Rule, the invalid interests are stricken and legal effect is given to what is left. *Example*: G conveys Blackacre "to Klamath Falls so long as used for a library, but if Blackacre ceases to be used for a library, then to A and her heirs." If the Rule did not apply, G would have conveyed to Klamath Falls a fee simple subject to a condition subsequent. (Language of both fee simple determinable and fee simple subject to a condition subsequent is present. Since there is an ambiguity and the law disfavors the automatic termination of estates, the estate would be a fee simple subject to a condition subsequent.) A would have a shifting executory interest. However, since Blackacre could clearly cease to be used for library purposes later than 21 years after a life in being at the time the future interest was created, the Rule does apply. Applying the Rule, we "blue pencil" the impermissible portion of the conveyance, leaving "to Klamath Falls so long as used for a library." This is a fee simple determinable with a possibility of reverter in G.

i. **Reforming the Rule Against Perpetuities.** As you have seen, application of the Rule can lead to undesirable results. There has been a trend in recent times to reform the Rule.

1) **The wait and see doctrine.** A majority of states apply the wait and see doctrine in different forms. For example, some jurisdictions wait to see if vesting occurs within the common law period (21 years); others wait and see the length of measuring lives of persons statutorily listed. The Uniform Statutory Rule Against Perpetuities provides a 90-year wait and see period.

2) **Cy pres.** Some courts will apply this doctrine and permit the conveying instrument to be modified to comply with the presumed intent of the grantor. Thus, if a contingent future interest would be void under the Rule ("then to A's children who reach 30"), the court will modify to comply with the apparent intent of the grantor. In the example, this will be changing the age from 30 to 21.

3) **Reformation.** Some states have enacted reformation statutes to cure violations of the Rule, *e.g.*, setting a realistic age for cessation of child-bearing.

C. CO-OWNERSHIP

1. **Common Law Concurrent Tenancies.** At common law, the three basic forms of concurrent tenancies were tenancies in common, joint tenancies, and tenancies by the entireties.

a. **Tenancies in common.** This form of concurrent ownership is the simplest of the three basic tenancies. It is created by an express conveyance or when the property is inherited. Each tenant (co-owner of an interest) has a stated share of the property. Moreover, each tenant has an undivided interest in the whole property. That is, each tenant has an equal right to possess the whole property. Thus, unless his co-tenants object, one tenant can enter and use the whole property. When one tenant dies, his interest goes to his heirs (there is no "right of survivorship"). Tenants in common can have unequal shares of the property and need not have the same estate. The significance of this will become apparent when examining joint tenancies.

1) **Presumption.** Unless otherwise stated, it is presumed that a conveyance creates a tenancy in common.

2) **Partitioning.** Tenants in common can petition the court to divide the property among them. The court will do so if it is in the interests of the tenants as a whole.

b. **Joint tenancies.** In this form of tenancy, each tenant has an undivided interest in the whole property, just as in the case of tenancies in common. The distinctive characteristic of this tenancy is the right of survivorship. When one tenant dies, the surviving joint tenants receive the decedent's interest in the property. The decedent's interest can never pass to his heirs (unless, of course, one of them happens to be a joint tenant).

1) **Special requirements in creating a joint tenancy.** At both common law and modern law, there are four requirements in creating a joint tenancy. These requirements are rooted in the old common law and are called the "four unities." If there is a failure of one of the four unities, the tenants are tenants in common, not joint tenants.

a) **Unity of title.** Every one of the joint tenants must acquire title by the same conveyance, be it a will or a deed. This requirement must be carefully scrutinized for its pitfalls. Often a husband will desire to convey property to himself and his wife as joint tenants. If he does this by "granting Blackacre to myself and my wife, as joint tenants," all he has created is a tenancy in common. The reason for this is that at common law no one could convey property to himself. Thus, the husband's conveyance to himself and his wife amounted to a conveyance to his wife of one-half of the property, with him retaining the other half. Hence, there was no unity of title. Modern statutes sometimes give this type of conveyance effect as a joint tenancy.

b) **Unity of time.** Each joint tenant's interest must vest at the same time. If G conveys Blackacre "to A for life, then to her heirs and the heirs of B as joint tenants," all that is created is a tenancy in common. The reason for this is that A's heirs are determined at the time of A's death and B's heirs at the time of B's death. There is thus a failure of the concurrent estate to vest in A's heirs and B's heirs at the same time.

c) **Unity of interest.** Each joint tenant's interest must be equal and must be the same type of estate. Thus, a conveyance of one-third of Blackacre to A for life and the other two-thirds to B in fee simple fails because (i) the interests are not equal (1/3 vs. 2/3) and (ii) because the estates are not equal (one is a fee simple, the other a life estate).

d) **Unity of possession.** When each joint tenant acquires his interest, he must have the right to possess the whole. Of course, after the tenancy is created, the tenants can agree that only one of them is to have actual possession of the property.

2) **Split conveyance.** A conveyance can be split. That is, it may create a joint tenancy in combination with some other tenancy. Thus G can convey Blackacre "one-half to A and B as joint tenants, the other half to B and C as tenants in common." This does not offend the unity of interest requirement.

3) **Grantor's intent.** At common law it was presumed that a grant to two or more persons was a joint tenancy. This presumption has been abolished. Currently the various jurisdictions require a clear intent on the part of the grantor to create a joint tenancy.

4) **Bank accounts.** It is common for holders of concurrent interests in bank accounts to be joint tenants. A special set of rules applies to joint interests in bank accounts. This topic is beyond the scope of this outline.

2. **Severance.** A joint tenant may sever the right of survivorship by severing any of the four unities. The common law viewed this strictly. Modern law generally requires that the joint tenant intend to sever one of the unities. Many states have enacted statutes providing that divorce converts a joint tenancy between spouses into a tenancy in common.

Riddle v. Harmon

a. **Elimination of common law fictions--Riddle v. Harmon,** 162 Cal. Rptr. 530 (1980).

1) **Facts.** Mr. Riddle (P) and his wife acquired a parcel of real estate as joint tenants. Mrs. Riddle decided to terminate the joint tenancy so she could dispose of her share by will. Her attorney had her execute a deed granting herself an undivided one-half interest in the real estate. The deed specifically stated that the purpose of the deed was to terminate the joint tenancy. The trial court quieted title to the real estate in P. Harmon (D), the executrix of Mrs. Riddle's will, appeals.

2) **Issue.** May a joint tenant terminate a joint tenancy by granting his or her one-half undivided interest to himself or herself?

3) **Held.** Yes. Judgment reversed.

a) A joint tenancy may be converted to a tenancy in common by destruction of one of the four unities: interest, time, title, and possession. Each joint tenant clearly has the right to destroy the joint tenancy without the consent or knowledge of the other joint tenant by conveying his or her separate estate by gift or otherwise. Even if the recipient reconveys the property to the joint tenant, the unities remain destroyed and there is no joint tenancy.

b) At common law, the only way for a person to create a joint tenancy with another person was to use a "strawman," who would receive the property, then reconvey it to the original owner plus the other joint tenants. California changed this rule by statute so that a joint tenancy conveyance may be made from a sole owner to himself and others.

    c) Prior cases have held that a joint tenancy cannot be terminated without using a strawman; *i.e.*, the joint tenant would have to convey the property to the strawman who would then reconvey to the former joint tenant. This is an outdated requirement that is easily met by using a trust or an associate of the attorney involved as the strawman. Because there is no reason other than tradition for following the feudal law requirements, the strawman procedure is no longer necessary.

    d) The elimination of the strawman requirement does not give new powers to a joint tenant, because such tenants had the power to destroy the tenancy by conveying to another person. Thus, one joint tenant may unilaterally sever the joint tenancy without using an intermediary.

4) Comment. The court noted that there are several alternative ways to create an indestructible right of survivorship. These include creating a joint life estate with a contingent remainder in fee to the survivor; a tenancy in common in fee simple with an executory interest in the survivor; and a fee simple to take effect in possession in the future.

b. Effect of a mortgage on a joint tenancy--Harms v. Sprague, 473 N. E.2d 930 (Ill. 1984).

    Harms v. Sprague

1) Facts. Harms (P) and his brother took title to some real estate as joint tenants with right of survivorship. P's brother obtained a mortgage on the joint tenancy. When his brother died, P sued Sprague (D), the executor and sole devisee, as well as the mortgagees, to quiet title and to obtain a declaratory judgment. D counterclaimed seeking recognition of D's interest as a tenant in common. The trial court found that the mortgage severed the joint tenancy and survived the death as a lien against D's one--half interest. The appellate court reversed, and D appeals.

2) Issue. If one joint tenant mortgages his interest in the joint property, is the joint tenancy severed?

3) Held. No. Judgment affirmed.

    a) Cases involving severance of a joint tenancy typically rely on the four unities of interest, title, time, and possession. The courts have held that a judgment lien on one joint tenant's interest does not sever the joint tenancy unless a deed is conveyed and the redemption period has passed.

    b) If a mortgage is merely a lien, and not a conveyance of title, the execution of a mortgage by a joint tenant would not destroy the unity of title. Early cases followed the title theory of mortgages and would have resulted in the severance of the joint tenancy in this case. However, this court has since characterized a mortgage as a lien. Consequently, a joint tenancy is not severed when one joint tenant executes a mortgage on his or her interest because the unity of title has not been severed.

     c)   Because the joint tenancy survived the execution of the mortgage, P became the sole owner of the property upon his brother's death. The mortgage does not survive. P takes the property through the conveyance which created the joint tenancy, not as his brother's successor. The mortgage was a lien on P's brother's interest, which was extinguished by his death.

Delfino v.
Vealencis

3. Partition--Delfino v. Vealencis, 181 Conn. 533, 436 A.2d 27 (1980).

    a.   **Facts.** The Delfinos (Ps) and D owned a 20.5-acre parcel of land as tenants in common. D occupies the land. Ps seek to develop the property into building lots. Ps brought an action to partition the property by sale; D moved for in-kind partition. The trial court held that petition in kind would result in material injury to the rights of the parties and ordered that the property be sold at auction and the proceeds distributed to the parties. D appeals.

    b.   **Issue.** Did the court properly order the sale, pursuant to statute, of the property owned by Ps and D as tenants in common?

    c.   **Held.** No. Judgment set aside and case remanded.

        1)   It has long been the policy of this and other courts to favor partition in kind but to allow partition by sale in emergencies or when division cannot be well made otherwise.

        2)   The burden is on the party requesting partition by sale to demonstrate that such sale would better promote the owners' interests.

        3)   The court must consider the interests of all parties and not only the economic gain of one party. The court failed to consider that D had actual and exclusive possession of a portion of the property for a substantial period of time; D made her home on the property and derives her livelihood from the operation of a business on this portion of the property.

Spiller v.
Mackereth

4. Rights and Duties of Co-ownership--Spiller v. Mackereth, 334 So. 2d 859 (Ala. 1976).

    a.   **Facts.** Spiller (D) and Mackereth (P) owned a building as tenants in common. When the lessee vacated, D entered the building, began using it as a warehouse and supplied new locks. P wrote a letter demanding that D vacate half of the building or pay half of the rental value. D refused. The court found for P. D appeals.

    b.   **Issue.** Is a co-tenant in possession liable to his co-tenants for the value of his use of the property in the absence of an agreement to pay rent or an "ouster"?

    c.   **Held.** No. Reversed.

1) Since there was no agreement to pay rent, ouster of a co-tenant must be established before D is required to pay rent to P. Ouster describes two distinct fact situations: (i) the beginning of the running of the statute of limitations for adverse possession, *i.e.*, a claim of absolute ownership and denial of the co-tenancy requirement; and (ii) the occupying co-tenant refuses a demand of the other co-tenants to be allowed into use and enjoyment of the land, regardless of a claim of absolute ownership. The second situation applies here.

2) P's letter was not a demand for equal use and enjoyment of the premises.

3) Whether a demand to vacate or pay rent is sufficient to establish an occupying co-tenant's liability has not been addressed here, but the majority view is that the occupying co-tenant is not liable for rent notwithstanding a demand to vacate or pay. The occupying co-tenant must have denied his co-tenants the right to enter. There is no evidence that D did so.

5. **Leasing the Property.** Special rules apply if one tenant leases the property to third parties without the consent of his co-tenants. At common law this effectuated a severance of the concurrent interest. The more modern view is contrary. The next case sets forth the modern trend and the principles surrounding it.

a. **Application--Swartzbaugh v. Sampson,** 54 P.2d 73 (Cal. 1936).

Swartzbaugh
v. Sampson

1) **Facts.** Swartzbaugh (P) and her husband owned as joint tenants 60 acres of land. Her husband entered into an option to lease this property to Sampson (D). P sued her husband and D to have the lease canceled. (Sampson leased the property in order to construct a boxing pavillion on it. P disapproved of this and would not sign any lease. Her husband and D then entered into the lease without P's knowledge. Subsequently the two men entered into a second lease involving the property.) P lost in the lower court and appeals.

2) **Issue.** Can one joint tenant who has not joined in the leases executed between her co-tenant and another maintain an action to cancel the leases where the lessee is in possession of all the leased property to the exclusion of the plaintiff?

3) **Held.** No. The lower court is affirmed.

a) An estate in joint tenancy can be severed by destroying one or more of the necessary unities, either by operation of law, by death, or by voluntary or certain involuntary acts of one joint tenant without the consent of the other. One of the essential unities is possession.

b) Ordinarily a joint tenant out of possession cannot recover possession of the property to the exclusion of the other. Further, one joint tenant cannot sue the co-tenant for rent as a result of occupancy of the property (*i.e.*, he cannot sue a co-tenant in possession for rent if the co-tenant lives on the property) or for profits derived from his own labor. He can compel the tenant in possession to account for rent paid by third parties.

c) During the lives of the co-tenants, the rules regulating the transfer of their interests are substantially the same whether they are tenants in common or joint tenants. Neither a joint tenant nor a tenant in common can do any act to the prejudice of his co-tenants in their estate. Thus, one tenant cannot without consent sell his co-tenant's interest.

d) Generally, one joint tenant cannot, without the consent of his co-tenant, bind or prejudicially affect the rights of the other.

e) An exception to this rule allows one joint tenant to lease all of the joint property without the consent of the co-tenant and put the lessee in possession. The theory behind this is that the one joint tenant is entitled to possession of the entire property and the lease merely gives to the lessee a right that he, the lessor, had been enjoying; thus, this is not prejudicial to the co-tenant. However, the lessor/joint tenant cannot convey that which he does not have (for example: he could not unilaterally give the lessee an option to purchase). The nonlessor co-tenant can recover from the lessor-tenant a pro rata share of the rents if the lessee refuses to allow him the use of his share of the estate.

f) Thus, we conclude that a lease such as the one here is not a nullity but is valid. Hence, P cannot cancel the leases. P's concern that D will obtain title to the land by adverse possession is without merit.

4) Comment. Under the rule in this case P could have tried to use one half of the land. If the lessee refused to let her do so, she could have recovered from her husband one-half of the rent. For purposes of this example, the effects of California law as a community property state were ignored.

b. Expenses. Each tenant must pay his share of the taxes, mortgage, etc. If one tenant is in actual possession of the property, he can make these payments and then turn around and sue his co-tenants for contribution. However, the co-tenant in possession cannot collect from the other tenants for improvements he makes to the property. Of course, rent from third parties must be divided among the co-tenants.

c. Ouster by exclusive possession. Sole possession by one tenant is not in itself adverse to the rights of a co-tenant. Even long, exclusive, and uninterrupted possession by one tenant, without any possession or claim for profits by the nonpossessory tenant, is not sufficient evidence of an actual ouster absent an explicit repudiation of the co-tenancy.

6. Marital Interests—the Common Law System.

a. Marital estates. At common law a system of marital estates evolved which had as their goal the protection of the surviving spouse. These estates were dower for the wife and jure uxoris and curtesy for the husband.

1) **Dower.** The wife had a one-third life estate in all land with which her husband was seised during the course of the marriage if that land would be inheritable by children born to the marriage. (There did not have to be children born to the marriage.) Thus, if the husband had a life estate, after his death the wife would have no dower claim (since the life estate terminated at the husband's death and hence could not be inherited by children of the marriage). Once the dower right attached (the moment the husband was seised of the land), any subsequent holder of the property (purchasers, creditors, etc.) took it subject to the wife's right to dower. Of course, the wife's dower interest was inchoate (not yet possessory) until her husband died.

2) **Jure uxoris.** For the period of the marriage, all of the wife's personal property (except clothes and ornaments) was the property of her husband. This included her earnings and the right to possess, manage, and take all the profit from her real property.

3) **Curtesy.** This is the equivalent of dower for the husband. It was subject to the same conditions and limitations as dower. The chief difference between dower and curtesy was that the husband did not have a right to curtesy unless children were born to the marriage.

4) **Rationale for common law marital estates.** At common law a surviving spouse could not inherit the decedent spouse's property. The only rights of the surviving spouse were dower or curtesy.

5) **Remarriage.** Rights to dower and curtesy did not terminate if the surviving spouse remarried.

6) **Curtesy and dower abolished.** By statute, curtesy, dower, and jure uxoris have been abolished in all but six United States jurisdictions. They have been replaced by modern statutes such as the Uniform Probate Code, which provides for an "elective share" of the decedent's estate to go to the surviving spouse.

b. **Tenancy by the entirety.** This form of tenancy can exist only between husband and wife. It is quite similar to a joint tenancy in that the four unities must be satisfied and there is the right of survivorship. However, severance by one of the tenants is impossible. In the states which still recognize this form of tenancy (many states no longer recognize it), it is rebuttably presumed that a conveyance to a husband and wife creates a tenancy by the entirety.

1) **Common law.** At common law the husband had the exclusive right to manage the property and collect all the rents and other profits. If he survived his wife, he received the whole of the concurrent estate. The husband could transfer his right of survivorship to third parties, including creditors. The wife, on the other hand, had only the right of survivorship. This right remained with the wife even if the husband conveyed away his entire interest in the property. Her creditors could not reach her right of survivorship.

2) **Modern law.** The Married Women's Property Acts, enacted in every state during the last century, changed this. It put the wife on equal footing with her husband in managing and disposing of real and personal property.

Various jurisdictions apply their Acts differently as to tenancies by the entirety.

3) **Application--Sawada v. Endo,** 561 P.2d 1291 (Haw. 1977).

a) **Facts.** Action to set aside conveyance of real property. Mr. and Mrs. Sawada (Ps) were struck by a car driven by Kokichi Endo (D). On the date of the accident, D owned as a tenant by the entirety a parcel of real property. Shortly after the accident, D and his wife conveyed, without consideration, the real property to their sons. The deed was recorded shortly before the auto accident trial. Ps won the auto accident trial and, after being unable to satisfy their money judgment from D's personal property, sought to have the above conveyance set aside so they could satisfy the money judgment. (Kokichi's wife died a few days after the auto accident trial.) Ps lost and appeal.

b) **Issue.** Is the interest of one spouse in real property, held in tenancy by the entirety, subject to levy and execution by his or her individual creditors?

c) **Held.** No. The trial court is affirmed.

(1) Nineteen states and the District of Columbia continue to recognize tenancy by the entirety as a valid and subsisting institution in the field of property law. These jurisdictions can be divided into four groups.

(2) Group I: Three states hold that the estate is essentially the common law tenancy by the entirety, unaffected by the Married Women's Property Acts. As at common law, the estate is subject to the husband's exclusive dominion and control. The husband may convey the entire estate subject only to the possibility that the wife may become entitled to the whole estate upon surviving him. In two of these states the use and income from the estate is not subject to levy during the marriage for the separate debts of either spouse. One state allows only the husband's creditors to levy against the estate.

(3) Group II: Five states allow the interest of the debtor spouse to be sold or levied upon for his or her separate debts, subject to the other spouse's contingent right of survivorship. One of these states by statute allows levying against a debtor spouse's interest unless the property is a "homestead."

(4) Group III: Eleven jurisdictions hold that an attempted conveyance by either spouse is wholly void, and the estate may not be subjected to the separate debts of one spouse only.

(5) Group IV: Two states hold the contingent right of survivorship appertaining to either spouse is separately alienable by him and attachable by his creditors during the marriage. The use and profits, however, may neither be alienated nor attached during coverture.

(6) Hawaii has long recognized that joint, common, and entirety tenancies are separate and distinct estates. In a tenancy by the entirety, both spouses are seised of the whole estate. Spouses do not take by moieties.

(7) The Married Women's Property Acts abrogated the husband's common law dominance over the marital estate and placed the wife on equal footing with her husband as regards the exercise of ownership over the whole estate. They also had the effect of insulating the wife's interest in the estate from the separate debts of her husband.

(8) Neither husband nor wife has a separate divisible interest in the property held by the entirety that can be conveyed or that can be reached by creditors. The estate is indivisible except by joint action of the spouses. Each spouse owns the entire estate.

(9) This holding is not unfair to creditors. They can require the signatures of both spouses, insist that debtors do not hold property as tenants by the entirety, etc.

(10) Were we to consider public policy we would reach the same result. By not permitting property held by tenants by the entirety to be subject to the individual spouse's creditors, the marital estate is secure for family purposes. This permits planning for children's educations, family emergencies, etc.

d) **Dissent.** I dissent on the ground that the majority misconstrues the Married Women's Act. A better interpretation is that since at common law the husband could alienate his right of survivorship, the Act enabled the wife to do likewise. Thus, the judgment creditors of either spouse may levy and execute upon their separate rights of survivorship. There is no logical reason to place a restriction upon the freedom of the spouses to deal independently with their respective interests.

4) **Civil forfeiture by innocent spouse--United States v. 1500 Lincoln Avenue,** 949 F.2d 73 (3d Cir. 1991).

United States v. 1500 Lincoln Avenue

a) **Facts.** The United States (P) sought civil forfeiture of property owned as a tenancy by the entireties and containing a pharmacy out of which Mr. Bernstein illegally distributed prescription drugs. Mrs. Bernstein averred that she had no knowledge of the criminal activity. She did not occupy the premises. P conceded that Mrs. Bernstein had a valid innocent owner defense to the extent of the interest in the property she was entitled to retain. P maintained that Mr. Bernstein's illegal use of the property resulted in severance of the entireties estate and that Mrs. Bernstein was entitled to a one-half interest. The district court dismissed P's complaint based on Mrs. Bernstein's defense and her right to an interest in all of the property as a tenant by the entireties. P moved to alter or amend the judgment, arguing that the court should enter an order granting forfeiture except to the extent of Mrs. Bernstein's interest should Mr. Bernstein survive or divorce his wife or should the tenancy be severed by other means. The district court denied P's motion, suggesting P file a lis pendens against the property. P appeals.

b) **Issue.** Is any interest in the subject property held as a tenancy by the entireties subject to forfeiture irrespective of an innocent owner defense?

c) **Held.** Yes. Reversed and remanded.

(1) There is no definitive guidance in the applicable statutes or the legislative history which shows precisely how Congress sought to balance the interest of forfeiture and the interest of an innocent owner. The interpretation we believe should be adopted is that which best serves the goals of 21 U.S.C. section 881 (a)(7): forfeiture of property used in drug offenses and preservation of innocent owners' property rights.

(2) Since the Bernsteins' and the district court's interpretation frustrates the government's interest in forfeiture of property used in committing drug crimes, we limit our consideration of the extent of forfeiture to the interpretation advanced by P and interpretations that would result in a lesser degree of forfeiture. There are two interpretations: (i) that P is not entitled to forfeiture of any interest now or at any future time, but P may preserve its rights by filing a lis pendens; and (ii) P is entitled to immediate forfeiture of Mr. Bernstein's interest with Mrs. Bernstein retaining exclusive use and possession during her lifetime, being protected against any conveyance without her consent or any attempt to levy upon the interest formerly held by her husband, and retaining the right to obtain title in fee simple absolute if she is predeceased by Mr. Bernstein.

(3) On remand, the district court should determine whether Mr. Bernstein's interest is subject to forfeiture irrespective of Mrs. Bernstein's innocent owner defense, and if it is determined that it is, the court should enter an order forfeiting that interest but preserving Mrs. Bernstein's rights.

c. **Dissolution.** Dissolution presents many difficult problems which are normally studied separately in a family law course. However, the division of marital property involves certain basic property law principles with which any attorney should be familiar. The basic purpose of property settlements is to allocate to each spouse what equitably belongs to him or her. The concepts of equity have changed over the years.

1) **Common law approach.** At common law, each spouse would retain the property to which she or he held title. A tenancy by the entirety would become a tenancy in common, and existing joint tenancies or tenancies in common would remain valid. Normally, the husband owned most of the property, but he would have to provide support, or alimony, to the wife.

2) **Modern approach.** With the acceptance of no-fault divorce, the states replaced the common law approach to property division with a rule of equitable distribution, permitting the court to exercise discretion in dividing the property. Some states permit division of all property owned by the spouses; others restrict it to marital property, which can include all property acquired by whatever means during the marriage, or merely the property earned by either spouse during the marriage. Alimony is commonly called "maintenance" and is paid only for a period long enough to allow the dependent spouse to obtain employment.

3) **Determining what property is subject to division--*In re* Marriage of Graham,** 574 P.2d 75 (Colo. 1978).

a) **Facts.** Mrs. Graham (P) put her husband (D) through one year of under-graduate school and three years of M.B.A. school by working full-time as an airline stewardess. He worked part-time while going to school. P contributed 70% of the family financial support. Following his graduation D got a job as an executive assistant with a large corporation. After six years of marriage they filed for divorce. (No marital assets were accumulated during the marriage.) The divorce court found that as a matter of law, the M.B.A. degree was jointly owned by P and D. The future earnings value of the M.B.A. were valued at $82,836. P was awarded $33,134 of this as her portion, with D to pay her at the rate of $100 per month. D appealed. The intermediate court held for D. P appeals. (Note, P did not claim financial support from D.)

b) **Issue.** Is a graduate degree marital property subject to division on divorce?

c) **Held.** No. Judgment affirmed.

(1) The applicable statute requires, without regard to misconduct, marital property to be divided in such proportions as it deems just after considering all relevant factors.

(2) It is clear that the statute intended for "property" to be broadly defined. Nonetheless, there are necessary limits upon what is "property."

(3) One helpful definition is "everything that has an exchangeable value of which goes to make up wealth or estate." For example, in one case we held that military retirement pay was not property for the reason that it did not have any of the elements of cash surrender value, loan value, redemption value, lump sum value, or value realizable after death.

(4) Even under the broad view of property, a graduate degree simply does not have an exchange value or any objective transferable value on an open market. It is personal to the holder. It is the result of many years of education, diligence, and hard work.

(5) We are unable to find any decisions, even in community property states, which hold that one spouse's education is a marital asset to be divided on dissolution; *e.g.*, a case has held that a physician's accrued goodwill in his medical practice is not property.

(6) This holding does not mean that a spouse who contributes to the other's education is without remedy. Contribution of financial support to a spouse getting a degree is a factor that may be taken into consideration in awarding the contributing spouse support. Here, P does not seek support from D.

d) **Dissent.** As a matter of economic reality, the most valuable asset acquired by either party during their six-year marriage was the graduate degree. By excluding the degree from the definition of "property," courts are impotent to provide a remedy for an obvious injustice. Future earning capacity is an asset considered in wrongful death actions; it should be the same in divorce actions.

  e) **Comment.** In awarding support (alimony), courts have broad discretion in considering relevant factors, such as contribution to one spouse's education. This case points out factors to be considered in determining whether or not something is "property."

Elkus v.   **4)** **Celebrity status or property--Elkus v. Elkus,** 169 A.D.2d 134, 572 N.Y.S.2d
Elkus   901 (1991).

  a) **Facts.** Frederica von Stade Elkus (P) had just embarked on her career in opera at the time of her marriage, and during her marriage her career succeeded dramatically. In 1973, she earned $621,878. P is known internationally, has received numerous awards, and has performed for the President of the United States. P's husband (D) traveled with P, attending and critiquing her performances, and photographed her. D was also P's voice coach and teacher for 10 years of the 17-year marriage. D claims he sacrificed his own career to devote himself to P, and since P's celebrity status increased during the marriage due in part to his contribution, he is entitled to equitable distribution of this marital property. P and D have stipulated to mutual judgments of divorce and to joint custody of their two minor children. Trial on the remaining economic issues has been stayed pending P's appeal. The supreme court found that the enhanced value of P's celebrity status was not marital property. D appeals.

  b) **Issue.** Is the enhanced value of P's career and/or celebrity status marital property subject to equitable distribution?

  c) **Held.** Yes. Order reversed; remanded.

    (1) To the extent D's contributions and efforts led to an increase in the value of P's career, this appreciation was a product of the marital property subject to equitable distribution.

    (2) Marital property is property acquired during the marriage regardless of the form in which title is held.

    (3) Marital property need not be an asset with exchange value, salable, assignable, transferable, or licensed. However, a medical license has been held to enhance earning capacity, so as to enable a spouse who contributed to its acquisition to share its value.

    (4) A marriage is an economic partnership to which both parties contribute. The enhanced skills of an artist such as P, albeit growing from an innate talent, which have enabled her to become an exceptional earner, may be valued as marital property. D's contributions and active involvement were direct and concrete. It is the nature and intent of the contribution by the spouse seeking equitable distribution, rather than the nature of the career, which should determine the status of the enterprise as marital property.

5) **Professional goodwill.** Most jurisdictions treat professional goodwill, *e.g.*, reputation likely to generate future business, as a divisible marital asset.

7. **Community Property.** Arizona, California, Idaho, Louisiana, Nevada, New Mexico, Texas, Washington, and Wisconsin are community property states. Basically, community property means that all the property acquired during the period of the marriage belongs equally to the spouses, each having equal right to manage the property.

   a. **Distinguishing separate property from community property.** In community property states property is divided into two classes, community and separate. All property acquired by a spouse before the marriage, or after marriage if the property was acquired by gift, descent, or devise, is that spouse's separate property. All other property acquired during the marriage is community property. This includes wages. Each spouse has a 50% interest in all community property.

   b. **Effect of commingling separate and community property.** While the exact rules vary from state to state, generally commingling causes separate property to become community property unless a contrary intent on the part of the couple can be proven.

   c. **Rights at divorce.** Upon divorce each spouse gets his/her own separate property and one-half of the community property. The division of community property need not be exactly 50-50. In addition, from the time of separation each spouse's earnings are his or her separate property.

   d. **Characterizing property when the couple moves.** If a couple moves away from a community property state to a common law state, problems arise in characterizing property as community or separate. Generally, the law of the state where the couple is domiciled at the time they acquire the property governs. The chief exception to this rule involves real property. In that case the law of the state where the land is situated governs. If a couple moves to a community property state from a common law state, then all property acquired after the move is governed by community property law. The character of the property acquired prior to the move does not change.

8. **Unmarried Cohabitation.** There has been a trend to divide property acquired during cohabitation among the cohabitants when they split up. Special rules apply to such cases.

   a. **Express contracts between unmarried cohabitants--Marvin v. Marvin,** 557 P.2d 106 (Cal. 1976).

   Marvin v. Marvin

      1) **Facts.** Michele Triola (P) and Lee Marvin (D) lived together for seven years without marrying. All property during this period was taken in D's name. P avers that in 1964, she and D entered into an oral agreement whereby P and D would combine their efforts and earnings and share any and all property accumulated as a result of their individual and/or combined efforts. P and D agreed to hold themselves out to the public as husband and wife and that P would render services as companion, homemaker, housekeeper, and cook to

D, who agreed to provide all of P's financial support and needs for the rest of P's life. P gave up her lucrative career in order to devote her full time to D. During the period 1964 through May 1970, P lived with D and fulfilled her obligations; the parties accumulated property worth over $1 million. In May 1970, D compelled P to leave his home and after November 1971, D provided no support for P. P sued to enforce the contract. The trial court granted judgment on the pleadings for D. P seeks declaratory relief.

2) **Issue.** Did the trial court err in finding that P's complaint failed to state a cause of action based upon an expressed contract?

3) **Held.** Yes. Reversed and remanded.

   a) We have an established principle that nonmarried partners may lawfully contract regarding property ownership acquired during the relationship.

   b) A contract between nonmarried partners is unenforceable only to the extent that it explicitly rests upon the immoral and illicit consideration of meretricious sexual services. Adults who voluntarily live together and have sexual relations are competent to contract respecting their property and earnings. Here, the contract as alleged does not rest upon any unlawful consideration.

   c) P also has a claim based upon principles of implied contract or equity. Courts may inquire into the conduct of the parties to determine whether that conduct evidences an implied contract or agreement of partnership or joint venture or other tacit understanding. When appropriate, the court may employ principles of constructive trust; quantum meruit may also be applied.

4) **Note.** On remand, the trial court found that D had no support obligation, that the parties had never agreed to combine earnings or share property accumulated during the period of their cohabitation. Because P had no visible means of support, however, D was ordered to pay P $104,000 "in equity" to enable her to rehabilitate. D appealed. The court of appeals reversed the judgment ordering payment, finding that P had not asked for "limited rehabilitative support" and there was no basis for such support.

9. **Same Sex Couples.** Some states and municipalities grant same sex couples many of the rights and benefits enjoyed by married heterosexuals. However, the argument that denial of the right to marry for same sex couples has yet to succeed.

   a) We have an established principle that nonmarried partners may lawfully contract regarding property ownership acquired during the relationship.

   b) A contract between nonmarried partners is unenforceable only to the extent that it explicitly rests upon the immoral and illicit consideration of meretricious sexual services. Adults who voluntarily live together and have sexual relations are competent to contract respecting their property and earnings. Here, the contract as alleged does not rest upon any unlawful consideration.

    c)   P also has a claim based upon principles of implied contract or equity. Courts may inquire into the conduct of the parties to determine whether that conduct evidences an implied contract or agreement of partnership or joint venture or other tacit understanding. When appropriate, the court may employ principles of constructive trust; quantum meruit may also be applied.

4)   **Note.** On remand, the trial court found that D had no support obligation, that the parties had never agreed to combine earnings or share property accumulated during the period of their cohabitation. Because P had no visible means of support, however, D was ordered to pay P $104,000 "in equity" to enable her to rehabilitate. D appealed. The court of appeals reversed the judgment ordering payment, finding that P had not asked for "limited rehabilitative support" and there was no basis for such support.

III. LANDLORDS AND TENANTS

A. LEASEHOLD ESTATES

1. **Introduction.** Landlord-tenant law has changed significantly in recent years as the courts and legislatures have recognized the inapplicability of traditional notions to modern circumstances. This area of law originated during the feudal ages when tenants were farmers who were primarily interested in the land. Buildings were maintained by the tenant, and the landlord typically had few duties other than to not evict the tenant. This agrarian model has proven inappropriate for the residential tenant, and the law has adapted to the needs of the modern tenant.

2. **The Types of Tenancies.**

   a. **Tenancy for years.** This type of tenancy is (i) for a fixed period of time (does not have to be measured in years) and (ii) the calendar dates for the beginning and ending of the lease period are ascertainable. For example, "one year from the date of signing of this lease," or "three years, five days after my thirtieth birthday." In both of these examples, once the lease is signed, the beginning and ending dates are ascertainable, so no notice is required.

   b. **Periodic tenancy.** This tenancy is for a fixed period of time until either the landlord or the tenant gives notice of termination. Examples of this are, "from month to month," "from year to year." Absent contractual provisions to the contrary, the terms and conditions carry over from period to period.

   c. **Tenancy at will.** It is easy to confuse the tenancy at will and the periodic tenancy. A tenancy at will lasts only so long as the landlord and tenant desire. Both are equally capable of terminating the lease at any time. The lease may provide for a given period of notice, such as 30 days, before the lease may be terminated.

   d. **Tenancy at sufferance.** A tenant who was rightfully in possession but wrongfully remains in possession after the tenancy expires becomes a tenant at sufferance. The tenant is not a trespasser and is not really a tenant because the possession is without the landlord's permission. The tenancy at sufferance lasts until the landlord either evicts the tenant or elects to hold the tenant to another term. The states apply varying rules as to the terms of the tenancy that apply if the landlord elects to hold the tenant to another term.

   e. **Construing lease terms--Garner v. Gerrish,** 473 N.E.2d 223 (N.Y. 1984).

      1) **Facts.** Donovan leased a house to Gerrish (D) for rent of $100 per month. The lease was to continue until D terminated the agreement at a date of his own choice. D moved in and lived there for over four years when Donovan died. Garner (P), Donovan's executor, served D with a notice to quit the premises. D refused, and P initiated an eviction proceeding on the claim that the lease created a tenancy at will. D claimed the

Garner v. Gerrish

lease was a tenancy for life, but the court granted P summary judgment, holding that since the lease term was indefinite, it was a month-to-month term. The appellate court affirmed and D appeals.

2) **Issue.** If a tenant has the right to terminate a lease at a date of his own choice, does the tenant have a determinable life tenancy?

3) **Held.** Yes. Judgment reversed.

   a) At common law, a lease at the will of the lessee was also deemed to be at the will of the lessor. This rule arose from the requirement of livery of seisin to convey a life estate; if livery of seisin did not take place, a tenancy at will resulted.

   b) Livery of seisin has been abandoned, so there is no reason to convert a lease granting a tenant the exclusive right to terminate at will into a tenancy at will terminable by either party. The rule adopted by the Restatement recognizes that a lease such as D's creates a determinable *life* estate in the tenant, terminable at the tenant's will or on the tenant's death.

   c) D's lease gives D the right to terminate the lease at a date he chooses. This is a common way to create a life tenancy terminable at the tenant's will. The lease is not indeterminate even though D could terminate it earlier than the time of his death.

f. **Holdover tenants.** A tenant who "holds over" (stays beyond the end of the lease period) is a tenant at sufferance. The period of "sufferancy" lasts until the landlord decides either to evict the holdover tenant (after which time the tenant becomes a trespasser) or to hold the tenant to another lease term (or one year, whichever is less). If the landlord elects to hold the tenant over for another term, it is under the same terms and conditions as in the original lease. At common law, there were *no* excuses for being a holdover tenant. Now some courts will accept excuses if it is apparent that the tenant did not intend to stay beyond the end of the term.

   1) **Rent increases.** If the landlord notifies that a higher rent will be charged for holding over, the tenant is liable for the increased rent unless he notifies the landlord that he will not pay it. This is one situation where silence on the tenant's part will be construed as consent to the rent increase.

   2) **Landlord's election--Crechale & Polles, Inc. v. Smith,** 295 So. 2d 275 (Miss. 1979).

      a) **Facts.** Crechale (P) brought suit for back rent and damages. P leased a store building to Smith (D) for five years. Near the end of the five years, D notified P that the new building to which D was moving was not completed and that D, therefore, wanted to stay over on a month-to-month basis for a couple of months. The facts are disputed, yet it appears clear that P initially told D that it would not extend the lease on a month-to-month basis, and that D had to move out at the end of the term. D stayed beyond the lease term. P accepted and cashed a check for the first holdover month's rent. P then

Crechale & Polles, Inc. v. Smith

Property - 57

refused D's check for the second holdover month's rent. Some three and one-half months after the end of the lease term, P notified D that it considered D a holdover tenant and that the lease had been renewed. D moved out and did not pay rent. P sued. P was awarded rent for the time D actually occupied the premises beyond the term of the lease. P appealed.

b) **Issue.** Once a landlord elects to treat a holdover tenant as a trespasser, may he rescind that election?

c) **Held.** No. The lower court is affirmed.

1) Generally, when a tenant continues beyond the end of the lease term, a landlord may do either one of the following: (i) treat him as a trespasser and evict him, or (ii) hold him over as a tenant for another term.

2) Once having chosen his remedy, the landlord may not rescind his election.

3) Here P elected to treat D as a trespasser. He should have stuck with his election and pursued his remedy of eviction. He could not later change his mind and choose to treat D as a holdover tenant.

4) By accepting the check for the first holdover month's rent, P, in effect, consented to the month-to-month extension of the lease.

d) **Comment.** Some courts allow a landlord to cash checks for holdover months' rent and still evict the tenant. The holdover term in this case would have been one year, since the five-year lease term is greater than the one-year maximum.

3. **The Lease.** As mentioned above, landlord-tenant law originated in an agrarian culture. At first, a lease was primarily contractual, but in the sixteenth century the courts began recognizing the tenant's interest as a possessory interest in the land. A lease was a conveyance of an estate in land as well as a contract between the landlord and tenant. In recent years, the courts and legislatures have emphasized the contractual nature of leases in order to better protect tenants.

a. **Conveyance.** To the extent that a lease is a conveyance, the tenant typically acquires the right of exclusive possession, and the landlord can reenter only if the tenant breaches a covenant. The tenant assumes the responsibility of caring for the property.

b. **Contract.** The contractual nature of a lease involves the respective promises, or covenants, between landlord and tenant. The parties may allocate risks, expenses, and duties as they see fit. The promises are mutually dependent, so that if one party does not perform, the other is excused from performance.

4. Selection of Tenants—Discrimination.

a. Familial status--Soules v. United States Department of Housing and Urban Development, 967 F.2d 817 (2d Cir. 1992).

Soules v. United States Department of Housing and Urban Development

1) **Facts.** Soules, Petitioner (P), a single woman with a 12-year-old daughter, sought housing from Downs, Respondent (R), a realtor. To comply with a New York State Health Department rule that required separate bedrooms for children of different sexes over five years old, R's lease application asked the number and ages of children who would be occupying a premises. R asked the applicants with whom she communicated on the telephone the same questions as appeared on the lease application. In March 1989, R signed an agreement with the owner of a two-family home to rent the second floor. The homeowner asked R to find a tenant who could "live harmoniously" with the elderly couple on the first floor because the husband suffered from poor eyesight and diabetes. During April 1989, R was caring for an elderly aunt, who lived an hour and 15 minutes from her home and frequently stayed overnight. P replied to a newspaper ad placed by R. When R interviewed P over the telephone, she asked P the age of P's child. P demanded to know why this question was being asked and R explained she did not want an upstairs tenant who would make too much noise. P continued to question R, but R stopped volunteering information and told P she would call her if the apartment were available. P contacted HOME, a non-profit organization which investigates allegations of discrimination. HOME sent two testers to apply for the apartment. The first tester said she would be living alone and R made an appointment for her to see the apartment; the tester then cancelled the appointment. The second tester said she had a seven-year-old son and a roommate. R asked if the child was quiet and told her about the elderly couple. R never contacted this tester to arrange a showing. Sometime later R told the tester the apartment had been rented. R met with P and, after arriving 20 minutes late for their appointment, showed P a less desirable apartment and told P no other apartments were available. R told the Perrys, a family with children, who were looking for a place to live, about the apartment. Finally, the apartment was rented to a single woman with no children under 18. P and HOME have petitioned for review of an order of an administrative law judge ("ALJ") dismissing P's discrimination claims brought under sections 3604(a) and (c) of the Fair Housing Act, 42 U.S.C. sections 3601 *et seq.* ("FHA"). The order became a final order of the Secretary of the United States Deptartment of Housing and Urban Development ("HUD") on October 21, 1991.

2) **Issues.**

   a) Did substantial evidence support the ALJ's decision to dismiss P's claims?

   b) Did the ALJ err by inquiring into R's intent regarding R's alleged statements indicating an impermissible preference, discrimination, or limitation in violation of section 3604(c)?

3)   Held. a) Yes. b) No. Affirmed.

a)   Section 3604(a) of the FHA, as amended in 1988, makes it unlawful "[t]o refuse to sell or rent after the making of a bona fide offer, or to refuse to negotiate for the sale or rental of, or otherwise make unavailable or deny, a dwelling to any person because of race, color, religion, sex, familial status, or national origin." "Familial status" includes "'one or more individuals (who have not attained the age of 18 years) being domiciled with' a parent or guardian."

b)   Once a plaintiff makes out a prima facie case showing she is a member of a protected class who applied for, was qualified to rent or purchase housing, and was rejected although the housing remained available, defendant is allowed to explain whether impermissible considerations motivated his actions. The ALJ employed this burden shifting procedure.

c)   D claimed that she did not want to rent to P because of P's negative and combative attitude and because she wished to secure quiet neighbors for the downstairs tenants. P claimed D's reasons were pretextual and cited D's treatment of the first and second testers in favor of her argument.

d)   However, D's treatment of the Perrys fully establishes that D was willing to rent to a family with children.

e)   An ordinary listener standard is an appropriate guide for measuring complaints with the FHA, and standing alone, the FHA is not necessarily violated when one asks whether a child is noisy.

f)   It was proper for the ALJ, after determining D's statements did not facially indicate a discrimination or preference, to examine D's reasons for making the statements. He resolved D's reason was to guarantee that the elderly tenants would continue to live in a quiet environment. D never asked only how old the child was; she always followed up with an inquiry whether the child was noisy.

Bronk v. Ineichen

b.   No reasonable accommodation for house pet--Bronk v. Ineichen, 54 F.3d 425 (7th Cir. 1995).

1)   Facts. Bronk and Jay (Ps), deaf women, leased a townhome from Ineichen (D). D had a no-pets policy he refused to modify to allow Pierre, a dog allegedly trained as a "hearing" dog by Bronk's brother, to live with Ps. Bronk testified she offered to show D a certificate regarding Pierre's abilities, but D was not interested. D threatened to raise Ps' rent and charge them additional security deposit if they brought the dog to the townhome. Ps filed a complaint with the Madison Equal Opportunities Commission ("MEEOC") pursuant to the 1988 Fair Housing Amendments Act, 42 U.S.C. sections 3601 *et seq.* ("FHAA"), alleging that D had discriminated against them on the basis of their gender and their disability. The MEEOC found probable cause to support only the disability claim and enjoined D from enforcing his no-pets policy against Ps. Later Ps relocated and subsequently filed suit in federal court. The jury returned a special verdict of no liability against D. Testimony indicated that Pierre had never been formally trained; no facility had certified him; Ps had lived together on previous occasions and did not require a "hearing" dog. Ps moved for judgment as a matter of law or a new trial. These motions were denied. Ps appeal.

2) **Issues.**

   a) Should the trial court have granted Ps' motions?

   b) Was the verdict fatally tainted by improper jury instructions?

3) **Held.** a) No. b) Yes. Reversed and remanded for a new trial.

   a) There is ample evidence to support the jury's finding of no liability. Judgment as a matter of law is appropriate "only when there can be but one conclusion from the evidence." Here, however, Ps offered no evidence that Pierre had any discernible skills. D impeached Ps regarding Pierre's certification and Ps' former roommate testified that she had seen no evidence Pierre was trained. A rational jury could reasonably conclude that Pierre was a simple house pet.

   b) However, the trial court instructed the jury as if there were one cause of action rather than three. After deciding that the appropriate question was whether D had "discriminated against [the plaintiffs] by failing to reasonably accommodate [their] disability," he provided instructions as to what accommodations are considered reasonable by borrowing standards from state and local law.

   c) The instructions took matters out of the hands of the jurors and implied that as a matter of law it was reasonable for D to demand Pierre's training credentials or to make Pierre's residence dependent upon Ps' accepting responsibility for damages caused by the dog.

   d) The federal statute says none of these things. Reasonable accommodation "must facilitate a disabled individual's ability to function, and it must survive a cost-benefit balancing that takes both parties' needs into account." Ps have the right to argue that Pierre had accumulated sufficient skills to aid the daily functions of a deaf person. Professional credentials, while a partial indicator of Pierre's skill level, are not the sine qua non. "An instruction that elevates specific levels of training to per se reasonable status instead of allowing the jury to evaluate Pierre's abilities and assigns its own weight to his lack of schooling essentially forecloses that argument."

4) **Comment.** In order to make out a prima facie case under the FHA, discriminatory effect is sufficient; a plaintiff need not prove discriminatory motive.

5. **Landlord's Duty to Deliver Possession.** The landlord must give the tenant at the beginning of the lease term the right of possession. If the landlord does not

then have the right of possession or if he fails to transfer it to the tenant, the landlord is in default.

a.   **Majority rule.** The majority rule (also known as the "English rule") imposes on the landlord the duty of giving the tenant both the legal right of possession and actual possession. If a prior tenant is holding over, it is the duty of the landlord to get him out.

b.   **Minority view ("American rule").** In a minority of jurisdictions the landlord need deliver only the legal right of possession. Holdover tenants become the new tenant's problem and he has to sue to get them out at his own expense.

Hannan v. Dusch

c.   **Application--Hannan v. Dusch,** 153 S.E. 824 (Va. 1930).

    1)   **Facts.** Dusch (D) leased some real property to Hannan (P) for a term of 15 years. When the term was to begin, the tenant who had possession prior to the agreement refused to relinquish the estate to P. D refused to take any legal action to remove the holdover tenant. P brought suit against D to recover damages resulting from D's inability to take possession of the leased land. The lower court held in favor of D. P appeals.

    2)   **Issue.** Does the landlord have the implied duty to deliver physical possession to the tenant at the beginning of the lease term?

    3)   **Held.** No. Judgment affirmed for D.

       a)   There is no implied covenant that leased premises shall be open for possession by the tenant at the beginning of his term. The only right that the new tenant has is the right to possession. When the lease makes no provision for physical possession at the beginning of the term, and there is a tenant who is in possession and refuses to relinquish the leasehold, the new tenant has a remedy against the wrongdoer but not against the landlord.

       b)   The rationale appears to be that the landlord should not be held liable for the wrongdoings of a third party.

    4)   **Comment.** The tenant's obligation to pay rent is dependent upon the landlord's fulfilling his obligation:

       a)   To provide the legal right to possession;

       b)   Not to interfere either directly or indirectly with the tenant's physical possession; and

       c)   In most jurisdictions, to place the tenant in actual possession.

6.   **Assignment and Subleasing.**

    a.   **Assignments.** Leases may be assigned by either the lessee or lessor absent some contractual provision to the contrary. The assignee (new tenant) is in privity of estate with the landlord, and unless otherwise provided, their obligations are the same as in the original lease.

b. **Subleases.** Subleases are different from assignments in that the tenant who subleases is a landlord to his sublessee. There is no privity of estate between the original landlord and the sublessee; neither one can sue the other. Certain rules apply in determining whether a transfer is a sublease or assignment.

1) **The effect of a reversion.** At common law, if the subleasing tenant conveyed to the sublessee anything less than the whole leasehold estate (retained a reversion), it was a sublease and not an assignment. Conversely, if the new lessee received the whole (and not one bit less) of the leasehold estate, an assignment was involved.

2) **The effect of retaining a right of entry.** If a transferring tenant retains a right of entry in the event the transferee breaches a condition of the lease, the common law regards the transfer as an assignment, not a sublease. The modern view would hold the transfer to be a sublease.

3) **Modern trend.** The modern trend is to examine the intention of the parties in determining whether a transfer is an assignment or a sublease. If the transferring tenant charges more rent than he has been paying, the courts view this as an indication of a sublease. If the transferee tenant pays a lump sum, the courts take this as an indication of an assignment.

c. **Construing terms of a sublease--Ernst v. Conditt,** 390 S.W.2d 703 (Tenn. 1964).

1) **Facts.** Ernst (P) leased land to Frank Rogers for a term of 53 weeks. Rogers operated a go-cart business on the land. A few months later, Conditt (D) desired to purchase Rogers' business. P, Rogers, and D negotiated a two-year modification of the original lease. In the modification, P consented to Rogers' "subletting" the premises to D. However, Rogers remained personally liable to P. After D occupied the land and paid the rent for a few months he quit paying rent. D remained in possession till the end of the lease term. P sued D to recover back rent. D contended that he had sublet the land from Rogers, so there was no privity between P and D. Consequently, P could not sue D. The chancellor found for P. D appeals.

2) **Issue.** Are the words "sublease" and "subletting" in a transfer document controlling in determining whether a transfer is a sublease?

3) **Held.** No. Judgment affirmed for P.

a) If a transfer is a sublease, there is no privity and the original landlord cannot recover directly from a sublessee. If a transfer is an assignment, there is privity and the landlord can recover from the assignee.

b) At common law, if a transfer conveyed the whole leased estate, it was an assignment. If it conveyed less than the whole, even one day less, it was a sublease. (Under a sublease the sublessor had a reversionary interest, a right to reenter).

c) The modern rule looks to the intent of the parties rather than to formalistic ancient rules.

d) Under either rule, the transfer to D was an assignment.

e) This is true in spite of Rogers' being personally liable. Under either sublease or assignment he still would have been personally liable to P absent a lease provision to the contrary. Rogers had no reversionary interest since he completely divested himself of the business and the leased property. Under the common law rule the transaction was an assignment.

f) The use of the words "sublease" and "subletting" in the modified lease is not controlling. Under the common law rule, the effect of the transfer was controlling, rather than the words. Under the modern rule, it is the intent of the parties that is controlling, not the words.

4) Comment. Courts distinguish between a sublease and an assignment in the following way: When a lessee transfers all of her interest under the lease, *i.e.*, the right to possession for the entire term remaining, an assignment results; when a lessee transfers anything less, a sublease results (*e.g.*, where there are three years remaining on the lease and the lessee transfers two years, she has subleased and retains a reversion at the end of the two-year period).

Kendall v.
Ernest Pest-
ana, Inc.

d. Commercial lessor's duty to act in good faith--Kendall v. Ernest Pestana, Inc., 220 Cal. Rptr. 818, 709 P.2d 837 (1985).

1) Facts. Ernest Pestana, Inc. (D) leased hangar space at an airport which was subject to a preexisting sublease with Bixler. Bixler arranged to sell his business to Kendall (P) and two other parties, but because Bixler's lease provided that the consent of the lessor was necessary for an assignment, Bixler sought D's consent. D refused to consent. Ps sued, claiming D's refusal to consent was an unlawful restraint on the freedom of alienation. The trial court sustained D's demurrer to the complaint and Ps appeal.

2) Issue. May a commercial lessor unreasonably and arbitrarily withhold consent to an assignment by the lessee?

3) Held. No. Judgment reversed.

a) The common law rule of free alienability of a leasehold interest is still valid, but parties are permitted to restrict this alienability by contract. Such restraints are strictly construed against the lessor, however, especially when the lessor can terminate the lease if it is assigned without the lessor's consent. The lease in this case contained such a provision.

b) The majority rule allows a lessor to arbitrarily refuse to consent to a proposed assignment, although in many cases the lessor is found by its conduct to have waived the right to refuse. An increasing minority has modified this rule by permitting a lessor to withhold consent only when it has a commercially reasonable objection to the assignment. This appears to be the better approach.

c) Because a lease is a conveyance, it is subject to the public policy favoring reasonable alienation. Conditions unreasonably restraining alienation are deemed void. The Restatement (Second), section 15.2(2), adopts the minority approach while permitting a lessor to object to a proposed assignment on reasonable commercial grounds. The lessor is also protected because the original lessee remains liable as a surety.

lease is a conveyance AND a contract

d) A lease is also a contract, and contracts include a duty to act in good faith and to deal fairly. Generally, a contract that gives one party discretionary power that affects the other party also imposes a duty to exercise that power in good faith. D here had discretionary power to disapprove an assignment. D must exercise that discretion in good faith.

w/ discretionary power comes duty to exercise power in good faith.

e) The reasonableness of the lessor's refusal to consent is a factual question. It would not be commercially reasonable to refuse consent solely because of the lessor's personal tastes, convenience or sensibility, or to charge a higher rent.

f) While a lessor may have the freedom to choose its own tenant, this freedom is preserved by allowing the lessor to disapprove assignments for commercially reasonable reasons. Even though the lessee did not insist on reasonableness language in the lease, the lease does not forbid assignment, so the parties must have contemplated that if the lessee obtained a satisfactory subtenant, the lessor would consent.

g) D claims it is entitled to charge higher rent to a sublessee because D is entitled to the benefit of increased property values. However, the lessee has already agreed to a particular rent. By ensuring a return to the lessor, the lessee assumes the risk of a decreased market value, and should also benefit from an increase in market value. D would get more than it bargained for if it were permitted to increase its rent.

e. **Landlord's remedies for defaulting tenants.** The landlord has various common law, statutory, and, typically, contractual remedies to ensure the tenant's compliance with the lease. Most leases contain rent acceleration clauses which provide that all the rent due under the contract is immediately due and payable if the tenant defaults. Of course, the landlord cannot accelerate the rent and take possession of the premises. Security deposits are also common in most leases. Common law remedies include "distress" (entry on the premises and seizure of the tenant's chattels in order to secure payment of the rent), although in some jurisdictions this has been either abolished or the entry must be peaceable. Statutory liens are also permitted in many jurisdictions. These statutes vary quite a bit, but basically, they allow the landlord a lien on the personal property of the tenant to secure payment of the rent.

1) **Eviction.** A tenant may be evicted if he breaches lease covenants or holds over beyond the lease term. There are two types of eviction, self-help and by judicial process. The self-help remedy has fallen into disfavor in recent years.

a) **By judicial process.** The most common judicial process for eviction is by a statutorily prescribed summary proceeding. In some places this is called "unlawful detainer," and in others, "forcible entry and detainer." Basically, this involves serving a tenant a notice to quit. If the tenant does not leave, the landlord files an unlawful detainer action, which is typically heard in five days or less. After the hearing, if the judge finds the tenant in breach of the lease, he will sign an order authorizing the sheriff to evict the tenant. Under these summary proceedings, a landlord cannot do anything more than obtain possession of the premises. He cannot get back rent. A landlord can also file a suit in ejectment, but this action does not get priority on the civil calendar and for that reason is seldom used. In Los Angeles County, for example, it could take five years for this to come to trial. No landlord wants a nonpaying tenant for that long.

b) **Self-help.** At common law, a landlord could use self-help to evict a tenant. In America, a landlord has traditionally been allowed to use reasonable self-help to remove a tenant (changing the locks is a good example). The modern trend, however, has been to hold a landlord liable for damages if he uses self-help. This harshness is felt appropriate in light of the modern availability of summary judicial proceedings.

Berg v. Wiley   c) **Application--Berg v. Wiley,** 264 N.W.2d 145 (Minn. 1978).

(1) **Facts.** Action for damages for wrongful eviction. Wiley (D) leased a restaurant to Berg (P) for 1970-1975. P, in violation of the lease, remodeled the restaurant without D's consent. P's restaurant was often cited for health code violations. This violated a lease provision regarding operating the business in a lawful manner. In 1973, D gave P two weeks notice to make remodeling changes or, pursuant to the contract, D would retake possession. At about the same time, the Health Department gave P two weeks to remedy the health code violations. On the last day of the two week period, P dismissed her employees, closed the restaurant and put up a "closed for remodeling" sign. While P was gone, D changed the locks. P sued for damages and lost profits, claiming that she had closed the restaurant for a month to remodel it to D's specifications. P sued for wrongful eviction and won $31,000 for lost profits. D appealed.

(2) **Issue.** May a landlord use self-help to regain possession of his property?

(3) **Held.** No. The trial court is affirmed.

(a) While the evidence is contradictory, it is sufficient to uphold the jury's determination that P was going to reopen the restaurant after remodeling.

(b) The second issue relating to a landlord's self-help is more difficult. At common law the landlord was legally entitled to retake possession if: (i) the landlord is legally entitled possession (such as where there is a reentry clause in the lease), and (ii) the landlord's means of reentry is peaceable.

(c) Public policy discourages landlords from taking the law into their own hands, especially where the self-help may result in breaches of the peace.

(d) Today, summary legal proceedings are available that can get the landlord possession in three to 10 days. This is a quick, easy, and safe way to retake a leased premises.

(e) Actual violence is not required for there to be forceful retaking. Changing the locks in P's absence is not a peaceable method of reentry but rather a forceful retaking.

(f) The modern trend to require landlords to use legal process, rather than self-help, is in direct contradiction to the common law.

(g) Thus, the only lawful means to dispossess a tenant who has not abandoned or voluntarily surrendered, but who claims possession adversely to a landlord's claim of breach of a written lease, is by resort to judicial process. There is no place and no need for self-help.

(4) **Comment.** The court here held that under either the common law or the modern rule, P had shown D's forceful eviction of P. The jury applied the common law in finding D's eviction of P wrongful. "Closed for remodeling" signs are a common ploy when a restaurant goes out of business and wants to delay its creditors.

d) **Self-help authorized by lease.** Typically, courts uphold contractual provisions permitting the landlord to use self-help. A minority hold such provisions void as offending public policy.

7. Abandonment.

a. **Landlord's options.** If the tenant abandons the premises during the lease term, the landlord may leave the premises vacant and sue the tenant for the rent. (In most jurisdictions the landlord need not mitigate by seeking a new tenant. A minority of jurisdictions hold contra.) Or he may retake the premises and try to lease again. The courts are in conflict as to whether this effects a surrender of the premises (in such an event the tenant would only be liable for rent to the day of termination).

b. **Application--Sommer v. Kridel,** 378 A.2d 767 (N.J. 1977).

Sommer v. Kridel

1) **Facts.** This case is a consolidation of two cases. Sommer in one and Riverview Realty Co. in the other (Ps) sued Kridel in one and Perosio in the other (Ds) for rent due. The facts of *Sommer v. Kridel* follow: D entered into a two-year lease agreement with P, with a rent concession for the first six weeks. Subsequent to the lease, but prior to occupancy, D wrote P a letter explaining that his expected wedding plans had been cancelled and that he could no longer afford to take the apartment. P made no reply to the letter. Thereafter, a third party went to look at the apartment and was ready and willing to move in, but she was told the apartment was rented. P did not

reenter nor attempt to lease the apartment for at least three months. P then rented to a new tenant under the same terms as before, including a six-week rent concession. The new lease began September 1. Prior to reletting the premises, P sued D demanding the total amount due for the full two-year term. After reletting the premises, P amended the complaint asking for rent due between May and September. The trial court found for D, holding that the landlord (P) had a duty to mitigate damages by attempting to relet the premises. The appellate division reversed. D appeals.

In *Riverview Realty Co. v. Perosio* the facts are: D, the tenant, entered into a two-year lease with P. D took possession and occupied the premises for one year. At that time D vacated the premises. P sued for rent due on the one year remaining of the lease term. The trial court granted P's motion for summary judgment against D. The appellate division affirmed. D appeals.

2) **Issue.** Is a landlord seeking damages from a defaulting tenant under a duty to mitigate those damages by making a reasonable effort to relet the premises?

3) **Held.** Yes. Both decisions of the appellate division are reversed.

(a) The minority view, which is based on antitrust law, is that a landlord does have an obligation to make a reasonable effort to mitigate damages where a tenant has surrendered and abandoned the premises prior to expiration of the lease.

(b) The majority rule, which is based on property law, is that a landlord is under no duty to mitigate damages caused by a defaulting tenant. This court finds the majority view antiquated and will follow the minority view.

4) **Comment.** This case illustrates the continuing trend by the courts to apply principles of contract law rather than pure property law to residential leases. In this particular case, however, the court's opinion leaves some doubt as to whether the landlord has a duty to mitigate when he is seeking damages from the defaulting tenant or when he is recovering unpaid rent. Most of the language goes primarily to the landlord's duty to mitigate if he is seeking damages. However, Ps in these cases were seeking unpaid rent, not damages. Only a few states still follow the common law rule. However, some states require mitigation only for commercial leases and others only for residential leases.

B. LANDLORD'S DUTIES

1. **Habitability of the Premises.** At common law, the landlord was under no duty to furnish habitable premises. Absent contractual provisions to the

contrary, the premises were leased "as is." However, if there were defects or dangerous conditions known to the landlord and not easily discoverable, the landlord had a duty to disclose the defect. These rules have undergone significant development in recent years.

a. Quiet enjoyment and constructive eviction.

breach by actual or constructive eviction

1) **Quiet enjoyment.** A tenant has the right to "quietly enjoy" the premises. This means that the landlord cannot interfere with the tenant's use of and enjoyment of the premises. This covenant is implied in every lease. Even at common law, where the general rule was caveat lessee, breach of this covenant absolved the tenant from his responsibility to pay rent. This covenant can be breached by either actual eviction or constructive eviction.

2) **Actual eviction.** If the landlord evicts the tenant from the entire leasehold, the tenant may treat the lease as breached and terminate it. He no longer has to pay rent. If the tenant is evicted from only a portion of the lease-hold, he may stay on the premises and refuse to pay rent until the landlord restores the entire premises to the tenant.

3) **Constructive eviction.** If, through the landlord's fault, the tenant's quiet enjoyment of the premises is substantially interfered with, the tenant may treat the lease as terminated and vacate the premises. He is no longer liable for the rent. The theory behind this is that the landlord has so interfered with the tenant's right of possession that he might as well have evicted the tenant. The necessary elements are:

   a) **Substantial interference.** The tenant's use and enjoyment of the premises must be substantially interfered with. Of course, if the tenant knows of the interference when he signed the lease, the court may hold that he waived the interference.

   b) **Notice to the landlord.** The tenant must give notice to the landlord of the defect and give the landlord a reasonable time to cure the problem.

   c) **Tenant must vacate.** The tenant cannot stay on and refuse to pay rent. He must vacate within a reasonable time.

   d) **Fault.** The interference to the tenant's enjoyment and use of the premises must be the fault of the landlord. He must act, or fail to act, to the tenant's damage.

4) **Damages.** After vacating, the tenant can recover damages for being wrongfully evicted. This would include damages for the additional cost of substitute premises, lost profits, increased expenses proximately caused by the eviction, etc.

5) **Measuring substantial interference--Reste Realty Corp. v. Cooper,** 251 A.2d 268 (N.J. 1969).

   a) **Facts.** Reste Realty Corp. (P) sued Cooper (D) for rent due under a lease. P's predecessor leased to D a portion of a basement for commercial purposes for a term of five years. After the first year, a new lease was executed for the entire basement for five years. At the execution of the lease, the lessor knew of the faulty construction of the driveway, which caused the basement to flood each time it rained. The lessor agreed at that time to correct the situation. D used the premises for sales training meetings and classes. For several years the basement flooded each time it rained, but the lessor promptly drained the water so it did not interfere with D's use of the premises. The original lessor then died. The rain continued to flood the premises, but the new lessor (P) did not respond to any of D's complaints. D then notified P of its intention to quit the premises with two years remaining on the lease. P subsequently sued for the two years' rent due under the lease. D asserted the defense of constructive eviction. The trial court entered judgment for D. The appellate court reversed. D appealed.

b) **Issue.** Does a tenant have the right to vacate if his quiet enjoyment of the premises is substantially interfered with by his landlord?

c) **Held.** Yes. The appellate court decision is reversed and the trial court judgment is reinstated.

(1) There is a covenant of quiet enjoyment, express or implied, the substantial interference with which by the lessor constitutes constructive eviction. The lessee then may vacate the premises, thereby relieving him of any further obligation to pay rent. A tenant's right, however, to claim constructive eviction is lost if he does not vacate the premises within a reasonable time after there has been a substantial breach of warranty of quiet enjoyment.

(2) The lease agreement exists as a contract between the lessor and the lessee; thus, the substantial breach of any condition therein constitutes a failure of consideration. As such, it is immaterial whether the violation of the lessee's right is expressed as a breach of a covenant of quiet enjoyment, or material failure of consideration, or material breach of an implied warranty against latent defects.

d) **Comment.** This case is another illustration of courts' move away from the doctrine of caveat lessee and toward viewing short-term leases as contracts.

6) **Partial constructive eviction.** Some courts have gone so far as to allow a tenant to recover for partial constructive eviction. This developed in light of judicial consideration for the situation of the modern city dweller.

b. **Illegal lease agreements.**

1) **Generally.** Some local housing codes prohibit rental of premises in violation of the code. In such circumstances, the tenant cannot be forced to pay rent.

2) **Limitations.** For the tenant to be able to defend against the landlord's action for rent, the illegal condition must have existed at the time the lease was signed. Also, although the tenant need not pay rent, he is still liable for the reasonable rental value of the premises. Usually, if the illegal condition is substantial (renders the premises unfit for human occupation), this will not be very much money.

c.   Implied warranty of habitability. — *abandonment not required*

1)   Traditional approach. At common law, the landlord had no duty to keep the premises in repair once the tenant moved in. Of course, the landlord and tenant could agree that the landlord will keep the premises in repair. This covenant, like contractual covenants in general, was independent. Thus, even if the landlord failed to keep the premises in repair, the tenant still had to pay rent, but could sue for breach of contract or specific performance.

2)   Implied warranty of habitability. One of the areas of major reform in the law in the last 20 years is in the area of implied covenants of habitability. Most courts will now imply, in every noncommercial lease, a covenant that the premises be delivered to the tenant in fit and habitable shape. The courts have further held that the landlord's fulfillment of this covenant is an antecedent condition to the paying of rent. While the exact application of this doctrine varies from state to state, typically the tenant can avoid the lease, or make the repairs and withhold the amount of the repairs from the rent. Several states have enacted statutes which codify this doctrine.

 a)   Commercial leases. Some courts have extended this implied covenant to commercial leases.

 b)   Standards applied. Courts and statutes differ on exactly what standard to use in assessing habitability. Some use the housing code standards, others follow a "fit for human habitation" standard. Some courts also require that the landlord be given notice of the unfit condition and time to make repairs.

 c)   Waiver. This implied covenant, according to the cases decided so far, cannot be waived by the tenant. Any waiver of it is held to violate public policy.

3)   Tenant need not abandon premises--Hilder v. St. Peter, 478 A.2d 202 (Vt. 1984).

 a)   Facts. Hilder (P) rented an apartment from St. Peter (D) for herself, her three children, and a new-born grandson. P agreed to pay $140 per month plus a $50 damage deposit. She paid the deposit and the first month's rent. P also cleaned up the apartment from the previous tenants in reliance on D's promise to refund the damage deposit, but D never refunded the money. P always paid her rent. P notified D of several problems, which D promised to fix but did not. These included a broken window, no key to the front door lock, a clogged toilet and inoperable bathroom electricity, falling plaster due to a roof leak, and raw sewage in the basement from a broken sewage pipe. P also paid for her own heat contrary to the rental arrangement. P finally sued for reimbursement of the rent paid and additional compensatory damages. The trial court awarded P the rent she paid of

$3,445, plus the $50 deposit, and $1,500 as additional compensatory damages. D appeals, claiming P should not have been reimbursed for the rent because she occupied the apartment the whole time.

b) **Issue.** When a landlord breaches the implied warranty of habitability, must the tenant abandon the premises in order to obtain reimbursement of the rent paid?

c) **Held.** No. Judgment affirmed in part and remanded on the damages issue.

(1) Traditionally, leases were deemed to be conveyances of real property, and possession by the tenant created a duty to pay rent. The landlord was not liable to make repairs unless the lease so specified. The modern approach, recognizing the inability of urban tenants to make effective repairs in complex apartment situations and the tenants' inferior bargaining position, treats leases as contracts. Thus, a tenant's duty to pay rent depends on the landlord's maintaining the premises in habitable conditions. The tenant does not have to abandon the premises in order to bring suit.

(2) All rentals of residential dwelling units include an implied warranty of habitability that applies to latent and patent defects. The tenant does not assume the risk of defects in place when the lease is entered, and the implied warranty of habitability cannot be waived in writing or verbally.

(3) Whether the implied warranty is breached depends on the circumstances of the particular case, but if the defect impacts the tenant's safety or health, there is probably a breach. Before suing, the tenant must notify the landlord of the defect and allow a reasonable time for correction. The defects in this case, and P's response thereto, satisfy these requirements, and D breached the implied warranty.

(4) When there is a breach, the tenant may pursue rescission, reformation, and damages. The basic measure of damages is the difference between the value of the residence as warranted and its value as it actually exists. The tenant may also recover for discomfort and annoyance, as well as any costs of repair. The tenant may choose to withhold future rent. Finally, punitive damages may be awarded to punish landlords who are morally culpable.

(5) In this case, the trial court awarded damages for the proper reasons but did not adequately explain the basis for the additional compensatory damages.

d. **Tort liability.**

1) **Conditions existing at time of lease.** The general common law rule was caveat lessee. The landlord was liable neither to the lessee nor his guests unless he failed to disclose a known, latent, dangerous condition or defect (one which the lessee probably could not discover). Once a latent defect was disclosed to the lessee, the landlord was no longer liable. If the latent, dangerous defect was discovered by the landlord after the tenant entered into possession, the landlord had a duty to disclose (but not repair).

a) **Modern rule.** Most courts now hold landlords liable if they fail to disclose dangerous defects. This extends to defects which the landlord should have discovered, even if he had no actual knowledge.

b) **Publicly used portions of the premises.** The landlord is liable for injuries occurring to the public on these portions of the premises if he knows, or should know, of the defect, has reason to think that the tenant will not fix the defect, and fails to use reasonable care to fix the condition. The landlord is not liable for the tenant's injuries under this rule. If the landlord does not know that that portion of the premises was going to be used by the public, he is not liable. A twist to this rule is that the landlord may be liable even if the tenant promises to make the repairs *if* the landlord has reason to know that the tenant will not make the repairs before admitting the public to that portion of the premises.

2) **Conditions arising after execution of the lease.** The general rule is no liability. It now becomes the tenant's job to keep the premises safe.

a) **Liability for voluntary repairs.** Even if the landlord is under no duty to make repairs, if he does do so he must use reasonable care. He is liable if the repairs are made negligently. This is in accord with the general principles of tort liability.

b) **Contractually obligated repairs.** Modern cases treat this about the same as liability for voluntary repairs. The old view, still adhered to in some places, absolved the landlord of tort liability, leaving the tenant to sue for breach of contract.

3) **Common areas.** If the landlord is in control of the common areas (hallways, walkways, elevators, swimming pool), he is liable for those injuries resulting from those defects of which he knew or which he reasonably could have discovered.

4) **Legal duty to repair.** In some locations, statutes or ordinances impose liability on landlords to make repairs. Sometimes liability is imposed by enforcing an implied covenant of habitability.

C. TENANT'S DUTIES AND OBLIGATIONS

1. Tenant's Affirmative Duties.

a.   **Duty to repair.** At common law a tenant has the duty to keep the premises in as good a condition as when he leases it. He does not need to make substantial repairs.

b.   **Duty not to commit waste.** A tenant is liable for waste. Waste is one of two types, ameliorating or damaging.

    1)   **Ameliorating waste.** If the tenant improves the premises (adds a room, paints the house, etc.), he commits ameliorating waste. At common law he was liable for this. The modern cases do not hold tenants liable for this as long as the value of the premises is not lessened.

    2)   **Damaging waste.** If a tenant substantially damages the premises, he is liable. The injury must be one which extends beyond the end of the lease term. In certain conditions a landlord may get an injunction to stop the damage. A tenant is not liable for ordinary wear and tear.

    3)   **Involuntary waste.** Also known as permissive waste, this occurs when the premises are allowed to fall into disrepair.

c.   **Duty to pay rent.** Traditionally, the tenant had the obligation to pay the rent called for in the lease whether or not the landlord performed his part of the lease. If the value of the rent is not specified, it is presumed the tenant must pay a reasonable rental value. If the lease is illegal, the tenant must pay a reasonable rental value. He need not pay the price called for in the lease. At common law, the tenant was liable for rent even if the premises burned to the ground. Today, most jurisdictions excuse further performance from both parties in cases of accidental destruction.

Albert M. Greenfield & Co. v. Kolea

d.   **Modern approach--Albert M. Greenfield & Co. v. Kolea,** 380 A.2d 758 (Pa. 1976).

    1)   **Facts.** Suit for rent due under two leases. Lessor (P) executed two leases with lessee (D), leasing to D a one-story garage and an adjoining vacant lot. About a year later, fire completely destroyed the building covered by the first lease. Thereafter, D refused to pay rent under either lease. P sued and won. The appellate court upheld the judgment. D appealed.

    2)   **Issue.** Is the common law rule that holds, absent contractual provisions to the contrary, the lessee liable for rent if the premises is destroyed, outmoded?

    3)   **Held.** Yes. Judgment reversed.

        a)   Generally, a tenant is under the duty to pay rent even if the entire premises is destroyed. There are two exceptions to this rule:

            (1)   If only a portion of a building is leased and the entire building is destroyed, the tenant need no longer pay rent. The theory behind this is that it is the use of the building which has been bargained for.

            (2)   The second exception is founded on the contract doctrine of impossibility of performance. Under this doctrine if a contract

contemplates the existence of specific property to carry out the purposes of the agreement, and if, without the fault of either party, the property is destroyed, all contractual obligations relating to the property end.

    (3)   "Impossibility" does not mean strict impossibility, but impracticability because of extreme and unreasonable difficulty.

    b)   It is obvious that the purpose of the lease of the building (lease 1) became impossible due to the fire. The reason for lease 2 (the vacant lot, which was used for car sales) was made impossible when the adjacent building was destroyed.

    c)   The lower court erred in applying the outmoded doctrine and making D pay rent for the vacant land. The law should change to conform with today's need. It is no longer reasonable to assume that, in the absence of a lease provision to the contrary, the lessee should bear the loss. In the future, the courts should look to the intent of the parties.

4)   Concurrences.

    a)   (Robert, J.). I concur because the majority reaches the same result as the Restatement (Second) of Property, section 5.4.

    b)   (Nix, J.). The old common law rule that the destruction of a building by accidental fire is no defense to a claim for rent is no longer viable. I concur with the majority since its view reflects section 5.4 of the Restatement (Second) of Property.

D.   GOVERNMENT INTERVENTION

1.   **Selection of Tenants.** Traditionally, a landlord could lease or not lease to whomever he pleased for whatever reason he chose. Discrimination based on sex, race, and the like were possible in every case. Changes began by laws passed shortly after the Civil War.

    a.   **Civil Rights Act of 1866.** This Act prohibited racial, and only racial, discrimination in the leasing and selling of real and personal property. An aggrieved party could sue the landlord or seller for an injunction or damages.

    b.   **Fair Housing Act of 1968.** This congressional Act prohibits discrimination in selling or renting based on race, color, religion, or national origin. The Act was amended to prohibit discrimination based on sex in 1974.

1) **Exceptions.** The Act provides for certain exceptions. In the case of single-family dwellings a seller or lessor can discriminate if he owns fewer than four such dwellings, does not use a broker, and does not advertise in a manner which indicates his intent to discriminate. "Mrs. Murphy's" exception permits a resident owner of a building with four or fewer rooms or apartments (depending on whether it is the room or apartment for lease) to discriminate. Note that "Mrs. Murphy" must live in one of the four units, and she cannot advertise that she discriminates.

2) **Remedies.** Only the United States Attorney General (if she wishes), HUD (in certain cases), or the aggrieved party may sue the discriminating landlord or seller.

3) **Prima facie case and burden of proof.** Once the aggrieved party makes out a prima facie case, the burden of proof shifts to the landlord or seller.

2. **Rent Control.** The shortage of affordable housing in many areas has led to an escalation in rent. Because of the serious impact on the public generally, many jurisdictions adopted rent control regulations. The courts have generally upheld these regulations, so long as the interests of landlords are fairly considered.

Chicago Board of Realtors, Inc. v. City of Chicago

3. **The Chicago Ordinance--Chicago Board of Realtors, Inc. v. City of Chicago,** 819 F.2d 732 (7th Cir. 1987).

a. **Facts.** In 1986 the Chicago Board of Realtors (Ps) challenged a newly enacted Residential Landlord and Tenant Ordinance which codified the implied warranty of habitability and established new landlord responsibilities and tenant rights. Ps argued that the ordinance violated the Contracts Clause, procedural and substantive due process, the void-for-vagueness doctrine, equal protection, the Takings Clause, and the Commerce Clause. The district court denied a motion for preliminary injunction. Ps appealed, contesting the court's ruling with regard to all but the Takings Clause and the Commerce Clause issues. The court of appeals affirmed. Ps appeal.

b. **Issue.** Is the ordinance sufficiently specific and, giving due deference to the legislative judgment, sufficiently reasonable in light of its stated purpose to promote public health, safety, and welfare?

c. **Held.** Yes. Judgment affirmed.

Note: The court's constitutional analysis written by Judge Cudahy is not presented; the policy analysis contained in a separately filed opinion follows.

1) Judge Cudahy's opinion does not make the strongest case that can be made for the reasonableness of the ordinance. The stated purpose of the ordinance is to promote the public health, safety, and welfare and the quality of housing in Chicago. This is neither its real purpose nor its likely effect.

2) Forbidding landlords to charge interest at market rates on large rent payments does not meet the purpose or improve the quality of the

housing stock. Its effect will be to reduce landlord's resources and the resources they devote to improving housing.

3) The provisions requiring that interest be paid on security deposits and that interest be kept in Illinois banks are equally remote from the stated purpose. Their only apparent rationale is to transfer wealth from landlords and out-of-state banks to tenants and local banks—making this an unedifying example of class legislation and economic protectionism rolled into one.

4) The ordinance is not in the interest of poor people. It puts no cap on rents. The beneficiaries will be middle-class people who buy housing because the supply will be increased as landlords convert rental to owner housing, people willing to pay higher rent, and more affluent tenants who will be less likely to be late with rent or to abuse the right of a tenant to withhold rent. Landlords, out-of-state banks, and the poorest class of tenants will be the losers.

5) The literature dealing with the effects of government regulation of the market for rental housing shows that the market for rental housing behaves as economic theory predicts; if price is depressed artificially, or if landlords' costs are increased artificially, supply falls and the poorer and newer tenants are hurt.

4. Government Subsidized Housing.

a. **Legislation.** The federal government became involved in housing in the 1930s. The United States Housing Act lets the local public housing authority ("PHA") sell tax-exempt government bonds to raise revenue. The revenue is used to construct local low-income housing. Currently this scheme is used by private parties who construct public housing.

b. **Regulations.** Of course, numerous regulations need to be complied with in building public housing. Building sites must be approved by the local government in accordance with federal guidelines. Regulations require that building sites be located outside areas of high minority concentration. PHAs, on the other hand, are more eager to locate the housing in racially segregated areas. The aid of federal courts has been invoked to force local compliance with the regulations.

c. **Local approval.** A state's constitutional requirement that a low-rent housing project can be developed only after approval by a majority of the local residents has been upheld. The court held that the constitutional requirement was neutral on its face and not in fact aimed at racial minorities. Economic, but not racial, discrimination is permissible.

d. **Admission to public housing.** The PHA is free to decide its own admission requirements with the exception that preference is to be given veterans and persons displaced by urban renewal. Some courts have held that a person is entitled to an informal hearing on his eligibility.

e. **Rent increases in public housing.** It has been held that a tenant's right to low-rent housing is a property right that is subject to due process. With this as a rationale, courts have held that tenants are entitled to exercise certain rights prior to rent increases.

f. **Eviction.** Tenants may be evicted for destroying property or for being loud and unruly, etc. They may not be evicted for belonging to a tenants' organization or for exercising their constitutional rights.

IV. VOLUNTARY TRANSFERS OF PROPERTY

A. SALES AND GIFTS

1. **Contracts of Sale.** Typically, the sale of land involves two steps. First a contract to sell/purchase the real property is signed. In it is specified the date for the second step, closing. At closing the seller gives the buyer a deed to the property and the buyer gives the seller the agreed-upon consideration. A discussion of this two-step method of conveying must begin with the basic premise that the transactions must conform to the Statute of Frauds which requires, in essence, that the agreement to sell/purchase be in writing.

   a. **Statute of Frauds.** The Statute of Frauds provides that no interest in real property can be conveyed, encumbered, etc., without a writing signed by the party to be charged. The "party to be charged" is the party against whom it is asserted there is a contract. The writing can consist of several documents which, when taken together as a whole, evidence an agreement affecting real property. Thus, formal contracts are not required.

   b. **Essential terms.** The writing must contain all the essential terms for the agreement. "Essential terms" are words of art meaning the following terms: description of the property sufficient to make clear what property the parties have in mind, price (some courts will imply a "reasonable price" or "market price"), the parties, and the other terms and conditions pertinent to the transaction (manner of payment, etc.).

   c. **Specific performance.** Since all real property is unique, courts will use their equity powers to compel a buyer or a seller to go through with a deal, rather than award damages. The aggrieved party must ask for specific performance.

   d. **Oral revocation.** Most states hold that the Statute of Frauds applies only to the making of a contract affecting an interest in land and will thus allow subsequent oral modification or revocation of the contract.

   e. **Time of performance.** Unless the contract specifies that time is of the essence, if the contract is not performed on the date called for in the agreement, each party has a "reasonable" time in which to complete its performance.

   f. **Who prepares the contract?--State v. Buyers Service Co.,** 292 S.C. 426, 357 S.E.2d 15 (1987).

State v. Buyers Service Co.

      1) **Facts.** Buyers Service (D) is a commercial title company that also assists prospective property buyers referred by local real estate agents. D prepares the closing package and conducts closings without an attorney present. The State (P) brought this action, alleging D has engaged in the unauthorized practice of law by: (i) providing reports, opinions, or certificates as to the status of titles to real estate and mortgage liens; (ii) preparing documents affecting title to real property; (iii) handling closings;

(iv) recording legal documents; and (v) advertising to the public that it may handle conveyancing and real estate closings. The circuit court issued a declaratory judgment that D has illegally engaged in the practice of law and D was enjoined from performing (i), (ii), and (v) above, and from giving legal advice during a closing. Both P and D appeal.

2) **Issue.** Did the court properly enjoin D from performing future acts deemed to constitute the practice of law?

3) **Held.** No. Affirmed in part and reversed in part.

a) The preparation of deeds, mortgages, notes and other legal instruments related to mortgage loans and other real property transfers requires skill, competence, and ethics. Only the state supreme court has the power to determine, through a bar examination, yearly continuing education requirements, and the Code of Professional Responsibility, who has that skill.

b) Preparation of title abstracts for persons other than attorneys constitutes the practice of law. The examination of title requires expert legal knowledge and skill. Such activities must be supervised by an attorney.

c) Real estate closings give rise to legal questions and there is no practical way of assuring that lay persons conducting a closing will not attempt to offer a few words of explanation. Closings should be conducted under an attorney's supervision.

d) The circuit court order permits D to continue to record documents. We agree with P that this constitutes the practice of law. Recording is an aspect of conveyancing and the appropriate sequence of recording is critical to protect a buyer's title.

Hickey
v. Green

g. **Specific performance--Hickey v. Green,** 14 Mass. App. Ct. 671, 442 N.E.2d 37 (1982).

1) **Facts.** The Hickeys (Ps) put a deposit on D's lot after orally agreeing to a sale for $15,000. D accepted the $500 check, marked on the back with "Deposit . . . Subject to variance from Town of Plymouth." No variance was required and Ps told D to fill in the name of the payee which had been left blank because of uncertainty as to whether D or her brother and agent were to receive the check. D held the check, did not indorse it, and did not fill in the payee's name. Ps sold their house and accepted a deposit check. D told Ps she had decided to sell the lot to another for $16,000; Ps offered D $16,000. D refused. Ps sought specific performance. D claimed the Statute of Frauds barred relief. The court found for Ps based on stipulated facts and documents. D appeals.

2) **Issue.** May a contract for transfer of an interest in land be specifically enforced if there was no compliance with the Statute of Frauds if the party seeking enforcement reasonably relied on the contract and has so changed her position that injustice can be avoided only by specific performance?

3) **Held.** Yes. Remanded.

a) The rule is set forth in Restatement (Second) of Contracts, section 129 (1981).

b) In the present case, D knew Ps were planning to sell their house and Ps did so rapidly without obtaining any adequate memorandum of the terms of what appears to have been a quick sale. Ps relied on D's oral promise and less than 10 days later accepted a deposit on their house.

c) Ps bound themselves so that to avoid transfer of their home they might have had to engage in costly litigation.

d) D does not deny that she made the oral contract and the promise on which Ps relied and that she promptly repudiated it. In equity, D's conduct cannot be condoned.

e) Neither party has shown expectation of a written agreement.

f) No public interest will be violated if D is held to her bargain by the principles of equitable estoppel subject to the following: (i) Ps have already conveyed or are still obligated to convey their property, and (ii) the case is remanded for the trial judge to require D to convey the property only upon payment to her in cash of the balance of the purchase price within a stated time. If Ps have no obligation to sell their house, the trial judge may require full restitution to P of all reasonable costs in respect to this transaction rather than specific performance.

2. **Marketable Title.** Absent an express provision to the contrary, it is implied in every contract for the sale of land that the seller will furnish buyer "marketable title" to the property at closing. This is a title which is reasonably free from doubts; one which a prudent person would be willing to buy. Marketable title does not mean perfect title; it means one that is good enough for a title insurance company to be willing to insure in the regular course of business.

a. **Good record title.** Less frequently contracts will call for the seller to furnish good record title. This means that the seller must furnish good title based on the documents in the chain of title. It precludes title by adverse possession.

b. **Defects in title.** There are numerous possible defects in title. Some of the more common ones include a defect in one of the instruments in the chain of title, private encumbrances, unrecorded easements, covenants, and restrictions on the use of the property.

c. **Curing title defects.** Normally, the seller has until closing to cure any defects in title. Minor defects such as an unrecorded release of lien may be remedied by the seller setting aside from the purchase price sufficient funds to cover the lien until he procures the release. Generally, the seller must deliver the property unencumbered (no outstanding mortgages or liens). If the seller is willing and able to discharge the mortgage at closing, then the mortgage does not render title unmarketable. Similarly, if an easement benefits the property, it does not make the title unmarketable. Zoning restrictions do not, except in unusual cases, make title unmarketable. Finally, easements and the like which are shown on official maps may make title unmarketable.

d. **Violations of building codes and zoning restrictions.** If there are violations of zoning restrictions for which the government can demand correction, title is usually held to be unmarketable. The policy behind this is that the law is loath to require someone to buy into the possibility of a lawsuit.

Lohmeyer
v. Bower

e. **Violation of public and private restrictions--Lohmeyer v. Bower,** 227 P.2d 102 (Kan. 1951).

1) **Facts.** Action to rescind contract to buy real property. Lohmeyer (P) contracted to buy a house. The contract provided that Bower (D), the seller, was to provide good merchantable title subject to all restrictions of record. In the event there were imperfections of title, D was to have a reasonable time to correct them. The abstract of title showed that the original subdivider imposed a restriction requiring that any home erected on the lot be two stories in height (the existing home was one story). Further, under a zoning ordinance no frame building could be erected within three feet of the lot line (the existing house was within 18 inches of the lot line). D offered to buy for P two feet of the adjoining lot so that the house was more than three feet from the new lot line. P refused this offer and brought suit to rescind the contract. D countersued for specific performance. The trial court found for D, awarding specific performance. P appealed.

2) **Issue.** Does the violation of private and public restrictions render title unmarketable?

3) **Held.** Yes. The trial court is reversed.

a) This case requires a determination of (i) whether the encumbrances to which the property was subject made the title unmarketable; and (ii) if so, did they fall within an exception provided for by the contract?

b) P does not base his suit upon the fact that there existed both a private restrictive covenant on the property (the limitation as to building height) and a public zoning restriction (the three-foot requirement), but upon the violation of the two restrictions.

c) Two general rules applicable here are (i) the existence of municipal restrictions, such as zoning, is not a ground for a buyer to rescind a contract, and (ii) private covenants or restrictions, such as the height requirement, may constitute encumbrances rendering title unmarketable.

d) A "merchantable" (or "marketable") title is one which is free from reasonable doubt, and a title is doubtful and unmarketable if it exposes the party holding it to the possibility of litigation. Of course, defects in title must be substantial, not minor. Immaterial defects do not diminish the value of the property and are no grounds for a buyer to rescind the contract.

e) It is clear that the two violations here exposed P to the hazard of litigation. Thus, D could not convey marketable title. While the contract provided that the conveyance was to be made subject to all restrictions, that provision referred to the existence of the restrictions. It did not permit the violation of the existing restrictions.

f) On these grounds, the trial court erred in not granting P the relief sought.

f. **Adverse possession and its impact on the marketability of title--Conklin v. Davi,** 388 A.2d 598 (N.J. 1978).

1) **Facts.** Counterclaim seeking rescission of a contract to purchase residential property. Seller (P) contracted to sell a house to Purchaser (D). The contract called for P to furnish marketable and insurable title. D discovered that P had obtained title to part of the property through adverse possession. D refused to go through with the deal, claiming that P should have either (i) obtained a deed to that portion from the present record title holder, or (ii) obtained record title by an action to quiet title. P sued D for specific performance. D counterclaimed seeking rescission of the contract. Prior to trial P dismissed its action for specific performance, leaving only D's counterclaim to be decided. At the conclusion of D's case, the trial court granted P's motion for judgment. D appealed. The intermediate appellate court reversed the trial court and ordered a judgment in D's favor rather than a new trial. P appealed.

2) **Issue.** Is a title obtained by adverse possession per se unmarketable?

3) **Held.** No.

a) When a prospective seller's title is grounded on adverse possession he may either:

(1) Perfect record title (obtain record title from former owner, action to quiet title, action to concede outstanding encumbrance, etc.); or

(2) Choose to enter into a contract of sale hoping to convince the purchaser or, if necessary, the court, that his estimate of the marketability of the title is justified. This is the course P chose.

b) The contract did not require perfect title of record, but rather "marketable" title.

(1) A title is marketable if it is free from reasonable doubt. It need not be free from every doubt.

(2) The law will imply that a title must be marketable even if a contract fails to so specify.

(3) Further, when a court is left to determine marketability of title, it does so not at the time of closing, but at the time of the final judgment. The question is, what kind of title will the purchaser get if the court forces title on him?

    c)   Evidence showed that a title insurance company was willing to insure the title to the property. Thus, that contractual provision was fulfilled.

    d)   If title by adverse possession is clearly established, the title is marketable. Hence, on retrial P must establish marketable title by adverse possession by proving:

        (1)   That the outstanding claimants, were they to assert a claim, would not succeed; and,

        (2)   There is no real likelihood such a claim will ever be asserted.

    e)   The judgment at the intermediate appellate court is reversed and a new trial ordered.

    4)   **Comment.** Since P had shown that the title was insurable, as required by the contract, the only remaining issue on retrial was the marketability of title. It is important to note that one prong of the test as to marketability is the likelihood of there being a lawsuit. Thus, if it is clear that the person claiming title by adverse possession would win, if a lawsuit on the title were filed, the court will not require a purchaser to buy the property. The seller still must show that such a suit is unlikely. This is consistent with the axiom of contract law that a court will not force a prospective buyer of goods to also "buy" a lawsuit with the goods.

3.   **Risk of Loss.** Because the property is subject to being damaged or destroyed between the time the contract is entered and the transaction is closed, allocation of the risk of loss is an important matter to be resolved.

    a.   **Equitable conversion.** The two-step method of conveying, mentioned above, causes certain problems. In order to solve these problems, the doctrine of equitable conversion is often applied by the courts. Between the date of the contract to sell and closing, the doctrine steps in and treats the buyer as having title to the property. The doctrine treats the buyer as the equitable owner of the land with the seller the legal owner. The seller's interest is deemed security for the debt owed him by the buyer. The buyer still does not have the right of possession until closing.

    b.   **Alternative approaches.** The majority rule is that once the buyer acquires equitable title, the risk of loss passes to him. Thus, if the building burns down after the signing of the purchase agreement but prior to closing, and the buyer does not have the premises insured, it is his loss. He must still pay full price for the property. The minority rule is directly contra. Risk of loss remains with the seller until closing. Under the minority view, if the damages are slight, the buyer must still go through with the sale but he is entitled to have the purchase price abated by the value of the damages.

Stambovsky v. Ackley

4.   **Duty to Disclose Defects--Stambovsky v. Ackley,** 572 N.Y.S.2d 672 (1991).

    a.   **Facts.** P discovered that the house he had recently contracted to purchase was possessed by poltergeists seen by D and her family for nine years.

The apparitions were reported in *Reader's Digest* and the local press, and D promoted the house's reputation, but P was not a local resident. P sought rescission of the contract for sale. The supreme court dismissed P's complaint, holding that P had no remedy at law in this jurisdiction. P appeals.

b. **Issue.** May the remedy of rescission be properly applied to the doctrine of caveat emptor where a condition that has been created by the seller materially impairs the value of the contract and is peculiarly within the knowledge of the seller or unlikely to be discovered by a prudent purchaser exercising due care with respect to the subject transaction?

c. **Held.** Yes. Reversed; cause of action reinstated.

1) The doctrine of caveat emptor imposes no duty on the vendor to disclose any information concerning the premises unless there is a confidential or fiduciary relationship between the parties or some conduct on the part of the seller which constitutes "active concealment."

2) The doctrine requires the buyer to act prudently and operates to bar the purchaser who fails to exercise due care from seeking rescission.

3) D is estopped to deny the existence of the apparitions and, as a matter of law, the house is haunted.

4) The reputation of the house goes to the very essence of the bargain between the parties, greatly impairing both the value of the property and its potential for resale. The extent of this impairment may be presumed for the purpose of reviewing the disposition of this motion and represents merely an issue of fact for resolution at trial.

5) The most meticulous inspection would not reveal the presence of poltergeists or unearth the property's ghoulish reputation. There is no sound policy reason to deny P relief for failing to discover a state of affairs that the most prudent purchaser would not be expected to even contemplate.

6) D's contention that the merger or "as is" clause in the contract of sale bars P's recovery is unavailing. Even an express disclaimer will not be given effect where the facts are peculiarly within the knowledge of the party invoking it. Here, the merger clause expressly disclaims only representations made with respect to the physical condition of the premises and as broad as its language is, it does not extend to paranormal phenomena. Finally, if the language of the contract is to be construed as broadly as D urges to encompass the presence of poltergeists in the house, it cannot be said that she has delivered the premises "vacant" in accordance with her obligations.

d. **Dissent.** The existence of poltergeists is not binding on D or on this court.

5. **Material Defect Known to Seller--Johnson v. Davis,** 480 So. 2d 625 (Fla. 1985).

a. **Facts.** The Davises (Ps) agreed to purchase the Johnsons' (Ds') three-year-old home for $310,000. Ps made a deposit of $5,000 and the contract required another $26,000 deposit to be made within five days. One provision of the contract permitted Ps to obtain a report from a roofer verifying that the roof was watertight. Ds were to pay for any necessary repairs to the roof. Before Ps made the $26,000 deposit, they noticed indications of leaks in the roof. Ps told Ds that the window had had a minor problem that had been corrected and Ps paid the deposit. Several days later, it rained heavily and Ps saw water coming in in the areas they had pointed out to Ds. Ds hired two roofers who stated they could fix the leaks for under $1,000; Ps' roofers discovered the roof was inherently defective and would require replacement for $15,000. Ps sued for breach of contract, fraud, and misrepresentation, seeking rescission. Ds counter-claimed for liquidated damages. The trial court awarded Ps their $26,000 but awarded Ds $5,000. Both parties appealed, and the appellate court reversed the trial court award for Ds. Ds appeal.

b. **Issue.** May the seller of a home who fails to tell the buyer of a material defect known to the seller be liable for damages caused by the fraudulent concealment?

c. **Held.** Yes. Judgment of appellate court affirmed.

1) The trial court did not make any findings of fact, but its judgment indicates that it found Ds did not breach the contract. The contract itself did not require Ds to do anything more than repair the roof. Ds never refused to make the repairs, and Ps never demanded that the leaks be repaired. Thus, Ds did not breach the contract.

2) Ds' statements about the indications of a leak were a fraudulent misrepresentation, however. Relief for fraudulent misrepresentation is available when (i) the seller makes a false statement concerning a material fact, (ii) the seller knows the representation is false, (iii) the seller intended that the buyer rely on the representation, and (iv) the buyer is injured by its reliance on the representation.

3) After Ps made the $5,000 deposit, Ds told Ps there was no problem with the roof. Ds then received the $26,000 deposit when Ps relied on Ds' representation. Ds were thus obligated to return the $26,000 deposit. The fact that Ds' misrepresentation was made after the contract was signed does not change the result because it was made before the contract was executed by conveyance of the property.

4) Under common law, there was no liability for nonfeasance. Ds failure to tell Ps of the latent defect would not be actionable. However, a failure to disclose a material fact when it is intended to induce a false belief is close to an affirmative representation. Modern notions of justice and fair dealing require that the doctrine of caveat emptor be restricted. Other jurisdictions have held a home seller liable for failing to disclose material defects of which he was aware. This is the better approach and should be applied in Florida. Ac-

cordingly, Ds' failure to tell Ps of the roof problems from the outset constitutes fraudulent concealment and Ps are entitled to the return of the $5,000 deposit.

6. **Warranties from the Seller.** The common law rigidly applied the doctrine of caveat emptor. Many modern courts have overruled the common law and held that there is an implied warranty that the building is fit for the use contemplated by both of the parties. This warranty is often implied in housing which was fairly recently constructed.

    a. **Implied warranty of workmanlike quality--Lempke v. Dagenais**, 130 N.H. 782, 547 A.2d 290 (1988).

        1) **Facts.** The Lempkes' (Ps') predecessors in title contracted with D to build a garage. The original owners sold the property to Ps within six months after construction. Ps noticed structural problems with the garage shortly after the sale. Ps contend that separation of trusses from the roof of the garage was a latent defect that could not have been discovered until the separation and bowing became noticeable from the exterior. Ps contracted D, who agreed to make repairs but never completed them. Ps brought suit; D filed a motion to dismiss which was granted. Ps appeal.

        2) **Issue.** May a subsequent purchaser of real property sue the builder/contractor on the theory of implied warranty of workmanlike quality for latent defects that cause economic loss, absent privity of contract?

        3) **Held.** Yes. Reversed and remanded.

            a) Privity of contract is not necessary for latent defects that manifest themselves within a reasonable time after purchase and that cause economic harm. To require privity would be to defeat the purpose of the implied warranty of good workmanship and could leave innocent homeowners without a remedy.

            b) *Ellis v. Morris*, 128 N.H. 358 (1986), upon which the trial court based its dismissal, remains controlling on Ps' claim for negligence, but denial of relief to subsequent purchasers on an implied warranty theory in *Ellis* was predicated on the court's adherence to the requirement of privity in a contract action and on the fear that to allow recovery without privity would impose unlimited liability on builders and contractors.

            c) Many other courts have found that implied warranty, whether based on contract or tort law, exists independently, imposed by the operation of law on the basis of public policy because of the parties' relationship, the nature of the transaction, and the surrounding circumstances. We agree.

            d) Recovery for purely economic harm in these circumstances has been allowed in other courts which have found that to draw a line between mere economic loss and personal injury is without merit. We agree that there is no rational reason for such a distinction. The vendee has a right to expect to receive that for which he has bargained.

e) Our extension of liability is limited to latent defects and to a limited period of time. The plaintiff has the burden to show that the defect was caused by the defendant's workmanship. The builder also has defenses such as the defects being the result of age and wear and tear, not attributable to him, or that previous owners have made substantial changes.

B. DEEDS

1. **Requirements.** Usually the instrument used for transferring an interest in land is a deed, although sometimes more informal instruments may satisfy the Statute of Frauds. In the case of deeds the grantor, and only the grantor, must sign the instrument. It is a very good idea to have the grantor acknowledge his signature before a notary public so that the deed will comply with the recording acts. If it does not so comply, it cannot be recorded. Often the signature of the spouse will be required. It is always a good idea to have the spouse sign. This avoids problems caused by the spouse's right to community property, homestead, dower, curtesy, etc. As for the exact words required, any words evidencing an intent to make a transfer will suffice. (The common law required certain words of art. These technicalities have been rejected everywhere.) Further, the deed must name an ascertainable grantee ("John," "all my surviving children," etc.). Finally, the property to be conveyed must be described.

   a. **Consideration.** A deed does not require consideration to support it. A grantor may give the property away.

   b. **Failures in the description of the property.** Land can be described by metes and bounds, recorded plat, the name of the property, and the street address. (One must be careful in describing property by street address. Often mistakes are made when assigning house numbers. "1234 Lombard St." may legally be the address of the house next door.) Extrinsic evidence is normally admissible to clear up any ambiguity in the description of the property conveyed. The common law classified ambiguities as either latent or patent. A patent ambiguity (one on the face of the deed) could not be resolved by turning to extrinsic evidence. A latent ambiguity (one not on the face of the deed) could always be resolved by turning to extrinsic evidence.

   c. **Example.** If a deed ambiguously describes property as "1234 Loma Linda Blvd." in one place and a paragraph or two later refers to the property as "2134 Loma Linda Blvd.," this constitutes a patent defect. If a deed refers to "my cabin in the mountains" and the grantor has two different mountain cabins, this is a latent ambiguity and extrinsic evidence would be admissible to show which cabin the grantor meant to convey.

   d. **Modern trend.** The modern trend is to admit extrinsic evidence to resolve both kinds of ambiguities.

2. **Warranties of Title.**

   a. **Introduction.** Almost all deeds contain what attorneys refer to as the "usual covenants." These covenants run from the seller of real property to the buyer. There are six "usual" covenants, although one of them is actually unusual in America.

   b. **Types of deeds warranting title.**

      1) **Warranty deed.** This is the usual type of deed and it contains the "usual" covenants. It warrants title.

      2) **Special warranty deed.** This type of deed contains the "usual" covenants but warrants title only from defects arising during the time the grantor has held the land. By contrast, a general warranty deed has no such limitation.

      3) **Quitclaim deed.** This form of deed does not warrant anything. It only transfers whatever interest the grantor has, or may have, in the property.

   c. **The usual covenants.**

      1) **Present covenants.** These are covenants which in essence state "I, the grantor, warrant that as of the date of this deed, I have not breached this particular covenant." Such covenants are breached, if at all, when the conveyance is made. Thus, the statute of limitations for these covenants begins to run as of the date of the conveyance.

         a) **Covenant of seisin.** The seller covenants he owns the property conveyed.

         b) **Covenant of right to convey.** The seller warrants that he has the right to convey the property. For example, this covenant would be breached if the seller had the property in an irrevocable trust which gave only the trustee the right to convey.

         c) **Covenant against encumbrances.** The seller promises that there are no easements, covenants, mortgages, or liens on the property. As a practical matter almost all property is subject to an encumbrance of some sort. What the seller will do is warrant against encumbrances "except as enumerated herein."

      2) **Future covenants.** These are continuing covenants that may be breached at the moment of conveyance or anytime thereafter. The statute of limitations does not run until there is an actual breach.

         a) **Covenant of quiet enjoyment.** The seller warrants that the buyer will not be disturbed in his possession of the property by the lawful claim of a third party.

         b) **Covenant of warranty.** This covenant meshes closely with the covenant of quiet enjoyment. The seller warrants that the title to the property is good and that, as grantor, he will defend at his own cost any suit from a party claiming paramount title.

    c)   **Covenant of further assurances.** This is the unusual covenant. It is rare in America and more common in England. By this covenant the seller promises to perform whatever acts are necessary to perfect the buyer's title to the property.

  3)   **Merger.** Because land sales in the United States involve two steps, sometimes there is a discrepancy between what is promised in the contract for sale and the deed. The general rule is that, absent provisions in the deed to the contrary, the contract of sale and the deed merge, leaving only those covenants which are contained in the deed. The modern trend is to hold that acceptance of the deed does not bar a suit on the contractual promises.

3.   **Breach of Covenants.** Present covenants are breached, if ever, at the time of the conveyance. Future covenants may be breached anytime in the future. Generally, present covenants are "personal" and hence do not run with the land. Future covenants do run with the land. A minority of courts hold that the covenant against encumbrances runs with the land. From the definitions of the covenants above, it is fairly clear what constitutes a breach of one of these covenants. For example, if there is an encumbrance at the time of the conveyance, the covenant against encumbrances is breached.

Brown
v. Lober

  a.   **Present versus future covenants--Brown v. Lober,** 389 N.E.2d 1188 (Ill. 1979).

    1)   **Facts.** The Bosts bought 80 acres of land in 1947, the owner retaining a 2/3 interest in the mineral rights. In 1957 the Bosts conveyed the land to the Browns (Ps) under a general warranty deed containing no exceptions. Ps were going to convey the mineral rights to Consolidated Coal Co. for $6,000. Upon discovering that they had only 1/3 of the mineral rights, Ps sold that 1/3 interest for $2,000 and sued Lober (D), executor of the estate of the Bosts (both deceased), for $4,000 for breach of the covenant of quiet enjoyment. The 10-year statute of limitations had run, barring suit on the present covenants. The trial court found for D. The intermediate appellate court reversed. D appeals.

    2)   **Issue.** Does the warranty of quiet enjoyment constitute a warranty that the grantor is the owner of the entire estate as conveyed?

    3)   **Held.** No. Judgment reversed.

      a)   The question is whether P has alleged facts sufficient to constitute a constructive eviction. P contends that when he, a covenantee, fails in his efforts to sell an interest in land because he does not own what his warranty deed purported to convey, he has suffered a constructive eviction. We reject this argument.

      b)   The covenant of quiet enjoyment only guarantees the covenantee (buyer) that his peaceable possession of the land will not be taken from him. It does not guarantee to the covenantee that there is no one with a paramount title. Thus, if the covenantee never attempts to occupy the land, his possession can never be other than peaceful.

c) To possess a mineral estate, one must undertake the actual removal of the minerals from the ground. Possession of the surface does not carry possession of the minerals. Since no one has undertaken to remove the minerals, the mineral estate is "vacant." Accordingly, until such time as one holding paramount title interferes with Ps' right of possession (*e.g.*, begins mining coal), there can be no constructive eviction, and no breach of the covenant of quiet enjoyment.

d) The protection of the covenant of quiet enjoyment should not be extended to an area governed by another covenant (that of seisin). Here, the fact that the Bosts had only a 1/3 interest in the mineral rights was of public record. Yet Ps failed to bring suit within the 10 years following delivery of the deed.

4) **Comment.** An action for breach of a covenant of seisin lies whenever there is a defect in title. In Illinois, the statute of limitations was 10 years for breach of that covenant.

b. **Latent land use violation--Frimberger v. Anzellotti,** 25 Conn. App. 401, 594 A.2d 1029 (1991).

Frimberger v. Anzellotti

1) **Facts.** D's brother and predecessor in title conveyed to D by quitclaim deed property upon which the brother had built a bulkhead, filled the property and constructed a dwelling encroaching on the tidal wetlands boundary. D conveyed the property to P by warranty deed, free and clear of all encumbrances but subject to all building, building line and zoning restrictions, easements and restrictions of record. P discovered a violation of a land use statute when he engaged an engineer to perform repairs. The Department of Environmental Protection (DEP) informed D that he would have to submit an application to DEP demonstrating the necessity of maintaining the bulkhead and fill within the tidal wetlands in order to correct the violation. Instead, P filed suit, claiming breach of warranty against encumbrances and innocent misrepresentation. The trial court determined that the area had been filled in without obtaining the necessary permits, and found for P. D appeals.

2) **Issue.** Does a latent violation of a restrictive land use statute or ordinance, that exists at the time the fee is conveyed, constitute a breach of the warranty deed covenant against encumbrances?

3) **Held.** No. Reversed.

a) Latent violations of state or municipal land use regulations that do not appear on the land records, that are unknown to the seller of the property, as to which the agency charged with enforcement has taken no official action to compel compliance at the time the deed was executed, and that have not ripened into an interest that can be recorded on the land records do not constitute an encumbrance for the purpose of the deed warranty.

b) Such a conceptual enlargement of the covenant against encumbrances would create uncertainty and confusion in the law of conveyancing and title insurance because neither a title search nor a physical examination of the premises would disclose the violation.

c) P never filed an application; thus any damages P may have suffered were speculative.

d) The proper way to deal with violations of governmental regulations is by contract provisions or language in the deed.

e) Because we have held that the warranty of a covenant against encumbrances was not violated, no misrepresentation was made.

c. **Remote grantees--Rockafellor v. Gray,** 191 N.W. 107 (Iowa 1922).

1) **Facts.** Doffing conveyed 80 acres to Rockafellor (P). P assumed Doffing's mortgage to Gray (D). P subsequently defaulted and D foreclosed on the mortgage. Connelly purchased the land at a sheriff's sale and was given a sheriff's deed. He in turn sold the land to Dixon for $4,000 by means of a deed containing the usual covenants of warranty. Dixon sold the land to Hansen & Gregory (H & G) for $7,000 by means of a deed containing the usual covenants of warranty. Subsequently P had the sheriff's deed to Connelly set aside and the foreclosure proceedings declared void. H & G sued Connelly, the remote grantor, for breach of warranty of seisin and recovered an award of $4,000. Connelly appealed on the ground that since he had no title to the land (due to the void foreclosure) and had never entered in possession, the warranty of seisin could not run with the land to a remote grantee.

2) **Issue.** Does covenant of seisin run to a remote grantee even if the original grantor never had actual possession of the land?

3) **Held.** Yes. Judgment affirmed.

a) We have previously adopted the minority rule (English Rule) and held that a warranty of seisin runs with the land to remote grantees and is broken the instant a defective conveyance is delivered. (The majority rule is called the American Rule.)

b) Because on the day Connelly conveyed the land to Dixon he had no title and no possession of the premises, the covenant of seisin was breached. The covenant ran with the land to H & G, Dixon's successors.

(1) H & G filed their cross-petition within the 10-year statute of limitations.

(2) The original convenantee, here Connelly, is bound even if he does not have title or actual possession at the time of the conveyance.

c) This still leaves the issue of whether the covenant of seisin runs with the land since the original covenantee, Connelly, was never in possession of the premises. Some courts hold that possession (seisin) itself is what causes the covenant of seisin to run with the land. We reject this hypertechnical theory.

d) As to the amount of the judgment ($4,000, with interest thereon from the date of the conveyance to Dixon):

(1) Proof of actual consideration would be admissible only in a suit between the grantor Connelly and the original grantee (Dixon).

(2) In all other cases the consideration recited in the deed is a conclusive admission by a defendant of the land's value. (Connelly contended that although the deed recited consideration of $4,000, the real consideration was nominal. Connelly had parol evidence to support this).

(3) The damages are limited to the amount paid by the original grantee to the original grantor ($4,000) plus interest. H & G cannot recover the amount it paid to Dixon ($7,000).

4. **Delivery.** One of the requirements of a deed is that it must be delivered by the grantor. If the grantor signs a deed and leaves it on his desk (fails to deliver it), the deed is ineffective.

a. **Delivery defined.** "Delivery" has two requirements: (i) the grantor, by words or conduct, must manifest an intent to make the deed effective and (ii) the grantor must immediately give it to the grantee. Some modern cases have relaxed the manual delivery requirement where it is clear the grantor meant for the grantee to receive the property.

1) **Evidence of intent.** Extrinsic evidence is admissible to prove delivery or nondelivery.

2) **Delivery cannot be cancelled.** Once delivery of the deed has taken place, it cannot be cancelled because the grantor's interest in the property has already passed to the grantee. To get the property back, it must be deeded back to the grantor.

3) **Estoppel.** Even if there is no delivery the grantor may be estopped from denying delivery if a subsequent good faith purchaser for value is involved.

b. **Types of delivery.** There are two types of delivery: (i) those involving only the grantor and grantee and (ii) those involving a third-party intermediary.

1) **Grantor-grantee delivery.** When the grantor has possession of the deed, a rebuttable presumption arises that there was no delivery. Likewise, it is presumed that if the grantee has the deed, there was delivery. If a deed is recorded, it is presumed there has been a valid delivery. If the grantor has acknowledged his signature, one of the

prerequisites to recording, then a presumption of delivery applies. Once delivery is shown, it is presumed to have taken place on the date of the grantor's signature.

2) **Delivery subject to a condition.** Assume the grantor delivers a deed to the grantee subject to a condition, such as "this deed to take effect only upon my death." If the condition is expressed in the deed, it is usually held that there has been a valid delivery of a future interest (the grantor retaining a life estate). Likewise, if the condition is that the grantee survive the grantor, the delivery is valid. The common law is contra. The modern trend is to give effect to deeds that reserve in the grantor the power to revoke the deed prior to the date it passes legal title to the grantee. Oral conditions attached to a deed valid on its face are invalid. The courts simply ignore the conditions.

Sweeney, **c.** **Unsuccessful conditional delivery--Sweeney, Administratrix v. Sweeney,** 11
Administratrix A.2d 806 (Conn. 1940).
v. Sweeney

1) **Facts.** Maurice Sweeney deeded his farm to his brother John Sweeney (D). Then, as security in the event D predeceased Maurice, D immediately deeded it back to Maurice. The first deed was recorded; the second was not. Maurice took both deeds to D, who kept them at his house. Maurice continued to possess the premises and leased part of the property to a third party. D never received any rent or made any repairs to the property. Maurice died. Sweeney, Administratrix (P), Maurice's estranged, but still lawful, surviving spouse, sought a declaration that the property was part of Maurice's probate estate. The trial court rendered judgment for D and P appealed.

2) **Issue.** May a delivery of a deed be deemed conditional when it is made to the grantee?

3) **Held.** No. Judgment reversed.

a) Maurice did physically possess the unrecorded deed that reconveyed the property to himself. Physical possession is not conclusive proof that it was legally delivered, however; to be effective, the delivery must have been made with the intent to pass title.

b) The parties executed the attestation clauses on the deeds, which constitutes prima facie proof that the deed was delivered to Maurice. No facts rebut this presumption. In fact, the very purpose of the reconveyance was to protect Maurice if D predeceased him. This purpose would have been frustrated if no present intent to deliver had existed, because in that case the reconveyance would have been ineffective. Therefore, present delivery must have been intended by D.

c) D claims that any delivery was only conditional on D's predeceasing Maurice. However, delivery to the grantee cannot be conditional. Delivery to a grantee vests absolute title in the grantee. Conditional deliveries can only be effected through the agency of a third person, who then delivers the deed to the grantee upon the occurrence of the condition.

d. No intent to part with the power to retake--Rosengrant v. Rosengrant, 629 P.2d 800 (Okla. 1981).

1) **Facts.** Harold and Mildred Rosengrant, a childless elderly couple with six nieces and nephews, attempted to convey their farm to Jay Rosengrant (D). In the presence of their banker, Harold and Mildred signed the deed to their property and informed D to leave the deed at the bank until their deaths when D was to record the deed. Harold handed the deed to D to "make this legal." D accepted the deed, then handed it back to the banker, who put it into an envelope marked "J.W. Rosengrant or Harold H. Rosengrant." When Mildred was close to death, D checked with a lawyer regarding the legality of the transaction. D was told "it should be sufficient" but if D anticipated there would be problems with his cousins, he should draw up a will. After Harold's death, D retrieved the deed and recorded it. A petition to cancel and set aside the deed was filed. The trial court found the deed was null and void for lack of legal delivery. D appeals.

2) **Issue.** Did the trial court err in its ruling?

3) **Held.** No. Affirmed.

a) The writing on the envelope indicates the deed was retrievable at any time prior to his death by Harold. Harold continued to farm the land, pay taxes, claim it as his homestead, and otherwise control the land.

b) Harold attached a condition to delivery of the deed that it would become operative only after his and Mildred's death. He was attempting to use the deed as a will. The delivery to D was a symbolic delivery. It did not carry "all the force and consequence of absolute, outright ownership at the time of delivery."

4) **Concurrence.** A valid delivery requires actual or constructive delivery of a deed to the grantee or third party and the grantor's intention to divest himself of the interest conveyed. The Rosengrants' subsequent actions indicate they intended to reserve a de facto life estate or retain the power to revoke the conveyance.

5) **Comment.** The lawyer from whom D sought advice should have suggested Harold and Mildred establish a revocable trust whereby they would hold their land in trust for their joint lives and the life of the survivor and upon the death of the survivor have title pass to D. They would have accomplished what they set out to do and avoided probate. Also, Harold and Mildred could have, under Oklahoma law, delivered the deed to a third party depository with instructions to deliver to Jay at their death, intending at time of delivery to give up all ownership, control or power to retake. [*See* Anderson v. Mauk, 67 P.2d 429 (Okla. 1937)]

e. Delivery to third parties (escrow). Occasionally a grantor may want to make the transfer conditional on the occurrence of some event. This requires the use of a third party.

1) **Escrow.** If the grantor delivers the deed to a third party with instructions that he deliver it to the grantee on the occurrence of certain conditions, this

is deemed an effective present delivery so long as the grantor does not retain the right to revoke the delivery. The third party is an "escrow agent" and the instructions given him are contained in an "escrow agreement." Typically the conditions are something like "deliver the deed to the grantee upon my death," or "deliver the deed to the grantee when he deposits the purchase price with you." Often commercial escrow companies are used. In order to avoid gaps in title, the grantee is deemed to have received title when the grantor delivered the deed into escrow.

2) **Reservation of the power to revoke.** The general rule is that by reserving the power to revoke, the grantor still has such control of the deed that there is no delivery. The modern trend is to recognize the delivery so long as there is no actual revocation. Some courts will consider the delivery valid only if the contingency is beyond the grantor's control.

f. **Estoppel of grantor.** When dealing with deed delivery problems, the practitioner must not forget that estoppel may operate to prevent the grantor from denying that he delivered the deed to the grantee. Assume, for example, that the grantor gives a deed to Blackacre to the grantee to examine and the grantee breaches the trust and records the deed and sells Blackacre to C. If C is a BFP (bona fide purchaser for value), the grantor will be estopped from asserting nondelivery. The grantor's remedy is to sue the grantee. In cases involving wrongful delivery by the escrow agent, the majority rule is that the grantor is not estopped from asserting nondelivery. The minority view is contra.

g. **Estoppel by deed.** If a grantor conveys an estate that he does not own, and later acquires the estate, the grantee gets that interest. This doctrine is founded upon the proposition that by conveying what he does not own, the grantor has impliedly promised to immediately convey it to the grantee when he does acquire it.

C. REAL ESTATE FINANCE

1. **Introduction.** In most real estate transactions, the buyer makes a relatively small down payment and finances the rest. The financing institution, usually a bank or savings and loan association, typically takes a note from the borrower as well as a mortgage. The borrower is personally liable on the note, but the mortgage gives the lender the right to sell the property to pay off the note if the borrower defaults. The lender is the mortgagee, and the borrower is the mortgagor.

2. **Mortgages and Foreclosure.** Under early common law, the lender would receive title in fee simple absolute if the borrower failed to pay promptly. Eventually, borrowers were given an equitable right to redeem the property. This right of redemption could be foreclosed by the lender through a judicial foreclosure proceeding, the result of which would be a decree that the property be publicly sold and the proceeds used to pay the debt, with any balance going to the mortgagor. Many state legislatures have enacted

statutes permitting mortgagors to redeem property from the purchaser at the judicial foreclosure sale.

3. **Mortgagee's Duty Upon Foreclosure--Murphy v. Financial Development Corp.,** 495 A.2d 1245 (N.H. 1985).

a) **Facts.** The Murphys (Ps) bought a house and financed it with a mortgage loan. They later refinanced the home, using Financial Development Corp. (D) as the mortgagee. D assigned the note and mortgage to Colonial Deposit Corp. About a year later, Mr. Murphy became unemployed and Ps began failing to pay their mortgage payments. Ds notified Ps of their intent to foreclose. Ps made up the mortgage arrearage, but did not pay certain costs and legal fees incurred due to the foreclosure. Ds postponed the sale to give Ps more time, but Ps did not make the necessary payments. Ds refused to postpone the sale further. The only parties present at the sale were Ps, Ds, and an attorney. Ds bid the amount owed on the mortgage, plus costs and fees, and acquired the property for $27,000. Later that day, one of the attorney's other clients offered to buy the property for $27,000. Ds refused, but made a counter offer to sell for $40,000. Ds sold the property to this person two days later for $38,000. Ps sued to have the foreclosure sale set aside, or alternatively for money damages. The trial court found for Ps on the ground that Ds had not exercised good faith and due diligence in obtaining a fair price at the foreclosure sale. The court awarded Ps $27,000, representing the difference between what it found to be the fair market value on the date of foreclosure, $54,000, and the price paid by Ds, $27,000. The court also awarded legal fees. Ds appeal.

b) **Issue.** Does a mortgagee who is foreclosing on a property have a duty to secure a portion of the mortgagor's equity if it is reasonably possible to do so?

c) **Held.** Yes. Judgment reversed in part and remanded.

1) A mortgagee who forecloses on a property has a dual role as seller and potential buyer. In its seller role, the mortgagee has a duty to act in good faith and with due diligence, in a fiduciary capacity. The mortgagee must use reasonable efforts to obtain a fair and reasonable price.

2) Inadequacy of price alone does not prove the mortgagee acted in bad faith in selling the property; the circumstances of the particular case are controlling. In this case, Ds did comply with the statutory requirements and did postpone the sale once to assist Ps. Ds did not sell the property with any awareness of the subsequent purchaser. Thus, Ds did not act in bad faith.

3) The evidence does demonstrate that Ds failed to use due diligence in obtaining a fair price. The home had been appraised at $46,000 about two years before the sale. Ds thus had reason to know that they could make a quick turnaround sale. This knowledge was demonstrated by their rejection of the $27,000 offer made the day of the sale and Ds' counter offer for $40,000. Ds should have done more to ensure a higher sales price.

4) A mortgagee does not necessarily have to secure a portion of the mortgagor's equity in all cases, but Ds did have a duty to do so here. Ds' officer testified that Ds were only concerned with making Ds whole, not with obtaining the fair market value for the property. Ds' advertising was ineffective since no one showed up at the sale. Compliance with the strict requirements of the law was not enough in this case.

5) Even though Ds failed to exercise due diligence, the award to Ps of the difference between the fair market value and the price actually obtained was improper. This measure of damages may be appropriate for a case of bad faith, but it produces greater damages than a measure based on a "fair" price which is the result of due diligence. Ps are only entitled to the difference between a fair price and the price actually obtained.

4. **Deeds of Trust.** Most states permit use of a deed of trust, under which the borrower conveys title to the property to a trustee. If the borrower defaults, the trustee can sell the property without going to court. This power of sale is subject to statutory and judicial restrictions with respect to notice and procedure, but it avoids the burdensome judicial foreclosure proceeding.

5. **Installment Contracts.** A seller may finance the sale of real estate instead of a third-party lender. The common instrument used for doing so is an installment land contract. The seller promises to convey title to the buyer once the purchase price is paid; in the meantime, the seller retains title. The buyer takes possession and assumes responsibility to pay taxes and insurance. The terms of the ordinary installment contract provide that if the buyer defaults, the seller can keep all payments already made, but the courts normally hold such forfeiture clauses invalid. Instead, the seller's interest is treated as a lien which may be satisfied only through a judicial sale.

Bean v. Walker

6. **Defaulting Vendee--Bean v. Walker,** 464 N.Y.S.2d 895 (1983).

a. **Facts.** The Walkers (Ds) purchased a home from Ps for $15,000 to be paid over a 15-year period. Ps retained legal title to be conveyed upon payment in full. Ds were entitled to possession and were obligated to pay taxes, assessments, water rates, and insurance. The contract provided that if Ds defaulted and failed to cure within 30 days, Ps could elect to call the balance due immediately or terminate the contract and repossess the premises. If Ps chose to terminate, the contract provided that Ps could retain all money paid as liquidated damages and the money paid would be considered payment of rent. Ds defaulted after nine years, during which time they had paid almost one-half of the purchase price plus interest. Ps commenced an action in ejectment and the court granted summary judgment.

b. **Issue.** Does a vendee under a land sale contract acquire an interest in the property of such a nature that it must be extinguished before the vendor may resume possession?

c. **Held.** Yes. Reversed and remanded.

1)   A vendee acquires equitable title and the vendor merely holds legal title in trust for the vendee, subject to the vendor's equitable lien for payment of the purchase price in accordance with the terms of the contract. The vendor may not enforce his rights by an action in ejectment but must foreclose the vendee's equitable title or bring an action at law for the purchase price.

2)   Forfeiture may be an appropriate result where a vendee abandons the property or absconds or where he has paid a minimal sum on the contract and upon default seeks to retain possession while the vendor is paying taxes, insurance, and other upkeep.

D.   THE RECORDING SYSTEM

1.   **Introduction.** Recording does not directly affect the rights of the grantor and the grantee vis-a-vis themselves. It does affect the right of people who subsequently receive the property from the grantee. The purpose of recording is to give notice to the public as to who has what interest in the property. Recording furnishes constructive (also called "record") notice to everyone.

2.   **Method of Recording.** To record, a grantee files the deed with the county recorder. Furthermore, the deed must be "acknowledged" (*i.e.*, it has to be signed in front of a notary public). The deed is typically filed one of two ways:

    a.   **Grantor-grantee index.** The conveyance is filed chronologically. Record of the filing is kept in two books, one for grantors and one for grantees. The names in the books are listed alphabetically. Typically, a new book is begun each year. Tracing title through grantor-grantee index books, especially if a date or two is missing, becomes quite laborious. One must first determine the year of the conveyance and look up the grantee's name. One can then determine from the book who his grantor was. After finding the grantor's name, one looks for his name as a grantee. When one finds it, one determines who his grantor was and looks for him as a grantee. The process is repeated until reaching the initial conveyance of the land.

    b.   **Tract index.** In localities using tract indexes, each plot of land is given a tract, block, and lot number (*e.g.*, "Tract A, Block 57, Lot 23"). Recorded documents are filed in chronological order under each tract, block, and lot number. This simplifies title searching considerably. One looks up the tract, block, and lot number and there will be a list of all the documents pertaining to that particular lot.

3.   **Effect of Failure to Describe the Property with Specificity--Luthi v. Evans, 576 P.2d 1064 (Kan. 1978).**   Luthi v. Evans

    a.   **Facts.** In 1971, Owens specifically assigned her interest in seven Coffey County, Kansas, oil and gas leases to defendant International Tours (T). Included in the assignment was a clause stating that Owens also assigned "all interest of whatsoever nature in all . . . oil and gas leases in Coffey County, Kansas." This instrument of conveyance was recorded. In 1975 Owens assigned her interest in an oil and gas lease known as the Kufuhl lease (which was located in Coffey County) to defendant Barris (B). Prior to this assignment B personally checked the records in the office of the register of deeds and after the assignment, B secured an abstract of title to the real estate in question. The controversy on this appeal is whether T or B owns the lease. T contends that it owns the oil and gas rights due to the language of the prior assignment which, it argues, gave constructive notice to all subsequent purchasers, including B. B contends the 1971 assignment was sufficient as between the parties to that instrument. B argues, however, that it was not sufficient to give constructive notice to subsequent innocent purchasers for value who did not have actual notice of the prior assignment, since the general language of the instrument failed to state with specificity the names of the lessor and lessee, the legal description, etc. The trial court found for B. The intermediate appellate court reversed.

b. **Issue.** Is a general assignment, when recorded, sufficient to give constructive notice to an innocent purchaser for value?

c. **Held.** No. Judgment reversed.

1) A clause in a conveyance describing the property to be conveyed as "all of the grantor's property in a certain county" is commonly referred to as a "Mother Hubbard" clause. Although they are seldom used in Kansas, they have been upheld for many years as binding between the parties to the instrument. At the outset it must be noted that:

   (a) Here, both B and T agree that the "Mother Hubbard" clause in Owens' assignment to T was valid as between the parties to that instrument.

   (b) Further, it is recognized that a single instrument may convey separate tracts by specific description and by general description capable of being made specific.

   (c) Finally, a subsequent purchaser who has actual notice or knowledge of an instrument takes subject to the rights of the assignee or grantor. This is not applicable here since B did not have actual notice.

2) The central issue is whether a "Mother Hubbard" clause constitutes constructive notice to a subsequent innocent purchaser without actual notice.

3) Kansas recording statutes evince a legislative intent that instruments of conveyance should describe the land conveyed with sufficient specificity to enable the register of deeds (i) to determine the correctness of the description from the numerical index and (ii) to make it possible to make any necessary changes in address records for mailing tax statements.

4) It seems obvious that the purpose of the recording statutes is to impart knowledge to subsequent purchasers of the instrument which affects one's title to a specific tract of land. Thus, we hold that the specific land conveyed must be described sufficiently to be identified. Hence, since the Kufuhl lease was not described in the instrument, recording that instrument

was not sufficient to be constructive notice to B, who did not have actual notice of the Kufuhl lease.

5) This does not mean that as between Owens and T the conveyance was ineffective, nor does it mean that a properly recorded but improperly indexed instrument is not constructive notice to subsequent purchasers.

4. **Misspelled Name--Orr v. Byers,** 198 Cal. App. 3d 666, 244 Cal. Rptr. 13 (1988).

Orr v. Byers

a. **Facts.** Orr (P) obtained a judgment against William Elliott. Elliott was identified erroneously as William Duane Elliot on the judgment, and on an abstract of judgment later filed, as William Duane Elliot and William Duane Eliot. Elliott obtained title to a parcel of property which became subject to P's lien. When Elliott sold the parcel to D, a title search failed to disclose the abstract of judgment and the judgment was not satisfied from the sale proceeds. P sued D and others, seeking a declaration of the rights and duties of all parties, requesting a judicial foreclosure of his lien. The court found for D. P appeals.

b. **Issue.** Does an abstract of judgment containing a misspelled name impart constructive notice of its contents under the doctrine of *idem sonans*?

c. **Held.** No. Affirmed.

1) The doctrine of *idem sonans* provides that although a person's name has been inaccurately written, the identity of such person will be presumed from the similarity of sounds between the correct pronunciation and the pronunciation as written. Therefore, absolute accuracy in spelling names is not required in legal proceedings, and if the pronunciations are practically alike, the rule of *idem sonans* is applicable.

2) The rule is inapplicable where the written name is material, as it is here.

3) The rule is viable for purposes of identification but not to give constructive notice to good faith purchasers for value.

4) To apply the doctrine here would place undue burden on the transfer of property.

5. **Types of Recording Acts.** At common law the first person to record had priority. All states have recording acts which replace the common law.

a. **Race statutes.** Few states have race statutes. Under the race statutes the first to record had priority, even if the person recording knew of prior unrecorded conveyances.

b. **Notice statutes.** Under these statutes, a subsequent purchaser for value (BFP) prevails over a prior grantee who has not recorded unless the BFP has actual or constructive notice of the prior conveyance at the time of the conveyance to him.

c. **Race-notice statutes.** Under these statutes, in order to cut off a prior grantee, the BFP must both record first and have no actual or constructive notice of the prior conveyance.

d. **Example.** G deeds Blackacre to A. Subsequently G sells Blackacre to B. Under a race statute, whoever records first (A or B) wins, even if both know of both conveyances. Under a notice statute, B will prevail provided he did not know of the prior conveyance at the time he bought Blackacre. Remember, notice can be either constructive or actual. Under a race-notice statute, in order to prevail against A, B must (i) not have notice of the prior conveyance and (ii) must record before A.

e. **Application--Messersmith v. Smith,** 60 N.W.2d 276 (N.D. 1953).

   1) **Facts.** On May 7, 1946, Caroline Messersmith executed a quitclaim deed to Frederick Messersmith (P), her nephew, on property of which both she and P were the owners of record. On April 23, 1951, Caroline deeded to Smith (D) an undivided one-half interest in the mineral rights of the same property. Smith discovered an error in the deed Caroline had signed in front of the notary, so he tore it up and took a corrected deed to Caroline. She signed it. Smith took the deed to the same notary, who acknowledged the deed without Caroline's being present (the notary called Caroline on the phone to see if she had voluntarily signed the deed). On May 9, 1951, Smith deeded his interest in the mineral rights to Seale (D). Both the deed to Smith and the deed to Seale were recorded May 26, 1951. In July 1951, P recorded his deed from Caroline. P claimed that since Smith's deed was improperly acknowledged, Smith's deed was a nullity and did not have priority over P's deed (North Dakota had a race-notice recording statute). At trial Seale won and P appealed.

   2) **Issue.** Is an improperly acknowledged deed capable of being recorded?

   3) **Held.** No. Judgment reversed.

      (a) Seale claimed title to the land under a statute which voided all unrecorded real estate conveyances (such as P's) if there was a subsequent purchaser (such as Seale) who (i) bought the land in good faith, and (ii) for valuable consideration, and (iii) recorded first.

      (b) However, Seale cannot prevail since the deed was improperly acknowledged (Caroline did not sign it in front of the notary) and as such was legally incapable of being recorded. Thus, Seale does not fall within the protection of the statute.

   4) **Rehearing.** This holding has a narrow scope. It applies to situations involving a prior unrecorded valid deed and a subsequent deed which was improperly acknowledged and thus not worthy of being recorded. This situation differs from a prior properly acknowledged deed not entitled to be recorded because of a latent defect.

   5) **Comment.** One of the important aspects of this case is that the court examined Seale's *entire* chain of title (which was defective because of Smith) and not just the conveyance from Smith to Seale. Many jurisdictions hold the direct opposite of this case.

6. **Effect of Recording.** By recording, all subsequent prospective purchasers are put on notice of the existence and contents of the recorded document. Thus, no subsequent purchaser can be a BFP since to be a BFP one must take the property without notice of prior conveyances. Recording does not make an invalid deed valid nor does it protect one from interests in the land arising by operation of law (tax liens, implied easements, etc.).

a. **Effect of not recording.** A subsequent BFP can cut off one's interest in the property, leaving one to sue his grantor.

b. **What is a BFP?** Only a BFP is protected under the notice and race-notice statutes. A BFP (i) must purchase the property (or be a creditor or mortgagee), (ii) must take the property without notice of prior conveyance (this means without either constructive or actual notice), and (iii) must give valuable consideration.

E. CHAIN OF TITLE PROBLEMS

1. **Introduction.** To give notice to subsequent would-be purchasers, an instrument must be recorded in the "chain of title." "Chain of title" refers to the title established by the grantor's predecessors up to the time of the conveyance to the grantee. Special problems arise when instruments are improperly recorded. The next case will illustrate what is included in a chain of title.

a. **Prior unrecorded deeds in chain--Board of Education of Minneapolis v. Hughes,** 136 N.W. 1095 (Minn. 1912).

Board of
Education of
Minneapolis
v. Hughes

1) **Facts.** On May 16, 1906, Hughes (D) offered to buy a lot from Hoerger, which offer was accepted and the deed forwarded by mail the next day to D. The name of the grantee was blank. On April 27, 1909, Hoerger quitclaimed the lot to certain real estate agents, Duryea & Wilson, who subsequently sold the lot to the Board of Education of Minneapolis (P) on November 19, 1909, under warranty deed which was recorded on January 27, 1910. D recorded his deed from Hoerger on December 16, 1910, shortly after he finally filled in his name as grantee. Duryea & Wilson recorded their deed from Hoerger on December 21, 1910. In the action to determine adverse claims to the lot, judgment was rendered for P, and D appealed from an order denying a new trial.

2) **Issue.** Is a record of a deed from an apparent stranger to the title notice to a grantee of a prior unrecorded conveyance by the grantor?

3) **Held.** No. Judgment reversed and new trial granted.

a) There is a conflict in authority, but the better rule is that because the deed was complete in all other respects, the insertion of D's name by him did not invalidate the otherwise valid deed. D had authority to fill in his name, which, if not express, could at least be implied from the circumstances. For that reason, the deed to D was operative once he inserted his name as grantee.

b) Because D's deed was only effective when he filled in his name as grantee, D was a subsequent purchaser. The record of the deed from Duryea & Wilson to P was not notice to D of the prior unrecorded conveyance by Hoerger; it was merely the record of a deed from an apparent stranger to the title. As a subsequent purchaser, D was protected by recording his deed before the prior deed from Hoerger to Duryea & Wilson was recorded.

c) The recording statute does not give priority to a prior recorded deed that shows no conveyance from a record owner. P's deed would only have priority if the deed to P's grantor had been recorded before D's deed.

b. Deeds recorded before grantor obtains title. As may be recalled, if a grantor does not have title at the time he conveys but subsequently obtains title, the doctrine of estoppel by deed applies. Under this doctrine the grantor must then convey the property to the grantee. The jursidictions are split as to whether a recorded deed taken from a grantor without title is in the chain of title.

c. Subdivision restrictions. The courts are also split as to whether subdivision restrictions contained in the deeds to the other lots in the subdivision are outside the chain of title. To hold that they are within the chain of title imposes on a would-be buyer the burden of searching all the deeds flowing from a common grantor.

Guillette v. Daly Dry Wall, Inc.

1) Application--Guillette v. Daly Dry Wall, Inc., 325 N.E.2d 572 (Mass. 1975).

a) **Facts.** Guillette (P) purchased a lot in a subdivision from Gilmore. P's deed contained restrictions imposed for the benefit of the other lots on the recorded subdivision plan and stated that the same restrictions were imposed on each of the lots owned by Gilmore. The restrictions were intended to maintain the subdivision as single-family dwellings. Four years later, Daly Dry Wall, Inc. (D) purchased a lot by a deed which made no reference to the restrictions. D sought to construct a multifamily apartment building on its lots and P and other landowners obtained an injunction to prevent all but single-family dwellings. D appeals.

b) **Issue.** Is a grantee bound by restrictions in deeds to its neighbors from a common grantor when it took without knowledge of the restrictions and under a deed which did not mention them?

c) **Held.** Yes. Judgment affirmed.

(1) The Statute of Frauds prevents enforcement of restrictions when the common grantor has not bound his land by writing. In this case, Gilmore did bind his remaining land by writing, so D as a subsequent purchaser from Gilmore takes title subject to the restrictions in P's deed.

(2) D claims it was only required to determine whether there were restrictions in prior deeds in its chain of title. However, P obtained not only one lot but also an interest in the rest of the land still owned by Gilmore. P's deed was properly recorded. Even though it may be burdensome for a title examiner to search all deeds given by a grantor in the chain of title while he owned the premises in question, it is not an impossible task.

(3) As a purchaser of part of restricted land, D took subject to those restrictions which could have been discerned from the records. D's deed referred to a recorded subdivision plan even though the restrictions were not mentioned.

d) **Comment.** Other courts hold that a restrictive covenant on one parcel created by a deed on a separate parcel is not in the first parcel's chain of title.

d. **Recorded instrument that refers to unrecorded instrument.** Generally, if a recorded instrument refers to an unrecorded instrument, the buyer must make inquiry into the contents of the unrecorded instrument.

e. **Recorded instrument that is defective.** Similarly, if the prior instrument is defective, inquiry must be made.

f. **Knowledge.** The courts are split on the question of constructive notice when a prior deed from an owner is recorded after a later deed from the same owner. In *Woods v. Garnett*, 16 So. 390 (Miss. 1894), Riley borrowed $3,500 from Pond in 1891 and secured the note with a deed of trust (Tranthorn as trustee). The acknowledgment of the deed of trust stated that Riley had "signed" the deed, but omitted the words "and delivered." These latter words were required by statute. A deed without them was defective. This defective deed of trust was recorded. In 1892 Riley owed Cocke & Co. $397.22 and secured the debt with a deed of trust on the same land. Cocke's agent (Lester) did a title search and discovered the 1891 deed of trust. Lester saw the defect in that deed and, being of the opinion that the deed was ineffective, accepted the 1891 deed of trust as security for the $397.22 debt. Pond assigned the note to Wood (P) pursuant to provisions of the 1891 deed of trust. About this time the defect in the 1891 deed was discovered. P had the deed of trust properly acknowledged and rerecorded it. Subsequently, on November 19, 1892, the land was sold under each of the two deeds of trust, sales being at different places. At the sale under the 1891 deed of trust, P was the purchaser. At the sale under the 1892 deed of trust, Garnett (D) was the purchaser. D had no notice of the other sale. Thus, P had the deed first made but junior in record. D had the deed second made but senior in record. P sued D as noted above. The trial court found for D. On appeal the judgment was reversed. The court found that a subsequent grantee is under the duty to make further inquiry if he has actual knowledge of a prior conveyance, even if that conveyance is defective; and if a person fails to make such inquiry, his grantee who has no actual knowledge of the prior instrument, but who buys after the defect in the prior instrument is cured (and the instrument is properly rerecorded), does not have an interest superior to that of the grantee of the prior instrument. Cocke & Co., the court said, was not a bona fide encumbrancer of the land without notice of the Pond mortgage.

Having actual knowledge of the prior defective deed, Cocke & Co. was under the duty of making further inquiry. Having failed to make such inquiry, Cocke & Co. was held to having the knowledge such inquiry would have revealed. *Morse v. Curtis*, 140 Mass. 112, 2 N.E. 929 (1885) is the leading case holding a purchase is not required to examine the record after the date of a recorded conveyance to discover a prior conveyance recorded at a later time. A recent case following *Morse* is *Rolling "R" Construction, Inc. v. Dodd*, 477 So. 2d 330 (Ala. 1985).

2. **Protected Persons.** Some statutes vary regarding which persons come within the protection of a recording statute. Although creditors and subsequent purchasers are often protected, donees and devisees are not. Thus, it has been necessary for courts to determine whether a person is a purchaser or a donee and what constitutes valuable consideration for purposes of the recording act.

Daniels v. Anderson

a. **Equitable conversion theory waived--Daniels v. Anderson,** 162 Ill. 2d 47, 642 N.E.2d 128 (1994).

1) **Facts.** Daniels (P) contracted to buy two parcels of land from Jacula. The contract also provided P with right of first refusal on an adjacent parcel. The sale contract was not recorded. The deed, which was recorded, did not mention the right of first refusal. Eight years later, Jacula contracted with Zografos to buy the adjacent parcel. Zografos paid Jacula $10,000 and provided him with a note for the balance. After Zografos made two more payments, P's wife told Zografos about P's right of first refusal. Zografos made the final payment and recorded his deed. P sued Jacula and Zagrafos (Ds) for specific performance. Zagrafos claimed he was a subsequent bona fide purchaser without notice. The trial court found for P, holding Zagrafos had actual knowledge of the option when he took title, and ordered Zagrafos to convey the parcel to P. P was ordered to pay Zografos the full purchase price plus property taxes Zografos had paid. The appellate court affirmed. Zografos appeals.

2) **Issue.** Was Zagrafos a bona fide purchaser because he took equitable title when he entered into the contract of sale prior to receiving notice from P's wife?

3) **Held.** No. Affirmed.

a) Zografos raised the theory of equitable conversion for the first time on appeal. It has been held that an issue not considered by the trial court cannot be raised for the first time on review. The doctrine of equitable conversion has been waived.

b) Regarding the point at which a buyer becomes a bona fide purchaser, it is well established that a "buyer who prior to the payment of any consideration receives notice of an outstanding interest, pays the consideration at his or her peril with respect to the holder of the outstanding interest." A "consummation of the purchase, after notice of the outstanding interest, is a fraud upon the holder of the interest."

b. Lis pendens recorded but not indexed--Lewis v. Superior Court, 30 Cal. App. 4th 1850, 37 Cal. Rptr. 2d 63 (1994).

1) Facts. In February 1991, the Lewises (Ps) contracted to buy property from Shipley. On February 24, Fontana recorded a lis pendens on the property, but it was not indexed until February 29. Ps paid Shipley $350,000 on February 25, and at the closing on February 28, gave Shipley a note for $1,950,000. The note was paid and additional money was spent renovating the property. In September 1993, Ps were served in the pending Fontana lawsuit and first learned of the lis pendens. Ps brought suit for summary judgment to have the lis pendens removed. The trial court denied the motion. Ps appeal.

2) Issue. Was the lis pendens properly recorded before it was indexed?

3) Held. No. Superior court to vacate its order and issue a new order granting Ps' motion for summary judgment.

a) *Davis v. Ward,* 109 Cal. 186, 41 P. 1010 (1895), the case upon which Fontana relies to assert that Ps were not bona fide purchasers because they did not make full payment for the property until after the indexing, does not apply to this case.

b) In *Davis,* Ward mortgaged property to Davis's predecessor. The mortgage identified the wrong land parcel. Ward later sold half of the property to Fleming, who paid cash, and half to Brown, who paid part cash and part notes. At trial to have the mortgage reformed and foreclosed, Fleming and Brown were shown to be bona fide purchasers because they could not have discovered the error by searching the record of the purchased property. Fleming and Brown won nonsuits. On appeal the supreme court reversed Brown's nonsuit, finding he was not a bona fide purchaser because he could not show the purchase price had been paid before notice.

c) *Davis's* payment of value rule cannot be reconciled with modern property law and should be strictly limited to its facts. "Any purchaser without notice who makes a down payment and unequivocally obligates himself to pay the balance has every reason to believe that, if he makes the payments when due, his right to the property will be secure."

d) *Davis* permits the correct result, but for the incorrect reasons. Davis should have prevailed, not because Brown was a good faith purchaser, but because Ward continued to hold an interest that, in equity, belonged to Davis.

c. Purchase not completed. In *Alexander v. Andrews,* 135 W. Va. 403, 645 S.E.2d 487 (1951), Alexander's (P's) father conveyed his interest in real estate to his daughter Sarah on May 8, 1946, the consideration for which was stated in the deed to be love and affection. Sarah did not record until July 8, 1946. On May 14, P's father conveyed the same interest to P and P's deed was recorded on the same day. The consideration for P's deed, as testified to, was P's obligation to bury his father and to take care of him during his declining years. P also paid his father $1,000. P sought to have his title quieted in a suit in equity. The trial court found for D. The applicable statute read: "Every . . . deed conveying . . . real estate . . . shall be void as to . . . subsequent purchasers for valuable consideration without notice, until and except from the time that it is duly admitted to record in the county wherein the property . . . may be." The money and other consideration paid by P was sufficient to give P the benefit of the statute had it been paid in full at the time P first received notice of the former deed. To sustain a plea of purchaser without notice, the court stated, the party must be a complete purchaser before notice; that is, must have obtained a conveyance and paid the whole purchase money. P's transaction was not a completed one.

3. **"Inquiry Notice."** The third form of notice (in addition to actual and constructive) is inquiry notice. It imposes on the grantee the duty to inquire of documents which are referred to by documents in the chain of title.

Harper v. Paradise

a. **Duty to inquire--Harper v. Paradise,** 210 S.E.2d 710 (Ga. 1974).

1) **Facts.** In 1922, Susan Harper deeded her farm to her daughter-in-law, Maude Harper, for life with remainder in fee simple to Maude's named children. This deed was lost. In 1957, it was found by Clyde Harper (one of the named children) and recorded. Maude died in 1972. Susan died sometime during the period 1925-1927. In 1928 all of Susan's heirs but one (John) quitclaimed any interest they might have in the property to Maude. This quitclaim deed mentioned that the 1922 deed had been lost or destroyed. In 1933 Maude executed a security deed to secure a $50 loan to her from Ella Thornton. The loan went into default and Thornton foreclosed, receiving a sheriff's deed in 1936. There was an unbroken chain of title from Thornton to Paradise (P). P claimed title through warranty deed executed and recorded in 1955 and by way of adverse possession. Harper and others (Ds) were the remaindermen under the 1922 deed. Ps sued to have title secured in them and won a directed verdict. Ds appealed.

2) **Issue.** Must a grantee make inquiry as to the provisions of any deeds referred to in his chain of title?

3) **Held.** Yes. Judgment reversed.

a) P contends that since both the 1922 and 1928 deeds emanate from the same source (*i.e.*, Susan), the 1928 deed has priority because it was recorded first. P further relies upon a statute which protects innocent purchasers without notice who purchased from heirs or legatees (etc.). Such purchasers were protected from unrecorded liens or conveyances created by the deceased person. [Ga. Code §67-2502]

b) A subsequent purchaser (P) from a life tenant (Maude) cannot defeat the later claim of a remainderman (Ds) who did not join in the conveyance to the purchaser.

c) The 1928 deed to Maude made reference to the 1922 deed. Thus, Maude is bound to have taken the 1928 deed with knowledge of the 1922 deed. The recitals of the 1928 deed make it clear that Susan's heirs did not have any interest in the property; indeed, the 1928 quitclaim deed actually served as a disclaimer by them of any interest in the land. Thus, since Susan's heirs claimed no interest, the 1928 deed does not come within the purview of Code section 67-2502.

    d)   Since the 1928 deed made reference to the 1922 deed, P had the duty to inquire as to the contents of the 1922 deed. Having failed to do so, P is a grantee with notice. A deed in the chain of title gives constructive notice to all other deeds to which it refers. Since P has not shown he made inquiry, it is presumed that due inquiry would have disclosed the existing facts.

    e)   The time period for obtaining adverse possession from remaindermen begins to run upon the death of the life tenant. (The theory behind this is that the time period for adverse possession does not begin to run until the remaindermen are entitled to possession.) Since Maude, the life tenant, died in 1972, the time period did not begin to run until then. P thus has failed to occupy the land for the requisite time period to establish title by adverse possession.

b.   Inquiry from the subdivision. A negative reciprocal easement may be implied from the neighborhood. Basically, if from the looks of the neighborhood a buyer could reasonably assume that there is some sort of restriction on lot use, the buyer is put on inquiry notice of the contents of deeds that come from the neighborhood's common grantor.

c.   Inquiry from possession. The majority view is that a buyer is chargeable with the knowledge that would be revealed by physical inspection of the premises. Thus, if it turns out that the person in possession has an unrecorded deed to the property, he cuts off a BFP. The minority view is contra.

d.   Possession of condominium--Waldorff Insurance and Bonding, Inc. v. Eglin National Bank, 453 So. 2d 1383 (Fla. 1984).

    1)   Facts. Waldorff Insurance and Bonding, Inc. (D) entered into a written purchase agreement for condominium unit 111 from Choctaw, one of its clients, in April 1973 for a total of $23,550. At that time, D paid a $1,000 deposit to Choctaw. Shortly thereafter, D began occupancy and paid all monthly maintenance fees, repairs, etc. Choctaw had executed an $850,000 promissory note and mortgage on the entire development in June 1972, which was assigned to Eglin National Bank (P) in January 1975 when the principal balance remaining was $41,562.61. In October 1973 Choctaw executed another note and mortgage for $600,000 in favor of P which covered D's condo and other units. Again in June 1974 Choctaw executed a note and mortgage for $95,000 in favor of P, covering D's condo and other units. Choctaw fell behind in insurance premiums owed to D and agreed to transfer condo 111 to D in return for cancellation of its debt to D of over $35,000. D agreed and recorded the deed in March 1975. In 1976 P started a foreclosure action against Choctaw, but the status of D's condo was not decided until 1983, when the trial court found that P's liens were superior to D's interest. The trial court found that D's occupancy was equivocal because other occupiers of condos were non-

Waldorff
Insurance and
Bonding, Inc.
v. Eglin
National Bank

owners and that D did not pay the agreed consideration to Choctaw because D wrote the debt off as a bad debt for tax purposes. D appeals.

2) **Issue.** Is actual possession of a condominium constructive notice of the occupant's interest in the property even if other occupiers are not owners?

3) **Held.** Yes. Judgment reversed.

    a) When D agreed to buy the condo, equitable title to the condo vested in D even though Choctaw retained legal title. Any subsequent successor to the legal title would have taken the title burdened with D's equitable interest of which it had either actual or constructive notice. If P had actual or constructive notice of D's equitable interest at the time of the October 1973 and June 1974 mortgages, then D's interest has priority.

    b) Generally, actual possession is constructive notice of whatever right the occupants have in the land. D was clearly in open, visible and exclusive possession of the condo. The trial judge found this possession equivocal because nonowners occupied other condos, but the status of these other possessors could not affect D's rights. The inconvenience to P of checking the various ownership interests in the condos does not remove the constructive notice based on possession.

    c) Even though D wrote off the debt from Choctaw as a bad debt for tax purposes, the consideration to Choctaw was relief from having to pay the debt, which D did provide. Thus, D did provide the agreed consideration and the transfer was valid.

    d) D has priority as to all the mortgages except the 1972 mortgage lien, which predated D's interest.

4. **Improving the Recording System.** There are many problems with the recording system. Consequently, many solutions have been proposed. The following examines some of the proposed solutions.

    a. **Marketable title acts.** Conceivably, someone can come along and assert that 100 years ago there was a defect in an instrument of title and as a consequence, they are entitled to the title to Blackacre. Thus, to prevent stale claims, marketable title acts have been passed. These acts forbid the assertion of stale claims. Stale claims are defined as those 30 to 50 years old (depending on the jurisdiction).

Heifner v. Bradford

    b. **Independent chain of title--Heifner v. Bradford,** 4 Ohio St. 3d 49, 446 N.E. 2d 440 (1983).

    1) **Facts.** In 1916, Sprague conveyed land in which grantors reserved oil and gas rights, to Fred Waters. The transaction was recorded. Sprague died testate in 1931; her will was probated and devised the rights to her two daughters, Rogers and Bradford. In 1936, Fred Waters, without mention of the reserved rights, conveyed the land to

Charles, Emma, Sarah, and William Waters. This transaction was recorded in 1936. Sprague's will was filed in 1957 and an affidavit of transfer was filed in accord with its terms evidencing transfer of the oil and gas rights by inheritance to her daughters, both of whom were then dead. Thus, each daughter's share was divided among her children. These conveyances were recorded in 1957. In 1980 Charles Waters et al. conveyed their interest to William and Shirley Waters. Heifner et al. (Ps) own three undivided fractional shares of the oil and gas rights and instituted suit to quiet title and partition the shares. Bradford et al. (Ds) are the remaining fractional oil and gas rights owners, and the record surface owners are the Waters, who also claim to own the oil and gas rights based on Ohio's Marketable Title Act. The trial court found for Ps; the court of appeals reversed, holding that the Waters owned both land and rights. Ps appeal.

2) **Issue.** Do the Waters, who have an unbroken chain of title of record for 40 years or more, have a marketable record title even though Ps' competing interest arose from an independent chain of title recorded during the 40-year period subsequent to the Waters' root of title?

3) **Held.** No. Court of appeals reversed.

   a) The Act defines marketable record title as a title of record which operates to extinguish such interests and claims existing prior to the effective date of the root of title.

   b) A root of title is that conveyance or other title transaction in the chain of title of a person, upon which he relies as a basis for the marketability of his title and which was the most recent to be recorded as of a date 40 years prior to the time when marketability is being determined.

   c) A title transaction is any transaction affecting title to any interest in land, including title by will or descent.

   d) The statute provides that one "who has an unbroken chain of title of record to any interest in land for 40 years or more, [sic] has a marketable record title to such interest . . . subject to . . . [a]ny interest arising out of a title transaction which has been recorded subsequent to the effective date of the root of title from which the unbroken chain of title of record is started; provided that such recording shall not revive or give validity to any interest which has been extinguished prior to the time of recording . . . ."

   e) Ps' root of title is the 1916 deed; Ds' root of title is the 1936 conveyance, which fails to mention the reservation of gas and oil rights.

   f) The drafters of the Model Marketable Title Act, identical to Ohio's Act in relevant part, intended the provision to be operative both where there is a single chain of title and where there are two or more independent chains of title.

g) The 1957 conveyance is a title transaction from an independent chain of title, and Ps' interest was not extinguished by the Act.

5. Title Registration.

a. Introduction. With respect to jurisdictions covered by a Torrens Act, once the county sets up a tract index, owners of real property may bring an action (Torrens action) against all the world to vest in the owner absolute title in the land. If the owner succeeds, he is declared absolute owner of the land and all prior interests are forever cut off. The owner's title is then registered and he is issued a certificate of title. The certificate of title is the title of the property. When the owner sells the land, the government cancels the old certificate and issues a new one. If someone, after stealing a certificate and forging the required signatures, sells the land to a BFP, the BFP has title since he has the certificate. The original owner can then seek compensation from a fund established to pay those who are defrauded of their certificates. Since the certificate is conclusive proof of who it is that has title, no one can acquire title by adverse possession.

b. Exception. There is one exception to the rule that he who successfully maintains a Torrens action is the absolute owner. That exception is made only when a party in actual possession of the premises claims an interest in the property.

6. Title Insurance.

a. Introduction. Because of the problems with public records, title insurance was developed to insure against any defects in these records. The insurance does not run with the land, but must be purchased by each subsequent purchaser. A mortgagee's policy does not insure the homeowner, who must take out a separate policy if she desires the protection.

Walker Rogge, Inc. v. Chelsea Title and Guaranty Co.

b. Title policy or title search--Walker Rogge, Inc. v. Chelsea Title and Guaranty Co., 116 N.J. 517, 562 A.2d 208 (1989).

1) **Facts.** On December 12, 1979, Rogge (P) purchased a tract of land from Kosa. Kosa had purchased the property from Aiello. Before P signed the sale contract, Kosa showed P a 1975 survey that indicated the land was 18.33 acres. The P-Kosa deed described the land by reference to this survey, but did not indicate the acreage and adjusted the price on the basis of $16,000 per acre for deviations from 19 acres. P hired D to handle the title work. D had issued two prior policies on the property. In the Aiello-Kosa deed, the property description was based on a survey done by Shilling, which said the property contained 12.486 acres. D had a copy of this deed in its files. D's title commitment or binder issued before closing, and the title insurance policy, described the property by referring to the 1975 survey, and did not indicate acreage. After closing, D issued a policy insuring the title with the exception that it did not insure "Encroachments, overlaps, boundary line disputes, and other matters which could be disclosed by an accurate survey and inspection of the premises." P paid the mortgage for six years. In 1985, when P sought

to acquire adjacent property, he hired a surveyor who discovered the property in question was 12.42 acres. P sued, alleging that the 5.5 acre shortage was an insurable loss and D was liable in negligence for failing to disclose documents in its file revealing the true acreage. The court found for P. The appellate court affirmed but remanded for damages. D appeals.

2) Issues.

a) Is the survey exception in the title policy vague and therefore unenforceable?

b) Does the issuance of the title commitment and policy place a duty on a title insurance company to search for and disclose to the insured any reasonably discovered information that would affect the insured's decision to close the contract to purchase?

3) Held.

a) No. b) No. Affirmed in part; reversed in part and remanded.

(1) In the absence of a recital of acreage, a title company does not insure the quantity of land. To obtain such insurance, P should have provided D with an acceptable survey which recited the quantity of land described or obtained from D an express guaranty of the quantity of land insured in the policy. From a search of relevant public records, a title company cannot ascertain the risks that an accurate survey would disclose.

(2) A title company's liability is limited to the policy and the company is not liable in tort for negligence in searching records. The duty of the title searcher does not depend on negligence but on the agreement between the parties.

(3) D made a title search for its own benefit; P was billed for the search; the real transaction between P and D was a policy of insurance. D did not issue a separate abstract of title for P.

(4) Some out-of-state courts believe that a title company should be liable in tort based on the notion that the insured has the reasonable expectation that the title company will search the title. However, the relationship between the parties is essentially contractual. Notwithstanding this, the company could be subject to a negligence claim if the act complained of was the direct result of duties voluntarily assumed by the insurer in addition to the contract to insure title.

(5) Because it restricted P's claim to the policy, the trial court did not determine whether D knew or should have known of the difference in acreage and of its materiality to the transaction.

Therefore, the court did not determine whether D assumed an independent duty to assure the quantity of acreage, whether it breached that duty, or whether the breach caused P damage.

Lick Mill
Creek Apart-
ments v.
Chicago Title
Insurance Co.

c. **Hazardous substances--Lick Mill Creek Apartments v. Chicago Title Insurance Co.,** 283 Cal. Rptr. 231 (1991).

1) **Facts.** In 1979, Kimball Small Investments (KSI) purchased property that had been toxically contaminated. The California Department of Health Services (CDHS) ordered KSI to remedy the contamination but KSI did not comply. Lick Mill (Ps) acquired Lots 1, 2, and 3 from KSI in two separate transactions and purchased title insurance from two title insurance companies (Ds). In both instances, Ds commissioned a survey and inspection of the property. The surveyor noted tanks, pipes and other improvements on the property. At the time of the survey, the presence of hazardous substances on the property was a matter of public record. Following its purchase of the property, Ps incurred costs for removal and clean-up and sought indemnity from Ds for the sums expended. Ds denied coverage. Ps filed suit; Ds demurred and the court dismissed Ps' complaint. Ps appeal.

2) **Issue.** Do the title insurance policies issued by Ds provide coverage for the costs of removing hazardous substances from Ps' property?

3) **Held.** No. Affirmed.

a)   The insuring clauses are identical and provide coverage against loss or damage sustained or incurred by the insured by reason of: (i) title being vested otherwise than stated in the relevant schedule; (ii) any defect or lien or encumbrance on such title; (iii) lack of a right of access to and from the land; or (iv) unmarketability of such title.

b)   We do not agree with Ps' contention that marketability encompasses the property's value. One can hold perfect title to land that is value-less; one can have marketable title to land while the land itself is unmarketable.

c)   The presence of hazardous material may affect the market value of Ds' land, but, on the present record, because no lien was recorded, it does not affect title.

d)   We also disagree with Ps' reasoning that because any transfer of contaminated land carries with it the responsibility for cleanup costs, liability for such costs constitutes an encumbrance on title.

e)   Encumbrances are taxes, assessments, and all liens on real property. And where an owner of contaminated land may be held fully responsible for cleanup costs and a lien may be imposed to cover such costs, there was no such lien here.

V. NUISANCE

A. INTRODUCTION

Nuisances are interference with a person's right to quiet enjoyment of her land. The interference must come from an invasion of the land. In turn, the invasion can be of particles (including gases), noise, vibration, etc. This all stems from the common law principle which held that one must use his land so as not to injure his neighbors. There are two types of nuisances, public and private.

1. **Private Nuisances.** There are three elements to private nuisances: (i) there must be a substantial interference with the plaintiff's use and enjoyment of her land caused by the defendant; (ii) the defendant must act intentionally (meaning intending to cause the action which produces the offense), or unintentionally and negligently (including wantonly, recklessly, etc.); and (iii) the plaintiff must be entitled to the use and enjoyment of the land; *i.e.*, she must be in possession, but need not be the owner.

   a. **Weighing the harm.** From the above rule it is evident that the extent of the harm must be evaluated. This includes looking at the extent and character of the harm, the burden it will cause the defendant to correct the harm, the social value of the land invaded and the suitability of the invaded land to the locality. See the Restatement (Second) of Torts for more details.

   b. **Nuisances at law.** A nuisance at law (nuisance per se) is one not permitted in the neighborhood in question. Thus, storing highly radioactive atomic wastes in barrels in a residential neighborhood is a nuisance per se.

   c. **Nuisances in fact.** A nuisance in fact (nuisance per accidens) is one which, due to the location or circumstances, is a nuisance. A business which may lawfully be conducted at the particular location is never a nuisance per se. It can only be a nuisance in fact.

2. **Public Nuisances.** This is a nuisance which adversely affects the public as a whole. A public nuisance may be a crime and penal sanctions may be available to curb it. Conversely, if the use is permitted by statute or ordinance, it is not a public nuisance. Private individuals can bring public nuisance suits only in limited circumstances. The private plaintiff must show that the nuisance is especially injurious to her and that the harm she suffers is different from the harm to the public generally. Finally, if the plaintiff meets this criteria, she need not have an interest in adversely affected land.

3. **Unintentional Act.** An unintentional act may be a nuisance. When an unintentional act is involved, the court must take into account not only the gravity of the harm (as in intentional act cases) but also the conduct of the defendant.

4. **Compared to Trespass.** An invasion of a plaintiff's land may be either a trespass or a nuisance. The chief distinction is that a nuisance involves interference with the quiet enjoyment of the land and trespass involves interference with the right to possess the land.

5. **Negligence Is Not Element If Act Is Intentional--Morgan v. High Penn Oil Co.,** 77 S.E.2d 682 (N.C. 1953).

    a. **Facts.** Morgan (P) has lived on nine acres about 1,000 feet from High Penn Oil Co.'s (D's) refinery since 1945. Beginning in 1950, for several hours a week, D dumped large quantities of nauseating gases and odor into the air. These nauseating gases invaded P's land. The gases were highly noticeable for up to two miles away. P sued to recover temporary damages for a private nuisance. P won $2,500 and D appeals.

    b. **Issue.** Is negligence a necessary element for a private nuisance?

    c. **Held.** No. Judgment affirmed.

        1) A nuisance per se (nuisance at law) is an act, occupation, or structure which is a nuisance at all times and under any circumstances regardless of location or surroundings. A nuisance per accidens (nuisance in fact) is that which becomes a nuisance by reason of its location or by reason of the manner in which it is constructed.

        2) An oil refinery is a lawful business and hence cannot be a nuisance per se. However, D errs in contending that an oil refinery cannot be a nuisance per accidens, absent it being constructed or operated in a negligent manner.

        3) Negligence and nuisance are two distinct fields of tort liability. While the same act or omission that results in negligence may also result in nuisance liability, such is not always the case.

        4) Basically a private nuisance is (i) any substantial nontrespassory invasion of another's interest in the private use of land, (ii) whether intentional or unintentional:

            a) If the invasion is unintentional the defendant's conduct must be negligent, reckless or ultrahazardous (e.g., blasting with dynamite).

            b) If an intentional invasion is involved, then the defendant's conduct must be unreasonable under the circumstances.

        5) Conduct is "intentional" if the defendant acts with the purpose of causing it or knows that it results from his conduct or knows that it is substantially certain to result from his conduct. Anyone who creates or intentionally creates or maintains a private nuisance is liable regardless of the degree of care or skill exercised by him to avoid such injury.

        6) D intentionally and unreasonably caused noxious gases and odors to escape onto P's land to such a degree as to substantially impair P's use and enjoyment of the land. Thus, D is liable in nuisance. D also intends to operate the refinery in the future in the same manner it has in the past. Thus, P is entitled to an injunction as part of its remedy.

B. REMEDIES

There are basically two types of remedies. One is an injunction forbidding the activity which causes the nuisance. The other is damages. A court may refuse to grant an injunction and instead award damages, as the next case indicates. An aggrieved party is entitled to use reasonable self-help to abate the nuisance. The party can use only reasonable force in doing this. Sometimes a party can bring a summary proceeding to abate the nuisance.

1. **Weighing the Value of the Offending Conduct.** Courts must weigh the value of the offending conduct. If the offending conduct is of good social value and may suitably be conducted at the particular location, and it is impractical to prevent the invasion, the court may award the plaintiff damages instead of abating the nuisance. [*See* Boomer v. Atlantic Cement Co., *infra*]

2. **Rule of Necessity--Estancias Dallas Corp. v. Schultz,** 500 S.W.2d 217 (Tex. Civ. App. 1973).

    Estancias
    Dallas Corp.
    v. Schultz

    a. **Facts.** The Schultzes (Ps) owned and lived in a house next to which Estancias Dallas Corp. (D) built a 155-unit apartment building. D's air conditioning equipment made noises described as sounding like a jet plane or helicopter. As a result Ps could not use their backyard, lost sleep, etc. Ps sued D, seeking to abate the nuisance. The trial court found for Ps, awarding a total of $10,000 ($9,000 to the wife and $1,000 to the husband) and granted an injunction. The issue on appeal was not whether the noise was a nuisance but whether the trial court properly balanced the equities.

    b. **Issue.** When balancing equities in a nuisance action, is the "rule of necessity" to be narrowly construed?

    c. **Held.** Yes. Judgment affirmed.

        1) Although the injury may be supported by facts sufficient to constitute a nuisance, there should be a balancing of equities to determine if an injunction should be granted.

        2) The doctrine of balancing of equities (also called the doctrine of "comparative injury") considers the injury that may result to the defendant and the public by granting the injunction. If the court finds the injury to the plaintiff slight and the benefit to the public from the nuisance significant, the court will not award an injunction. This leaves the plaintiff to bring an action at law for damages.

        3) We do not find that the trial court abused its discretion in balancing the equities in P's favor.

        4) Here it is clear that P's enjoyment of his land was substantially impaired. On the other hand, D testified that the apartments were not suitable for renting without air conditioning; that the air conditioning system cost $80,000 new; and that it would now

cost $150,000 to $200,000 to change the system. Nevertheless, private financial benefit is not sufficient in this case to justify applying the rule of necessity for D's benefit.

5) There is no evidence before us that indicates that the necessity of others compels P to seek relief by way of an action for damages. The trial court's granting of the injunction is affirmed.

d. Comment. This court viewed strictly the "rule of necessity" and, although P's injury was only $10,000 and D's cost potentially $150,000, it granted an injunction. Also, D had tried unsuccessfully to abate the air conditioning noise.

Boomer v.
Atlantic
Cement Co.

3. Economic Considerations--Boomer v. Atlantic Cement Co., 257 N.E. 2d 870, 309 N.Y.S.2d 312 (1970).

a. Facts. Atlantic Cement Co. (D) was operating a large cement plant near a large community. Suit was brought by Boomer and others (Ps), as neighboring landowners, for injury to land due to smoke, dirt, and vibration. A nuisance was found at trial, with temporary damages, but the lower courts refused to enjoin continued operation of the plant because of the large disparity in economic consequences between the nuisance and an injunction. This left Ps with the option of bringing successive suits as further damage occurred. The court also found an amount of permanent damages to guide a settlement. Ps appeal.

b. Issue. Where a nuisance is shown with substantial damages, must an injunction be allowed as a matter of course, regardless of economic consequences?

c. Held. No. Judgment reversed on other grounds.

1) The general rule adhered to with great consistency has been that where damages are substantial, injunction will lie to abate a nuisance. However, to grant injunction in the instant case would require the court to close down a business that is important to commerce and that cannot at present be operated in a different manner.

2) The drastic remedy of closing down D's plant can be avoided in various ways. One way would be to grant the injunction but make the effective date far enough in the future to allow technological development sufficient for D to eliminate the nuisance. Another way would be to grant the injunction conditioned on D's payment to Ps of permanent damages.

3) To grant permanent damages in lieu of injunction would more justly balance the equities in this case. D will be required to pay the damages, or an injunction will lie.

d. Dissent. We should not change the longstanding rule that an injunction should issue to stop a nuisance that causes substantial continuing damage. This approach licenses a continuing wrong and impairs the incentive for D to eliminate the nuisance.

4. Preexisting Lawful Industries--Spur Industries, Inc. v. Del E. Webb Development Co., 494 P.2d 700 (Ariz. 1972).

    a. Facts. Spur Industries, Inc. (D) had owned and operated a cattle feedlot for a number of years prior to the development of the housing subdivisions owned by Del E. Webb Development Co. (P). P began constructing retirement villages and other housing units a couple of miles away from D's cattle feedlot, and as the housing units began to spread in the direction of the feedlot a problem began to develop because of the noxious odor and flies around the feedlot. P began to encounter strong sales resistance to those houses that were closest to the cattle yard. Therefore, P brought suit to enjoin the operation of the feedlot because it constituted a public nuisance. The trial court held that the cattle feedlot was a public nuisance and issued an injunction. D appeals, claiming that it should not be required to close down, and that if it is required to close down it should be indemnified by P.

    b. Issues. Where the operation of a lawful business becomes a nuisance by reason of the encroachment of a nearby residential area, may the business operation be enjoined?

    c. Held. Yes. Judgment affirmed in part.

        1) A change in the surrounding area can make a preexisting lawful use into a nuisance. A state statute provides that anything that constitutes a breeding ground for flies and is injurious to the public health is a public nuisance. A business which is not a public nuisance per se may become such by being carried on at a place where the health, comfort and convenience of a populous neighborhood begins to be affected.

        2) A party that "comes to the nuisance" usually cannot get an injunction against any prior use, on the theory that he knows of the nuisance and accepts the area as it is. But in this case, because the nuisance is injurious to the public health, an injunction is appropriate.

        3) Because P brought people to the nuisance, to the foreseeable detriment of D, P must indemnify D for the reasonable expense of moving or shutting down.

VI. EASEMENTS, SERVITUDES, AND THE LIKE

A. EASEMENTS

1. **Introduction.** An easement is a right afforded a person to make a limited use of another's property. A common example is a right-of-way across the land of another. An easement may endure for years, for life or in fee. It is more than a mere covenant or promise; it is a nonpossessory interest in land.

   a. **Easements, profits, and licenses.** An easement is not a profit although the two are similar. A profit is the right to enter onto the land of another (such entry is implied under an easement) and take something off of the land, be it wild animals, timber, or coal. An easement is not a license. A license is merely the permission to enter upon or do acts upon the land of another. Most licenses may be revoked at will by the landowner.

2. **Various Types of Easements.** Leaving aside profits, there are two types of easement. It is important to be able to categorize which type of easement is involved as the rules that apply to them vary. The land subject to an easement is called "servient" land.

   a. **Affirmative easement.** This is what most people think of as an easement. It is the right to go onto the land of another and use it, *e.g.*, a right of way.

   b. **Negative easement.** This is the right to make the owner of the servient land not do something which he would otherwise be entitled to do, such as build a swimming pool within 20 feet of the neighbor's yard. These easements are disfavored by the court and, except in the case of easements for light, air, subjacent (and/or lateral) support, and flow of an artificial stream, are not recognized. Instead the courts will construe them to be covenants or servitudes.

3. **Easements Appurtenant.** An easement which confers a benefit upon a dominant tenement is appurtenant to the dominant estate. The burdened land is called the servient tenement. Assume, for example, A has the right to cross B's land in order to get to A's farm. This right of way is appurtenant to the dominant tenement (A's land). The burdened land (B's land) is the servient tenement.

4. **Easements in Gross.** Easements which are personal to their owner (easements which are not appurtenant to a dominant tenement) are easements in gross. The servient land is burdened but there is no benefited land. Common examples involve utility right of ways and billboards on private land. In case of ambiguity, the courts favor easements appurtenant. Negative easements are always appurtenant to a dominant tenement.

5. **Creation of Easements.** Easements may be created by written instrument or by implication, necessity, or prescription.

a. **Reservation of an easement.** Generally easements are created by grant, that is, party A grants party B an easement across A's land. What happens when A conveys Blackacre to B and reserves in himself an easement across Blackacre? At common law, this was a nullity. An easement could never be reserved. Modern American law recognizes the reservation of an easement.

b. **Reservations in favor of third parties--Willard v. First Church of Christ, Scientist,** 7 Cal. 3d 473 (1972).

Willard v. First Chuch of Christ, Scientist

1) **Facts.** McGuigan, a member of the First Church of Christ, Scientist (D), sold a lot adjoining the church building to Petersen. A clause was inserted in the deed giving D an easement on the lot for parking during church hours. Petersen recorded that deed. A few days later Petersen sold the land to Willard (P). The deed to P did not mention the easement for church parking. Upon discovery of that easement, P commenced this action to quiet title in himself on the ground that McGuigan could not reserve an easement for the benefit of a third party (D). The trial court found for P, holding that one could not reserve an interest in property to a stranger to the title, *i.e.,* D.

2) **Issue.** May a grantor reserve an easement to the benefit of a stranger to the title?

3) **Held.** Yes. Judgment reversed.

   a) At common law a grantor could not, by reservation, vest an interest in land to the benefit of a third party. We reject the common law rule.

   b) The court's primary objective is to construe conveyances to give effect to the intent of the grantor. Here, it was clearly McGuigan's intent to reserve an easement for D's benefit. She even testified that she discounted the price she charged Petersen by one-third because of the easement.

   c) P relies upon a common law rule which courts in other states hold in disdain and have circumvented. P claims that the common law rule should be upheld because grantees and title insurers have relied upon it. P has produced no evidence to support this contention. Further, D was using the land for church parking throughout the period when P was purchasing it and after he acquired title; thus, P cannot claim that he was prejudiced by lack of use of the land for an extended period of time.

   d) Finally, we must balance the injustice which would result from refusing to give effect to a grantor's intent versus the injustice, if any, which might result by failing to give effect to reliance on the old rule. Although other cases may warrant application of the common law rule to presently existing deeds, we find no reason to apply the common law in this case.

4) **Comment.** The majority of jurisdictions follow the common law. Under the common law, a reservation or exception could not be created in favor of a stranger to a conveyance. However, the same result could be

achieved indirectly. Using the above case as an example, McGuigan could have deeded the land to D who in turn deeded it to Petersen, reserving an easement.

c. **Licenses.** Licenses may become irrevocable in certain circumstances. One form of irrevocable license is a license coupled with an interest. For example, if you buy a car and the former owner gives you permission to pick it up anytime, you may enter upon his property to remove the car. The seller cannot revoke the license as long as you have an interest. Many states will estop the grantor of a license from revoking it if the licensee has relied upon the license to his detriment.

Holbrook
v. Taylor

1) **Licensee's reliance--Holbrook v. Taylor,** 532 S.W.2d 763 (Ky. 1976).

    a) **Facts.** In 1941 D purchased the land over which P claims an easement. From 1944 until 1949, D gave P the right to construct a mining road on D's land for which D was paid a royalty. In 1957 D built a rental house on the land. The mining road was used by both D and the tenants. The rental house burned down in 1961 and was not replaced. In 1964 P purchased a three-acre parcel adjoining D's land, building a residence thereon in 1965. At all times prior to 1965 the road was used with D's permission. Subsequently P brought suit to establish a right to use a roadway, claiming that its right to use the road had been established by either prescription or estoppel. The trial court found that P had acquired a right to use the road by estoppel. D appeals.

    b) **Issue.** Is a licensor estopped from revoking a license to use a roadway if the licensee has expended money in reliance upon the license?

    c) **Held.** Yes. Judgment affirmed.

        (1) An easement may be established by: (i) express agreement; (ii) implication; (iii) prescription; or (iv) estoppel. Only the last two are asserted by P.

        (2) To establish an easement by prescription, one must show that he has openly, peaceably, continuously, and under a claim of adverse right to the owner of the soil, and with his knowledge and acquiescence, used a way over the land. Here, P has failed to show his use of the road was either adverse, continuous, or uninterrupted.

        (3) One may acquire a license to use a roadway where, with the knowledge of the licensor, he has, in the exercise of the privilege, spent money in improving the way (or for other purposes connected with its use) on the further strength of the license. Here, D acquiesced to P's use of the road. P had constructed a $25,000 house, using the road as ingress and egress. Thus, there were substantial grounds for the trial court to find that D is now estopped from revoking the license. The parties' actions resulted in the creation of an easement by estoppel.

d) **Comment.** Evidence showed there was no other location upon which a roadway could reasonably be built to provide an outlet for P.

6. **Creation by Implication.** An easement may be implied when necessary to carry out the intent of the parties or when required by public policy.

   a. **The two types of implied easements.** Implied easements are one of two types: (i) easements by necessity or (ii) intended easements based on quasi-easement.

      1) **Easements by necessity.** If, at the time a grantor divides a tract of land and conveys part of it to another (say to B), the only means of ingress and egress is over the remaining land, then an easement will be implied for B's benefit across the remaining land. This form of easement terminates when the necessity terminates.

      2) **Intended easement based on quasi-easement.** Assume at the time a tract of land is divided into two (or more) parcels there is an existing quasi-easement reasonably necessary for the enjoyment of the property which the court believes was intended by the parties to continue. The court will then hold that there is an implied intended easement based on a quasi-easement. For example, suppose A has two lots, #1 and #2, with lot #1 adjacent to a public road and lot #2 not adjacent to any road. Further suppose a lane leads across lot #1 to lot #2. If A sells lot #1, whoever has lot #2 will have an easement across lot #1. This is different from an easement by necessity in that the quasi-easement already existed at the time of the sale of lot #2 and, in the case of intended easements based on quasi-easement, the easement need only be reasonably necessary. The test for easements by necessity is more strict.

   b. **Prescription.** Just as by adverse possession one may obtain title to property, so by prescription one may obtain an easement. The elements are the same as for adverse possession. Similarly, if the would-be pre-scription user has the permission of the owner, he cannot obtain a prescrip-tive easement. For an example of an easement by prescription, *see Othen v. Rosier, infra.*

   c. **Equity--Van Sandt v. Royster,** 83 P.2d 698 (Kan. 1938).

Van Sandt
v. Royster

      1) **Facts.** In 1903, common grantor (Bailey) built a sewer that ran under all of her property and tied into a public street line. In 1904, common grantor conveyed by general warranty deed a part of the land to Jones and another part to Murphy, retaining a third part. Jones's parcel was the lowest in elevation. There was no reservation of an easement for the sewer line in the Bailey-Jones deed. Both Bailey and Murphy were tied into the line which ran through the Jones property. In 1920, Jones conveyed part of his parcel to Rey-nolds, who built a house upon the land, with a basement that was near the underground sewer line; Reynolds did not tie into the line. Reynolds conveyed to Van Sandt (P) in 1924. Royster and Gray (Ds) are successors in interest to Murphy and Bailey, respectively. Their sewage floods P's basement. P sought an injunction against contin-

ued use of the sewer that ran under his land. The trial court denied the injunction and P appeals.

2) Issue. May a court of equity recognize an easement that exists, if at all, only by virtue of an implied reservation?

3) Held. Yes. Judgment affirmed.

a) Quasi-easement: When a landowner uses a portion of his estate to the benefit of the remainder of his estate, a use in the nature of an easement arises, even though the landowner does not specifically "grant" the use to himself.

b) Necessity: In circumstances of necessity, such as sewer drainage, a reservation of use may be implied in favor of the prior quasi-dominant estate, even though no reference is made to it in the deed out of a portion of the prior estate (quasi-servient estate).

c) Notice: In fairness to the grantee of the quasi-servient estate, the reserved use must be such as to give notice of its existence and necessity (in this case these requirements were satisfied by the apparent topography and public record information as to the location of the public sewer line). Here, the court finds that the cost to successors of prior users by necessity to replace the existing sewer with an alternative line exceeds the inconvenience to P of occasional flooding.

4) Comment. There is a difference between an implied grant and an implied reservation. In the former, the dominant tenement is the parcel conveyed to the grantee, while in the latter it is the parcel retained by the grantor. The requirements for a finding of an implied reservation are the same as those for an implied grant, with the exception that the greater "necessity" is required, even approaching strict necessity. The implied reservation doctrine is recognized in only about half of the jurisdictions.

Othen v.
Rosier

d. Easement of necessity--Othen v. Rosier, 226 S.W.2d 622 (Tex. 1950).

1) Facts. In 1897 Hill deeded 60 acres which, after mesne conveyances, came to be owned by Othen (P). In 1899 Hill deeded 53 acres which, through mesne conveyances, also came to be owned by P in 1913. In 1896 Hill deeded 100 acres and in 1899, 16.3 acres, which through mesne conveyances came to be owned by Rosier (D) in 1924. P's land was not near a highway, so for years he had to travel across both the 16.3-acre and 100-acre plots to get to the road. Erosion was injuring D's land so he constructed a levee to stop it. The impounded water from the levee turned the lane used by P to get to the highway into a muddy mess for weeks at a time. P sued D to enjoin D from interfering with his use of the lane. The trial court found that P had an easement of necessity and enjoined D from interfering with P's use of the lane. The Court of Civil Appeals first affirmed the trial court's determination as to the existence of the easement but found the injunction to be too vague and uncertain to be enforceable. On rehearing, the Court of Civil Appeals found that P had no easement of necessity or prescription and rendered judgment for D. P appeals.

2) **Issue.** For there to be an easement of necessity, must the necessity for the easement have existed at the time the original grantor severed the two estates (*i.e.*, the servient and the dominant estates)?

3) **Held.** Yes. Judgment affirmed.

a) Before an easement of necessity can be implied it must be shown that: (i) there was a unity of ownership of the alleged dominant and servient estates; (ii) the roadway is a necessity, not a mere convenience; and (iii) the necessity must have existed at the time of severance of the two estates.

b) Hill did not part with his title to the 16.3 acres across which P claims an easement until two years after he sold the acreage (which P now owns). Thus, no easement can exist as to this land. One (Hill) cannot have an easement across land (the 16.3 acres) to which he has the fee simple title.

c) As to the 100 acres, P has failed to prove that the necessity to cross the 100 acres existed in 1896 when Hill deeded the land which P later bought. Thus, no easement of necessity arises on that land. The mere fact that P's land is completely surrounded by the land of another does not, of itself, give P an easement of necessity over D's land since P and D were not in privity of ownership.

d) P does not have a prescriptive easement across D's land.

(1) An essential element in acquiring a prescriptive right is the adverse use of the easement. Use by express or implied permission, no matter how long continued, cannot ripen into a prescriptive easement. Evidence shows that D consented to P's use of the lane and hence P does not have a prescriptive easement. It was shown that D's 100 acres had been fenced in 1906 and P had been permitted to use the gates in entering and leaving the land.

(2) P insists that by using the lane for 10 years before the fence was erected (in 1906), he acquired prescriptive rights. P errs. No evidence supports his contention that he used the lane for 10 years, since he moved onto his farm in 1900.

(3) Finally, P did not discharge his burden of proving that his predecessor's adverse possession was in the same place and within the definite lines claimed by him. Thus, he cannot tack the time his predecessor used the lane to the time he used the lane.

7. **Easements by Prescription.**

a. **Introduction.** Unlike adverse possession, an easement by prescription involves the use of land, not its possession. Over time, rights may be acquired through use of land. The time period for prescriptive easements is set by statutes which generally require open and notorious, continuous, adverse use under a claim of right.

b. Public trust doctrine--Matthews v. Bay Head Improvement Association, 95 N.J. 306, 47 A.2d 355 (1984).

1) **Facts.** Bay Head borders the Atlantic Ocean; a strip of beach runs along its entire length, bordered by 76 parcels of land. All but six of the parcels are owned by private individuals. The Association (D) controls and supervises the beach property, which it owns or leases from property owners. It regulates beach membership, limiting it to Bay Head residents. The public is allowed to use the beach only from 5 p.m. to 10 a.m. during the summer and with no hourly restrictions between Labor Day and mid-June. The Borough of Point Pleasant, which borders Bay Head on the north, instituted this suit but ceased pursuing it; a public advocate (P) became the primary moving party. D was joined by more than 100 individuals who either owned or had interests in oceanfront property in Bay Head. P claimed that D prevented Point Pleasant inhabitants from gaining access to the ocean and the beachfront in Bay Head.

2) **Issues.**

   a) Does the public, ancillary to its right to enjoy the tidal lands, have a right to gain access through and use the dry sand area not owned by a municipality but by a quasi-public body?

   b) Should the dry sand area D owns or leases be open to the public to satisfy the public's rights under the public trust doctrine?

3) **Held.** a) Yes. b) Yes. Judgment for P; judgment of dismissal against the individual property owners affirmed.

   a) The public trust doctrine acknowledges that the ownership, dominion and sovereignty over land flowed by tidal waters, which extend to the mean high water mark, is vested in the state in trust for the people. Public uses include navigation, fishing, and recreational uses, including bathing.

   b) We have held that this doctrine applied to municipally-owned dry sand areas, since enjoyment of rights in the foreshore is inseparable from use of dry sand beaches.

   c) The public interest in privately owned dry sand beaches may take one of two forms: (i) the right to cross privately owned dry sand beaches in order to gain access to the foreshore; and (ii) the right to sunbathe and enjoy recreational activities.

   d) Without some means of access, the public right to use the foreshore would be meaningless and seriously impinge on, if not eliminate, the rights of the public trust doctrine. The public interest is satisfied as long as there is reasonable access to the sea.

e) The bathers' reasonable enjoyment of the foreshore and the sea cannot be realized unless some enjoyment of the dry sand area for intermittent periods of rest and relaxation is also allowed.

f) While a private owner's interest is not identical to that of a municipality, where use of dry sand is essential or reasonably necessary for enjoyment of the ocean, the doctrine warrants the public's use of the upland dry sea area subject to an accommodation of the interests of an owner. Such accommodation will depend upon the circumstances.

g) There is no need to apply the notions of prescription. D's activities parallel those of a municipality in its operation of the beachfront; its quasi-public nature is apparent. Therefore, membership must be open to the public at large and thereby D's beach must be open to the public.

4) Comment. For a discussion of a possible problem involving a Fifth Amendment "taking without just compensation," *see Presault v. United States, infra.*

8. **Assignability of an Easement in Gross--Miller v. Lutheran Conference & Camp Association,** 200 A. 646 (Pa. 1938).

a. **Facts.** Miller (P) obtained the exclusive rights for recreational use of a lake and assigned one fourth of that interest to R. Miller. P and R. Miller together operated a recreation area for the public until the death of R. Miller. P continued to rent boats. R. Miller's executors and heirs licensed use of their interest to the Lutheran Conference & Camp Association (D). P sued to enjoin development by D because D wanted to rent boats in competition with P. P won at trial. D appeals.

b. **Issue.** Is an easement in gross divisible into jointly held interests?

c. **Held.** Yes. Judgment affirmed.

1) An easement in gross is similar in nature to a profit in gross. Where it is the intent of the parties to allow assignment of the interest, it will be assignable, especially when it is designed for commercial exploitation. Thus, R. Miller's interest was assignable to D.

2) An easement in gross may be divisible, but it must be exercised jointly. If such joint exercise were not required, it would result in a surcharge on the easement.

3) P and D are entitled to separate interests but D may not use its interest unilaterally. D cannot use the lake in a manner inconsistent with P's use of the lake without P's consent.

9. **Scope of Easements.**

a. **Introduction.** The scope of an easement depends on what type of easement is involved. An excessive or improper use of an easement normally justifies injunctive relief, as well as provable damages, but does not usually extinguish the easement.

1) **Express easements.** The scope of use permitted by an express easement depends first of all on the language used in the easement. Reasonable changes in the dominant estate may support changes in the use permitted. Subdivision of the dominant estate may give each transferee the right to use the easement as long as the burden is not thereby increased. Finally, an easement appurtenant to one parcel cannot be used for the benefit of a separate parcel.

2) **Easements by necessity.** The permitted use of an easement created by necessity depends on the extent of the necessity.

3) **Other implied easements.** The scope of use of other easements created by implication depends on the quasi-easement use, as changed by reasonably foreseeable changes in the use of the dominant estate.

4) **Prescriptive easements.** The scope of use of a prescriptive easement is normally limited to the original use.

Brown
v. Voss

b. **Attempt to expand scope of use of easement to nondominant tenement--Brown v. Voss,** 715 P.2d 514 (Wash. 1986).

1) **Facts.** Parcel B, the dominant tenement, was located between parcels A and C. A was the servient tenement because the owner of parcel B had a private road easement across A for ingress to and egress from B. C was an unrelated nondominant tenement. Voss (D) purchased parcel A. Brown (P) subsequently bought parcels B and C from different owners. P intended to remove the house on B and replace it with a house that would extend from B to C. P spent $11,000 in developing the property before D sought to prevent P from using the easement. When D blocked the road, P sued to have the obstructions removed, sought an injunction against further interference, and sought damages. D counterclaimed for damages and an injunction preventing P from using the easement for access to C. The trial court awarded each party $1 in damages and granted P's injunction, limited to use of the easement for access to a single-family residence. The trial court found that P had reasonably developed the property, that the new house involved no increase in traffic over the easement, that without the injunction P could not use parcel C, and that D's counterclaim was filed as leverage. The court of appeals reversed on the ground that the easement could not be used for access to parcel C. P appeals.

2) **Issue.** May a court grant an injunction against the owner of a servient tenement which allows the owner of the dominant tenement to use the easement for access to a nondominant tenement?

3) **Held.** Yes. Judgment reversed.

a) The easement was created by express grant and did not give P any rights to access to parcel C. Normally, an easement cannot be extended by the owner of a dominant estate to other parcels owned by him. Thus, by using the easement for access to land to which the easement is not appurtenant, P misused the easement.

b) The fact that P misused the easement does not necessarily entitle D to injunctive relief. D did not appeal the damages award. When considering equitable relief, the trial court has discretion to act so as to fit the particular facts, circumstances and equities of the specific case.

c) The trial court found that P's misuse of the easement did not increase the volume of use of the easement and did not increase the burden on D's estate, that P acted reasonably in developing the property, that D did not act until after P spent $11,000, and that D's counterclaim was for leverage. D's injunction would have worked a considerable hardship on P but its denial would not damage D. P's injunctive relief was limited to access to a single-family residence. Accordingly, the trial court did not abuse its discretion.

4) **Dissent.** By extending this easement to nondominant property, P clearly misused the easement. This constitutes a trespass, and if P builds the planned house, P's use of the easement will be a continuing trespass. It does not matter that the extension would not increase the burden on D's estate. Injunctive relief for D is the appropriate remedy. P should acquire access to parcel C and could do so by condemning a private way of necessity in accordance with state law.

c. **Negative easements.** An owner of the dominant estate may have a right to prevent the owner of the servient estate to refrain from acts on the servient estate. The traditional negative easements are those for (i) light, (ii) air, (iii) subjacent or lateral support, and (iv) the flow of an artificial stream. Hostility to negative easements in England produced the doctrine of equitable servitudes, and American courts generally followed this approach, limiting negative easements to the four traditional types.

10. **Termination of Easements.**

a. **Introduction.** An easement may be terminated in several ways. If one person acquires title to both the dominant and servient tenement, the easement is extinguished. A subsequent separation of the tenements does not revive the easement. One may release an easement by a written instrument or an oral agreement accompanied by an act done in reliance on the oral agreement. An easement is abandoned if the easement owner indicates clear intent to abandon the easement and acts in a way that indicates that intent (*e.g.*, not using the easement and permitting another to build over it). An easement by necessity terminates when the necessity no longer exists. An easement in a structure will terminate if the structure is destroyed.

b. **From commercial to recreational use--Presault v. United States,** 100 F.3d 1525 (Fed. Cir. 1996).

Presault v. United States

1) **Facts.** The Presaults (Ps) own a fee simple interest in land in Vermont made up of several parcels. An 1899 railroad right-of-way ran across parcels A, B, and C. The railroad acquired Parcels A and B by exercising a power of eminent domain given it by the state. Parcel C was acquired by the railroad via warranty deed appearing to

be the standard form used to convey a fee simple. In order to abandon a railroad line, a railroad must have permission of the Interstate Commerce Commission ("ICC"). In 1983, Congress enacted the Rails-to-Trails Act to preserve discontinued railway corridors for future use and to permit public recreational use of discontinued railroad rights-of-way. The Act permits the ICC to authorize abandonment or permit discontinuance. Here, the railroad stopped service in 1970 and removed the tracks going through Ps' parcels in 1975 but did not apply to the ICC for abandonment. In 1985, the ICC, Vermont and Burlington, Vermont, agreed Burlington would maintain the former track strip as a public trail. The ICC approved in 1986. Ps sued. The United States Supreme Court held the Act to be constitutional as an appropriate exercise of Congressional power, but held further that Ps may have a Fifth Amendment remedy for the taking of their property as defined by Vermont law. Ps sued the United States (D1) in the Court of Federal Claims; Vermont entered an appearance as co-defendant (D2). The court rendered summary judgment against Ps. Ps appeal.

2) **Issue.** Does the conversion to a public recreational trail, under the Act and pursuant to the ICC, of a long unused railroad right-of-way constitute a taking of the property of the owners of the underlying fee simple?

3) **Held.** Yes. Judgment reversed.

   a) The first question to be determined is whether in 1899 the railroad acquired only easements or a fee simple interest in Ps' property. In Parcels A and B, taken by eminent domain through a Commissioner's Award which fixed damages, it was determined by the trial court judge that the railroad acquired an easement under Vermont law. It is well established Vermont law that a railroad acquiring land for laying track acquires no more than that needed for its purpose, typically an easement, not a fee simple. Parcel C was conveyed by warranty deed, but, again pursuant to Vermont law, the railroad took only so much estate therein as was necessary, *i.e.*, an easement.

   b) The second question to be determined is the scope of the easements, whether they were sufficiently broad in scope to permit use for a public recreational trail—assuming said easements were still in effect in 1986. Vermont follows common law property principles which recognize the scope of an easement may be adjusted if the change is consistent with the original grant. "[T]he parties are presumed to have contemplated such a scope for the created easement as would reasonably serve the purposes of the grant ... This presumption often allows an expansion of the use of the easement, but does not permit a change in use not reasonably foreseeable at the time of establishment of the easement." Here, the use as a public recreational trail is clearly different from the original use. The burden on the property as a public trail is greater and the whim of many individuals in contrast to its former burden of having an occasional train crossing the land. Further, the easements in this case are limited by their terms and as a matter of law to railroad purposes.

   c) Even if the original conveyances could permit trail use, the question remains whether the easements were abandoned, and thus extinguished, in 1975, thereby mandating payment of the just compensation required by the Constitution. Something more than nonuse is needed to extinguish an easement. Under Vermont law, "acts by the owner of the dominant tenement conclusively and unequivocally manifesting either a present intent to relinquish the easement or a purpose inconsistent with its future existence" must accompany nonuse. Here, the railroad removed all of its equipment, including switches and tracks, in 1975 and, in the years following the shutting down in 1970 and the removal of equipment in 1975, neither the state nor the railroad made any move to reinstate service or replace the equipment necessary to return the line to service. The railroad had effected an abandonment of the easements in 1975.

d) Ps are entitled to recover Fifth Amendment compensation if the easements were in existence when the public recreational trail was established because its establishment could not be justified under the terms and within the scope of the original easements for railroad purposes. Alternatively, when the easements were abandoned in 1975, Ps held the property unencumbered in fee simple. The subsequent taking by Burlington pursuant to federal authorization was a physical taking of the right of exclusive possession that belonged to Ps. The federal government put into play a series of events which resulted in a taking of private property through a state agent and requires just compensation be paid.

B. REAL COVENANTS

1. **Introduction.** Real covenants are promises to use or not to use land in a specified way. These covenants run with the land but they are not an interest in land. As in the case of easements, covenants can be affirmative or negative.

Real covenant - runs w/ the land

a. **Benefits and burdens.** "Benefited" land is comparable to "dominant tenement" and "burdened" land is comparable to "servient tenement."

b. **Writing required.** The common law required real covenants to be in writing. Real covenants can be contained in a deed; the grantee is bound even if he does not sign the document containing the covenants.

Writing required - no signing needed by grantee.

c. **Enforceability.** These covenants are enforceable by the parties to them. Problems arise when third parties try to enforce them. Their enforceability depends upon whether a party is asserting that it is the benefit that runs with the land (and hence to the third party) or the burden that runs with the land.

no notice or horizontal privity required for benefit to run.

d. **Determining whether burdens run with the land.** A burden runs with the land if (i) it is the intent of the contracting parties that it do so, (ii) there is privity of estate (discussed in detail below), and (iii) the covenant "touches and concerns" the land. If the assignee of the promisor gave valuable consideration, there is an additional requirement that he have notice of the covenant.

to enforce, need
- privity of estate
- intent
- notice (burden)
- touch & concern

e.   Privity. Privity of estate between the two parties to the promise is horizontal privity. Privity of estate between the promisor and his successors in interest (those to whom it is asserted the burden ran) is vertical privity. For the burden to run, all courts require vertical privity, and some courts also require horizontal privity.

f.   Determining whether benefit runs with the land. For the benefit to run: (i) the original parties to the promise must intend that it run with the land, (ii) there must be vertical privity of estate, and (iii) the covenant must touch and concern the land.

2.   Equitable Servitudes. An equitable servitude is defined as a covenant enforceable at equity against the assignees of the burdened land. It does not matter whether the covenant runs with the land.

a.   Writing. Most courts feel that an equitable servitude is an interest in land and for that reason require that it be in writing. However, some courts will, in spite of the lack of a writing, imply an equitable servitude in cases involving restrictions in subdivisions.

b.   Reciprocal negative or restrictive equitable servitudes. If there is a reciprocal scheme in the neighborhood, a court may enforce it. It has to be reciprocal (*i.e.*, other property in the neighborhood must have a similar restriction), it must be either negative or restrictive (it cannot be affirmative), and it must be part of the developer's scheme of development. Not all courts recognize these types of servitudes in residential subdivisions.

c.   Equitable servitudes may be enforced by third parties. Enforcement is conditioned on the following requirements: (i) there must be an intent that the servitude be binding on assignees; (ii) vertical (not horizontal) privity is required; (iii) the covenant must touch and concern the land; and (iv) a BFP without notice does not take subject to the covenant. Again, notice can be actual, constructive or inquiry, as will be seen in the next case.

d.   The running of benefits to prior buyers. Because of the nature of equitable servitudes, it is possible for the benefit to be enforceable by prior buyers. In the case of implied equitable servitudes, the prior buyer can only enforce the building scheme that was in effect at the time he made his own purchase. There are two distinct theories used to justify this power of enforcement: first, that the prior purchaser receives an implied reciprocal servitude in the remaining land owned by the common grantor, so that subsequent purchasers take with notice; and second, that the prior purchaser may enforce the restrictions as a third-party beneficiary.

Tulk v.
Moxhay

3.   Enforceability By and Against Subsequent Assignees--Tulk v. Moxhay, 41 Eng. Rep. 1143 (1848).

a.   Facts. P sold land with a covenant that a certain portion of it was to remain open for use of tenants. D received the land through mesne conveyances of P's vendee and now threatens to build on the land. D had notice of the restrictive covenant even though his deed did not speak to it. P brought an action to enjoin D, with judgment for P at trial.

b. **Issue.** May D, not being in privity of estate with P, disregard a previous covenant restricting use of land even though he had notice of said covenant?

c. **Held.** No. Judgment for P.

   1) Generally a covenant that does not run with the land will not be enforced against a subsequent vendee.

   2) But where a vendee purchases property with notice of a covenant restricting use, it may be enforced against him.

d. **Comment.** This was the first case to hold that a written covenant was enforceable against a subsequent purchaser who acquired title to the burdened land *with notice* of the covenant.

4. Inquiry Notice--Sanborn v. McLean, 206 N.W. 496 (Mich. 1925).

   a. **Facts.** McLean (D) owned a lot in a strictly residential neighborhood and started to construct a gasoline station on part of the lot behind the residence. Sanborn and other neighbors and occupants of lots and dwelling houses on that street (Ps) sued and obtained an injunction against D, staying the construction. Ps and D obtained title through a common grantor with some of the deeds containing restrictions while others did not. D appeals.

   b. **Issue.** Will lots conveyed by a common grantor, some conveyed with restrictions and some without, all be impressed with the restrictions?

   c. **Held.** Yes. Judgment affirmed.

   1) If the owner of two or more lots, situated in such a way as to bear relation to one another, places restrictions on use of one lot for the benefit of the lot retained, a reciprocal negative easement arises on the lot retained and runs with the land to purchasers with notice.

   2) D was put on notice of inquiry where all lots were uniform in use, although there were no restrictions in D's chain of title.

5. Affirmative Covenant--Neponsit Property Owners' Association, Inc. v. Emigrant Industrial Savings Bank, 278 N.Y. 248 (1938).

   a. **Facts.** In 1911, Neponsit Realty Co. filed a residential subdevelopment plan. A 1917 deed of a parcel of the development to Deyer contained covenants which the grantee made for himself, his heirs, successors, and assigns with the intention that they run with the land. The covenants bound the grantee to pay a fixed annual charge for the maintenance of certain common property of the subdivision, which was dedicated to public purposes. The Emigrant Industrial Savings Bank (D) acquired the Deyer interest in a foreclosure sale. D refused to pay the charges under the covenant. The original parties had agreed that the charges were to become "liens" upon the land, to the extent unpaid. Rights to enforcement were expressly created in the covenantee and its successors and assigns. The Neponsit Property Owners' Association (P) is the successor to the original

Sanborn
v. McLean

Neponsit
Property
Owners'
Association,
Inc. v. Emi-
grant Indus-
trial Savings
Bank

grantor. P brought an action to foreclose on the basis of the liens that arose from nonpayment of the assessments. The trial court denied D's motion for summary judgment on the pleadings, and D appeals.

b. **Issue.** Are subsequent purchasers bound by an affirmative covenant to pay money for use in connection with, but not upon, the land which is subject to the burden of the covenant?

c. **Held.** Yes. Judgment affirmed.

1) A covenant will run with the land if (i) the parties intend the covenant to run with the land; (ii) the covenant "touches" the land which it concerns; and (iii) there is privity of estate between the party claiming the benefit and the party burdened with the covenant.

2) The test of whether a covenant runs with the land is whether it imposes a burden upon an interest in land which also increases the value of a different interest in the same or related land. Because the payment of the maintenance fee is essential to enjoyment of the property, the covenant "touches" the land, and is binding on subsequent purchasers.

3) Because P represents all the property owners, the corporate entity is recognized for what it is, a representative form. It succeeds to the estate of the owners and privity of estate is established.

C. SERVITUDES IN GROSS

1. **Introduction.** A benefit may be personal to the covenantee yet the burden may touch and concern the covenantor's land. The enforceability of such a servitude in gross depends on which approach is adopted.

a. **English rule.** Under the English rule, an easement in gross was not binding on assigns of the burdened land; because an equitable servitude was analogous to a negative easement, the burden of a servitude in gross would not run to assignees of the land. A servitude would run only if there was both a servient and a dominant tenement.

b. **American rule.** The American approach to easements in gross permits the burden to run with the land. One would expect that the burden of a servitude in gross would likewise run with the land, and some courts so hold, but many follow the English rule anyway.

2. **Restatement View.** The Restatement (Third) of Property, Servitudes, section 3.2 (T.D. No. 2, 1991) looks at a servitude both at its inception and after subsequent events have taken place. The Restatement position has moved from the touch and concern requirement to other tests of enforceability. The determination that a servitude is invalid often implies that although a servitude was valid at the time of its inception, subsequent events may indicate that it should no longer be enforced. A servitude may not be enforceable at its inception because it violates public policy (*i.e.*,

the public's interest in maintaining the privacy of the home, protecting the stability of neighborhoods, preventing the wealthy from foreclosing housing opportunities for others). Subsequently, a servitude may become unenforceable because it imposes an unreasonable direct or indirect restraint on alienation; imposes an unreasonable restraint on trade, or is unconscionable. *Eagle Enterprises, Inc. v. Gross*, 384 N.Y.S.2d 717, 349 N.E.2d 816 (1976), is cited in the Restatement as an example of the way the touch and concern test confuses the questions of initial validity and later unenforceability. In *Eagle Enterprises*, a subdivider conveyed realty in 1951 via a deed wherein the subdivider agreed to supply water to the purchasers for six months of the year for $35 per year. The deed also contained language that the covenant ran with the land. Eagle (P) was successor in interest to the subdivider and Gross (D), after several intervening conveyances, was the successor in interest to the purchasers. D refused to accept and pay for the water and had his own well. P commenced an action to collect the fee specified in the covenant and claimed D was bound to accept the water. The court found the promise of the original grantees to accept and make payment for seasonal water supply from the well of their grantor did not run with the land and become enforceable against subsequent grantees. In order for a covenant to run with the land: (i) the original parties must have intended that the covenant run with the land; (ii) privity of estate must exist between the party claiming the benefit of the covenant and the right to enforce it and the party upon whom the burden of the covenant is to be imposed; and (iii) the covenant must be deemed to touch and concern the land with which it runs. The court found the covenant in Eagle Enterprises did not substantially affect the ownership interest of landowners in the subdivision. The obligation to receive water from P resembled a personal, contractual promise. The court was also reluctant to enforce this covenant since the affirmative covenant is disfavored in the law for fear this type of obligation imposes undue restriction on alienation or an onerous burden in perpetuity.

3. **Personal Covenants Do Not Run with the Land--Caullett v. Stanley Stilwell & Sons, Inc.,** 170 A.2d 52 (N.J. 1961).

   a. **Facts.** Caullett (P) purchased a one-acre lot from Stanley Stilwell & Sons, Inc. (D), a builder. The deed stated that D reserved the right to build the original dwelling on the lot and that this right ran with the land. Negotiations between P and D on building the house broke down and P sued to quiet title. The trial court found for P on summary judgment, striking the aforementioned clause from the deed. D appeals.

   b. **Issue.** Does a servitude in gross, whereby the benefit is personal but the burden is placed upon the land, run with the burdened land?

   c. **Held.** No. Judgment affirmed.

      1) Restrictive covenants are to be construed realistically in light of the circumstances under which they were created. Nonetheless, they will not be enforced unless their meaning is clear and free from doubt. The deed here in question is too vague to be enforced. It failed to describe the type of structure to be built, the cost thereof, or the duration of P's obligation.

      2) Even assuming the clause was not too vague and indefinite, it still cannot operate as a covenant running with the land. The primary re-

quirement of the covenant did not touch and concern the property. It did not exercise any direct influence on the occupation, use, or enjoyment of the premises. The clause failed to define in some measurable and reasonably permanent fashion the proscription and limitation upon the use of the land. It only casually regarded the land, and was merely a personal arrangement between P and D.

3) Even if the covenant were construed to prohibit construction by P unless performed by D, the covenant would not run with the land at law. The benefit was in gross, or personal to D. A covenant cannot generally run with the land unless both burdened and benefited properties exist. An exception applies when the burden is in gross and the benefit attaches to property, because the benefit helps the alienability of the benefited property. But if the burden attaches to the land and the benefit is personal, the burden does not run with the land because of the hindrance on the alienability of the burdened property.

4) Even when a covenant does not run with the land at law, equity may enforce a servitude so that the owner of benefited property may enforce covenantal rights against the successor to the burdened land. The covenant in this case, however, is not enforceable as an equitable servitude because the benefit is in gross and it neither affects land retained by the grantor (D's other lots) nor is part of a neighborhood scheme. Some other courts have permitted attachment of equitable servitudes in gross, but in this jurisdiction, the existence of a dominant estate is essential.

d. **Comment.** The benefit involved in this case was D's getting to build a house on the lot sold to P and presumably thereby make money doing it. The burden was the restricting of the lot so that only D could build on it. Covenants which touch and concern the land typically involve minimum setbacks, proscribed architectural forms, minimum square footage of the building, etc. A covenant limiting who can build does not fit into the traditional definition of "touching and concerning" the land.

Hill v. Community of Damien of Molokai

4. **Restrictive Covenant in Violation of FHA--Hill v. Community of Damien of Molokai,** 911 P.2d 86 (N.M. 1996).

a. **Facts.** The Community (D), a nonprofit corporation providing homes to people with illnesses, leased a residence in Albuquerque in a planned subdivision for use as a group home for four (4) unrelated individuals with AIDS. Other neighborhood residents (Ps) noticed an increase in traffic going to and from the home and believed the home to be in violation of one of the restrictive covenants applicable to all homes in the subdivision. The covenant provided no lot or house shall be used for other that a single-family residence or residence purposes. The covenant restricts the land from being used for rooming houses or hospitals, among other things. Ps filed for an injunction to enforce the covenant and prevent further use of the group home. The trial court held the restrictive covenant prevented such use and issued a permanent injunction. D appeals.

b. **Issues.**

1) Does the restrictive covenant preclude use of the home as a group house for unrelated individuals with AIDS?

2) Would enforcement of the restrictive covenant violate the Fair Housing Act ("FHA"), 42 U.S.C. sections 3601-3631 (1988)?

c. **Held.** 1) No. 2) Yes. Judgment reversed. Injunction vacated.

1) In enforcing a restrictive covenant, we look to four general rules of construction: (i) if the language is unclear or ambiguous, the covenant is resolved in favor of free enjoyment; (ii) restrictions on use or enjoyment will not be read into the covenant by implication; (iii) the covenant must be interpreted reasonably; and (iv) words must be given their ordinary and intended meaning.

2) Insofar as "use" for single-family residence purposes, the home is intended to provide its occupants with a traditional family structure, setting and atmosphere. The residents share meals, provide social, emotional and financial support for each other and receive spiritual guidance together. Residents contract with a private nursing service for health care workers who do not reside in the home. D provides administrative assistance, organizes the health care workers' schedules, and receives donations of food and furniture on behalf of the residents. D collects rent from the residents. When the primary purpose of a group home is to create a normal family atmosphere unlike that found in traditional health care facilities, the purpose of the home is distinguishable from a commercial or institutional facility; thus, D's is used for purposes in compliance with the restrictive covenant.

3) Since the word "family" is not defined in the covenant, resulting in that term as used in the covenant being ambiguous, we must resolve the ambiguity in favor of free enjoyment of the property. Further, an Albuquerque zoning ordinance provides a definition at odds with Ps' definition of a "family" as individuals related by birth. The ordinance defines "family" as "[a]ny group of not more than five [unrelated] persons living together in a dwelling." Finally, there is a strong public policy in favor of including small group homes within the definition of "family." The legislative history of the FHA reflects this policy. We agree with the New Jersey court in *Open Door Alcoholism Program, Inc. v. Board of Adjustment*, 200 N. J. Super. 191, 491 A.2d 17 (App. Div. 1985), which noted "the controlling factor is considering whether a group of unrelated individuals living together as a single housekeeping unit constitutes a family . . . is whether the residents bear the generic character of a relatively permanent functioning family unit." D's use of the property does not violate the restrictive covenant.

4) The purpose of the covenant is to regulate the structural appearance and use of the homes. An increase in traffic, therefore, is not relevant to our determination since the covenant was not directed at controlling traffic or on-street parking.

5) The FHA creates three distinct claims for violations of section 3604(f)(1), which makes it unlawful "[t]o discriminate in the sale or rental, or to

otherwise make available or deny, a dwelling to any buyer or renter because of a handicap . . . ."

6) **Discriminatory Intent:** D must show that the residents' handicap was in some part the basis for Ps' actions. D argues that Ps knew the use of the property, were antagonistic to that use, and decided to enforce the covenant. D's evidence that Ps' traffic complaints followed a newspaper article describing the group home is insufficient to support a claim for discriminatory enforcement of the covenant.

7) **Disparate Impact:** D need only show that enforcing the covenant will actually result in discrimination or have a discriminating effect, and D has shown that Ps' attempt to limit group homes has the discriminatory effect of denying housing to the handicapped. Balancing both Ps' and D's interests, we conclude the negative effects of increased traffic are outweighed by D's interest in maintaining its group home for handicapped individuals.

8) **Reasonable Accommodation:** D charges that Ps failed to make a reasonable accommodation. Reasonable accommodation includes "changing some rule that is generally applicable so as to make its burden less onerous on the handicapped individual." In order to implement this requirement of the FHA, it is necessary only that the restriction serve as an impediment to an individual plaintiff who is handicapped and denied housing. Since Ps' interpretation of the restrictive covenant has the effect of denying access to the handicapped residents, Ps would be required to reasonably accommodate the group home provided that it would not require a fundamental alteration in the nature of the restrictions or impose undue financial or administrative burdens. Ps have not claimed allowing the group home to operate would impose any financial or administrative burden on them. Thus, a reasonable accommodation would have been not to seek enforcement of the covenant.

Shelley v. Kraemer

5. **Judicial Enforcement of Discriminatory Private Agreement--Shelley v. Kraemer,** 344 U.S. 1 (1948).

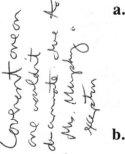
Covenant were on are valdait documents. due to Mr. Murphy's stepatur.

a. **Facts.** Shelley (D), a black person, purchased residential property that, unknown to D, was encumbered by a restrictive agreement that prevented ownership or occupancy of the property by non-Caucasians. Kraemer (P), a neighbor and owner of the other property subject to the restriction, brought suit to restrain D from possessing the property and to divest title out of D. The trial court denied relief and the Supreme Court of Missouri reversed. D appeals.

b. **Issue.** Does the Fourteenth Amendment Equal Protection Clause prohibit judicial enforcement by state courts of restrictive covenants based on race or color?

c. **Held.** Yes. Judgment reversed.

1) Property rights clearly are among those civil rights protected from discriminatory state action by the Fourteenth Amendment. Early decisions invalidated any government restrictions on residency based

on race. Here the restrictions are purely private and, standing alone, are not precluded by the Fourteenth Amendment.

2) Actions of state courts are state actions within the meaning of the Fourteenth Amendment. Judicial enforcement of these private racial restrictions constitutes state discrimination contrary to the Fourteenth Amendment and denies D equal protection.

D. TERMINATION OF SERVITUDES

1. **Introduction.** There are several methods by which covenants and servitudes terminate. They can be abandoned, the benefited party can acquiesce to their violation or be estopped from enforcing the covenant, the neighborhood can so change that enforcing the covenant will no longer benefit the neighborhood and, finally, the hardship on the burdened party may be too great for the court to sanction enforcement of the covenant.

2. **Merger.** If the benefited estate and the burdened estate come to be held by one owner, the covenant or servitude merges into the estate.

3. **Test for Determining If the Covenant Fulfills Its Original Purpose-- Western Land Co. v. Truskolaski,** 495 P.2d 624 (Nev. 1972).

   Western Land Co. v. Truskolaski

   a. **Facts.** In 1941 Western (D) subdivided a 40-acre tract. The lots received restrictive covenants which limited the land use to single-family dwellings and prohibited any stores of any kind. In time the area developed and the road bordering the subdivision became a main thoroughfare. In about 1969, D decided to construct a supermarket on the remaining undeveloped 3.5-acre tract. Truskolaski and other homeowners in the subdivision (Ps) sued to enjoin construction on grounds of the restrictive covenant. The trial court found for Ps and D appeals.

   b. **Issue.** As long as the original purpose of the restrictive covenant can be accomplished to the benefit of the restricted area, will the covenant be enforced?

   c. **Held.** Yes. Judgment affirmed.

      1) As long as the original purpose of the covenants can still be accomplished and substantial benefit will inure to the restricted area by their enforcement, the covenants will stand even though the subject property has a greater value if used for other purposes.

      2) There is ample evidence that shows, in spite of the growing commercial area next to the subdivision, that the restriction substantially benefits the residents of the subdivision. Thus, the trial court will be affirmed.

      3) Further, the fact that the Reno city council indicated a willingness to change the zoning for the 3.5-acre parcel is not significant. A zoning ordinance cannot override privately placed restrictions.

4) Even if this property is more valuable for commercial rather than residential purposes, this does not entitle D to be relieved of the restrictions it created since substantial benefit inures to the restricted area by their enforcement.

5) D argues that the restrictive covenants are no longer enforceable due to their abandonment. D showed that some people had built houses on lots less than the required 6,000 sq. ft. minimum; that someone ran a business out of his home in the late 1940s, etc. Even if the alleged occurrences and irregularities could be construed to be violations of the restrictive covenants, they were too distant and sporadic to constitute general consent by the property owners to abandon the restrictive covenants.

Rick v. West   **4.   Change of Conditions--Rick v. West,** 34 Misc. 2d 1002, 228 N.Y.S.2d 195 (1962).

    a.   Facts. Chester Rick subdivided 62 acres in 1946 and filed a declaration of covenants, restricting the land to single-family dwellings. In 1956 Rick sold to West (D) a half-acre lot upon which D built a house. Subsequently, Rick contracted for the sale of 45 acres to an industrialist, conditioned on the tract being rezoned. The tract was rezoned, but D would not release the covenant and the sale fell through. In 1961, Rick conveyed to Ps who were likewise prevented by D from selling 15 acres to a hospital. Ps sued, claiming the covenant was no longer enforceable because of change of conditions. The court held for D. Ps appeal.

    b.   Issue. Is the covenant nonenforceable due to a substantial change in the general neighborhood?

    c.   Held. No. Judgment affirmed.

       1) Ps' predecessor elected to promote a residential development and in furtherance of his plan imposed residential restrictions where there were previously none.

       2) D relied on the restrictions and has a right to continue to do so.

       3) Justice Cardozo in a similar case stated:

> By the settled doctrine of equity, restrictive covenants in respect of land will be enforced by preventive remedies while the violation is still in prospect, unless the attitude of the complaining owner in standing on his covenant is unconscionable or oppressive. Relief is not withheld because the money damage is unsubstantial or even none at all.

> Here, in the case at hand, no process of balancing the equities can make the plaintiff's the greater when compared with the defendant's, or even place the two in equipoise. The defendant, the owner, has done nothing but insist upon adherence to a covenant which is now as valid and binding as at the hour of its making. His neighbors

are willing to modify the restriction and forgo a portion of their rights. He refuses to go with them. Rightly or wrongly, he believes that the comfort of his dwelling will be imperiled by the change, and so he chooses to abide by the covenant as framed. The choice is for him only.

4) Our statute provides no basis for awarding pecuniary damage when the restriction is not outmoded, and when it affords real benefit to the person seeking its enforcement, no consideration can and should be given to any award of pecuniary damages to D in lieu of enforcement of the restrictions.

5. **Attempted Abandonment of Fee Simple--Pocono Springs Civic Association, Inc. v. MacKenzie**, 446 Pa. Super. 445, 667 A.2d 233 (1995).

Pocono Springs Civic Association, Inc. v. MacKenzie

a. **Facts.** The MacKenzies (Ds) purchased property at Pocono Springs (P) in 1969. In 1987, after Ds unsuccessfully tried to sell their lot, believing the property to be worthless, they attempted to abandon it. Ds unsuccessfully tried to sell or gift the lot to P, ceased paying taxes, informed all interested parties they intended to abandon the property, and ceased visiting the lot or using P's services. P argued that Ds had not abandoned the property and were obligated to pay association fees. The trial court granted summary judgment for P. Ds appeal.

b. **Issue.** Was the real property owned by Ds abandoned?

c. **Held.** No. Judgment affirmed.

1) Under Pennsylvania law, abandonment applies only to property with imperfect title. Ds have perfect title to their property. They are owners of a fee simple with a recorded deed.

E. HOMEOWNERS' ASSOCIATIONS

1. **Introduction.** Various types of organizations made up of homeowners have been developed to satisfy particular needs. Members subject themselves to certain restrictions and obligations in return for the protection of knowing that the other homeowners also assume the same obligations. Subdivision associations are a common type of homeowner association, made up of individual landowners. Condominiums and cooperatives involve some degree of joint ownership.

a. **Condominiums.** Condominiums are fairly common in modern society, but they were very rare in the United States until the 1960s. Each individual owner owns in fee simple the living unit, while the land, exterior walls, and common areas are owned by all the unit owners as tenants in common. The unit owners join an association which has authority to manage the common areas and establish and enforce rules and maintenance charges. This type of ownership is governed by statute as well.

Nahrstedt v.
Lakeside
Village
Condominium
Association,
Inc.

b.   Cooperatives. A resident in a housing cooperative typically has a long-term renewable lease to the living unit, and owns shares in the corporation that actually holds title to the land and improvements. The resident is a tenant of the corporation in which he has an ownership interest.

2.   No Cats Allowed--Nahrstedt v. Lakeside Village Condominium Association, Inc., 33 Cal. Rptr. 2d 63 (1994).

a.   Facts. Nahrstedt (P) sued Ds to obtain a declaration that she is entitled keep her three cats in her condominium notwithstanding the restrictions imposed by recorded covenants, conditions and restrictions; P further contends that she is not liable for fines assessed against her for her refusal to removal her cats. The trial court sustained, without leave to amend, demurrers to P's five causes of action. The court of appeals reversed and directed the trial court to determine whether P's acts interfered with the peace and quiet enjoyment of other homeowners. Ds appealed to the supreme court.

b.   Issue. Does enforceability of a pet restriction depend on proof of interference with the right of quiet enjoyment of other homeowners?

c.   Held. No. Judgment reversed and remanded.

1)   Because recorded use restrictions are essential to a stable and predictable living environment for common interests residential projects, the legislature has provided a presumption of validity to restrictions. The standard applicable to equitable servitudes requires a challenger to demonstrate the unreasonableness of the restriction. Restrictions that are arbitrary, against public policy, or that impose a burden on use that greatly outweighs any benefit will not be enforced.

2)   Enforcement of a restriction does not depend on an individual owner's conduct, but rather its reasonableness. This is determined by examining the restriction's effect on the common interest of the entire project.

3)   Some courts afford greater deference to restrictions contained in a master deed in order to promote stability and predictability and to benefit the majority of owners in their expectations. Enforcement also operates to discourage costly legal challenges to restrictions. Our "social fabric" is best preserved by uniform and predictable judicial enforcement of written instruments.

4)   The recorded pet restriction prohibiting cats and dogs, but allowing some other pets, is not arbitrary. It is rationally related to health, sanitation, and noise concerns. Neither is the burden on P disproportionate to the benefits to the community as a whole.

d.   Dissent. The majority has narrowly interpreted the statutory presumption of validity so as to contribute to the "fraying of our social fabric." The restriction is arbitrary and places a great burden on P by depriving her of the benefits of pet ownership within the confines of her home.

VII. ZONING

A. INTRODUCTION

1. **Zoning Power.** Only the state has the power to zone. This power has been delegated to cities and counties by statutes called "enabling statutes." Hence, all local zoning activity must abide by the enabling statutes.

2. **Goals of Zoning.** Zoning has as its goal the orderly development of the community. It promotes economic growth, community health, welfare, and safety.

3. **How Zoning Works.** One of the fundamental characteristics of zoning is that it segregates uses of land into geographic regions. Thus, high-rises may only be permitted downtown rather than in rural areas. It can be used to foster commercial districts as well as residential districts. For health and safety reasons, zoning can regulate the density of human population. This can be achieved by limiting building heights, providing for minimum and maximum yard sizes, yard setbacks, etc.

4. **Constitutional Considerations.** As with other areas of the law, zoning is affected by the Constitution. For instance, if the zoning in an area is going to be changed, due process requires that the landowners in the area be given a hearing. Zoning restrictions must be for a legitimate governmental objective. The Equal Protection Clause requires that all landowners who are similarly situated be treated equally, unless there is a legitimate reason for not doing so. Of course, as with eminent domain, if zoning regulations amount to a taking, just compensation must be given by the state.

   a. **Taking.** The local government properly exercises its police power when it phases out uses which are inconsistent with newly enacted zoning changes. For example, a city can change the zoning where a cement plant is located and give the plant a couple of years to move before it will be cited for violation of the new zoning. A use which, due to a zoning change, is no longer permitted is a nonconforming use. Most courts say that the landowner must be given a reasonable time to cease his nonconforming use. The length of time for ceasing the nonconformity may be based on the dollar value of the improvements of the land.

   b. **Leading case--Village of Euclid v. Ambler Realty Co.,** 272 U.S. 365 (1926).

      Village of Euclid v. Ambler Realty Co.

      1) **Facts.** The Village of Euclid (D) enacted a comprehensive zoning ordinance restricting uses of property according to areas found on a master plan. Ambler Realty Co.'s (P's) land fell into three different categories though it consisted of one continuous parcel. P brought suit to enjoin enforcement of said ordinance. At trial P won on the grounds that the statute was unconstitutional. D appeals.

      2) **Issue.** Is a comprehensive zoning plan restricting uses of properties according to areas designated by a legislative body

(where it divides one continuous parcel into three different uses) unconstitutional for violation of Due Process and Equal Protection Clauses of the Constitution?

3) **Held.** No. Judgment reversed.

a) The ordinance under review and all similar ones must find justification under the police power of the state asserted for the public welfare.

b) If the validity of a legislative classification for zoning purposes is fairly debatable, the legislative judgment must be allowed to control.

c) It is reasonable for a legislature to regulate building to avoid nuisances and promote safety, and if some harmless type of building is also excluded, this will not invalidate an otherwise good law.

d) Complete restriction of all industry and apartment buildings from a purely residential district is proper in that fire and health protection is thereby more fairly suited to the task, traffic congestion and street accidents are reduced, and a safer, cleaner, and more enjoyable place for detached housing development is provided. Apartment buildings or industry, taken as a whole, would negate these benefits.

e) If the provisions of a law are applied to a specific property, they may be found to be arbitrary and unreasonable. The Court will not examine each line of the ordinance and enjoin the enforcement where no injury is shown other than a general allegation that property values were affected.

f) In the development of constitutional law, the Court will not speculate with general rules beyond the immediate question presented.

4) **Comment.** Zoning laws are now presumptively valid.

B.   ADMINISTRATION OF ZONING ORDINANCES

1. **Introduction.** Zoning ordinances present numerous opportunities for abuse and for objection by affected landowners. Administration of zoning ordinances thus creates the potential for considerable litigation.

2. **Comprehensive Plans.** Enabling acts inevitably require the local zoning authority to adopt a comprehensive plan (which can be revised from time to time). The zoning must conform with the plan. The plan serves to limit the local zoning board's whims.

3. **Nonconforming Use--PA Northwestern Distributors, Inc. v. Zoning Hearing Board,** 526 Pa. 186, 584 A.2d 1372 (1991).

PA North-
western Dis-
tributors,
Inc. v.
Zoning Hear-
ing Board

a. **Facts.** After PA (D) opened an adult bookstore, the town amended its zoning ordinances to regulate "adult commercial enterprises" and included an amortization provision requiring preexisting uses which conflicted with the amendment to come into compliance within 90 days from the date of the ordinance. P's bookstore cannot meet the ordinance's restrictions because it is not located within an area designated for adult commercial enterprises. After being notified that it was out of compliance, P appealed to D, challenging the validity of the amortization provision. D upheld the validity of the provision; two lower courts dismissed P's appeals. P appeals.

b. **Issue.** Is a zoning ordinance which requires the amortization and discontinuance of a lawful preexisting nonconforming use confiscatory and violative of the state constitution as a taking of property without just compensation?

c. **Held.** Yes. Judgment reversed.

1) The lower court based its dismissal on the opinion in *Sullivan v. Zoning Board of Adjustment*, 478 A.2d 912 (1984), which is not a correct statement of the law of this Commonwealth. *Sullivan* presents a standard whereby the property interests of an individual are balanced with the health, safety, morals, or general welfare of the community at large.

2) Zoning involves governmental restrictions upon a property owner's constitutionally guaranteed right to use his or her property, unfettered by governmental restrictions, except where the use violates any law, creates a nuisance or the owner violates any covenant, restriction, or easement.

3) A lawful nonconforming use establishes in the property owner a vested property right which cannot be abrogated or destroyed, unless it is a nuisance, it is abandoned, or it is extinguished by eminent domain.

4) If the effect of a zoning law or regulation is to deprive a property owner of the lawful use of her property, it amounts to a taking for which she must be justly compensated.

d. **Concurrence.** A blanket rule against all amortization provisions should be rejected. The instant provision is confiscatory but the *Sullivan* standard should be upheld.

4. **Variances.** Zoning by its nature is general; it does not take into account the particularities of every lot in the zone. For that reason, boards of zoning adjustments have been established locally. They are empowered to grant variances for conditions that are unique to a particular lot or two. If the condition is not unique, a change in zoning should be sought. Suppose, for example, that when a tract of land was changed from a commercial zone to a residential zone, a 20-foot side yard requirement was imposed. If there

were a few lots that, due to their shape, could not be used for housing if the 20-foot side yards were required, the zoning adjustment board could grant a variance.

a. **Special exceptions.** A special exception is not the same thing as a variance. Where a particular use is compatible in theory with the surrounding zoning if certain conditions are met, a special exception can be issued to the landowner. Criteria must be established for granting special exceptions.

1) **Example.** A gas station may be compatible with a residential neighborhood if the gasoline storage tanks are placed underground. The ordinance regarding special exceptions would have to set forth the requirements for permitting a gas station in a residential neighborhood.

Commons v. Westwood Zoning Board of Adjustments

b. **Justification for refusing variance request--Commons v. Westwood Zoning Board of Adjustments, 410 A.2d 1138 (N.J. 1980).**

1) **Facts.** Commons (P) owned a lot with a 40-foot frontage. The zoning ordinance required a 70-foot frontage before a single-family house could be built. P sought a variance. Many neighbors opposed the variance. The Westwood Zoning Board of Adjustments (D) refused to grant the variance. D based its denial upon the ground that P had failed to prove hardship, but did not specify its reasons. P sought judicial review of D's action. Both the trial court and the intermediate appellate court affirmed the denial of the variance request. P appeals again.

2) **Issue.** Must a zoning board specify its reasons for refusing a variance request?

3) **Held.** Yes. Judgment reversed.

a) "Undue hardship" involves the notion that no effective use can be made of the property in the event the variance is denied.

(1) An owner is not entitled to have his property zoned to its most profitable use.

(2) If the owner, or his predecessors in title, created the nonconforming condition, then the hardship is said to be self-imposed. Related to the self-imposition of hardship are the efforts that the owner has made to bring the property into compliance with the ordinance's specifications.

b) Once an undue hardship is found to exist, then the local board of adjustment (such as D) must be satisfied that the granting of the variance will not substantially impinge upon the public good and the intent and purpose of the zoning board and ordinance.

(1) There lurks in the background of cases such as this the possibility that the denial of a variance will zone the property into inutility so that an exercise of eminent domain is called for and compensation will have to be paid.

(2) In viewing variance requests, there is a conflict between the right of the owner to use his land as he pleases, the right of

the public to restrict the exercise of property rights, and the rights of the property owners in the immediate vicinity.

    c) Here, D erred in concluding that P had failed to demonstrate any hardship. P showed a substantial difference between the offering and asking price for the land. (He had once been offered for the lot much less than the value of the land as a building lot.)

        (1) Although the house would be smaller than others in the neighborhood, the minimum floor requirements in the zone are not per se related to the public health, safety or morals. On these grounds, D could not refuse the variance request.

        (2) The burden of proof is on an applicant such as P. However, if the applicant complies with the variance ordinance's criteria, the local zoning board must specifically state why the request is denied; otherwise, a reviewing court cannot determine whether the board acted within its limits.

4) Comment. This case also illustrates the need for local zoning authorities to comply with the state enabling act's concern for public health, safety, and morals.

c. Excessive discretion granted to local zoning board--Cope v. Inhabitants of the Town of Brunswick, 464 A.2d 223 (Me. 1983).

Cope v. Inhabitants of the Town of Brunswick

1) Facts. The Copes (Ps) sought an exception to the local zoning ordinance so they could construct eight six-unit apartments on land then classified for suburban A residential use. The ordinance permitted the Brunswick Zoning Board of Appeals (D) to grant an application for an exception if the applicant proves, inter alia, that (i) the use requested will not adversely affect the health, safety, or general welfare of the public and (ii) that the use requested will not tend to devalue or alter the essential characteristics of the surrounding property. D found that Ps' project complied with the ordinance except for these two factors. D denied Ps' application. The reviewing court upheld the denial and Ps appeal.

2) Issue. Does a local zoning board have authority to take action based on general statements of policy contained in the zoning ordinance?

3) Held. No. Judgment reversed.

    a) Local zoning boards and municipalities themselves have no inherent authority to regulate the use of private property. This authority may only be conferred by the state, and only with such a detailed statement of policy that those to whom the law is to be applied may reasonably determine their rights. The determination of rights may not be left to the purely arbitrary discretion of the administrator; the administrator may not have discretion as to whether to grant the permit if the conditions stated in the ordinance exist.

    b) The two factors upon which D rejected Ps' application were so general that they did not limit D's discretion. Instead, they gave D discretionary authority to approve or disapprove applications as D thinks best serves the public interest. The lack of sufficiently detailed standards would permit a discriminatory application of the law, so the ordinance is unconstitutional.

c)   An exception allows the owner to use his property as the ordinance expressly permits. Whether a use would comply with the public health, safety and welfare and with the essential character of an area is a legislative question. In authorizing exceptions, the legislature makes a determination that the use would not ordinarily be detrimental to the neighborhood within the zone. The delegation to D under this ordinance permits D to decide that same legislative question again.

d)   Because D found that Ps complied with all the requirements of the ordinance except for the two invalid ones, Ps should receive the exception.

5.   **Amending Zoning Ordinances.** The local legislative body has power to amend the zoning ordinances. It need not follow the zoning board's recommendations.

a.   **Spot zoning.** This occurs when the local legislative body amends the zoning ordinance to permit a new zone which is limited in size (although it can be more than one lot) and does not conform to the comprehensive plan.

Fasano v. Board of County Commissioners of Washington County

b.   **Application--Fasano v. Board of County Commissioners of Washington County,** 507 P.2d 23 (Or. 1973).

1)   **Facts.** Fasano and others (Ps) were homeowners opposing a zoning change which allowed construction of a mobile home park. The planning commission denied the change; the county commission reversed and approved the change; on writ of review the trial court reversed and denied the change. The court of appeals affirmed the trial court. County Commission (D) now appeals.

2)   **Issue.** Must a change in zoning conform to the comprehensive plan?

3)   **Held.** Yes. Judgment affirmed.

a)   The standards for a comprehensive plan are that it shall be designed to promote the public health, safety, and general welfare and shall be based on the following considerations: (i) various characteristics of various areas in the county; (ii) suitability of areas for particular uses; (iii) trends in land improvement; (iv) density of development; (v) needs of economic enterprises; (vi) needed access; (vii) natural resources and development thereof; and (viii) public need for healthful, safe, aesthetic surroundings.

b)   In order for a change in zoning to be valid, it must be proved that the change will be in conformance with the above standards, *i.e.*, in conformance with the comprehensive plan. Proof must show that there is a public need for the change and that the need will best be served by changing the zoning of this particular piece of property.

c) The burden of proof to show that the above standards have been met is upon the one seeking the change (in this case the planning commission).

d) The more drastic the change, the greater will be the burden of showing that it is in conformance with the comprehensive plan, that there is a public need for the kind of change, and that the need is best met by the proposal under consideration. As the degree of change increases, the burden of showing that potential impact upon the area in question was carefully considered and weighed will also increase.

e) If an action produces a general rule or policy, it will be treated as a legislative act and be accorded a full presumption of validity and shielded from less than constitutional scrutiny by the theory of separation of powers. But if it entails the application of a general rule or policy to specific individuals or situations, it will be treated as quasi-judicial, and be subject to ordinary judicial review.

c. **Modification by voter initiative--Arnel Development Co. v. City of Costa Mesa,** 169 Cal. Rptr. 904, 620 P.2d 565 (1980).

Arnel Development Co. v. Costa Mesa

1) **Facts.** Arnel Development Co. (P) proposed a comprehensive 50-acre development including 539 apartments. Neighbors objecting to the proposal circulated an initiative to rezone the property, together with another 18 acres, as single-family residential use. The voters approved the initiative and P sued, claiming the zoning of small parcels of privately owned property was adjudicatory, not legislative, in nature and not subject to initiatives. The trial court upheld the initiative, but the court of appeal reversed. The City of Costa Mesa (D) appeals.

2) **Issue.** May the voters of a jurisdiction modify the zoning of relatively small parcels of private property through the initiative process?

3) **Held.** Yes. Judgment reversed.

a) It is well established that enactment of a zoning measure is a legislative act. The cases do not distinguish between zoning measures based on the size of the property in question. Yet P claims the initiative process deprived it of due process.

b) The Supreme Court has recognized that rezoning of even a single eight-acre parcel is a legislative act. [Eastlake v. Forest City Enterprises, Inc., 426 U.S. 668 (1976)] P still has the option of seeking administrative relief from the initiative zoning, and can seek judicial invalidation if the zoning is arbitrary and unreasonable. P has not been denied due process.

c) P claims the initiative was adjudicatory because it only affected three landowners, but P ignores the thousands of prospective tenants, the existing residents, and the future of the entire community. Zoning ordinances must be treated uniformly as legislative acts to avoid uncertainty in land use planning. Variances, by contrast, are adjudicative.

    d)   P did receive a hearing before the electorate. An initiative is not a simple process but requires considerable organization and is normally only used when significant public issues are involved. Even a zoning change adopted by initiative must comply with the city's general plan. These limitations on the power of the initiative are sufficient to prevent a few voters from imposing their interests on the city.

6.   Contract and Conditional Rezoning.

    a.   **Introduction.** This involves the local zoning authority granting a landowner's request for a variance or change in zoning on the condition that the landowner sign a contract to do certain things. For example, the city might require a developer to renovate a traffic intersection adjacent to his property in return for its changing the zoning so that he can build a grocery store.

Collard v.
Incorporated
Village of
Flower Hill

    b.   **Condition that owner create restrictive covenant--Collard v. Incorporated Village of Flower Hill,** 439 N.Y.S.2d 326, 421 N.E.2d 818 (1981).

    1)   **Facts.** Collard (P) bought property that, as part of an earlier deal to get the property rezoned, was subject to a recorded condition that no structures on the property could be altered unless the Incorporated Village of Flower Hill (D) consented. P applied to D for approval to enlarge the existing structure, but D refused to approve. P sought an order directing D to issue the required building permits. D moved to dismiss the complaint, but the trial court denied D's motion. The appellate court reversed, and P appeals.

    2)   **Issue.** May a city rezone a parcel of land on the condition that the owner execute a private declaration of covenants that restricts the use of the rezoned parcel?

    3)   **Held.** Yes. Judgment affirmed.

    a)   Conditional rezoning has been rejected in most jurisdictions, but New York has permitted the practice. Courts have rejected conditional zoning on the ground that it is illegal spot zoning that violates the legislative mandate for a comprehensive plan.

    b)   This criticism is not well founded for three reasons: (i) conditional rezoning removes restrictions on land use, and the limiting conditions adversely affect the land rezoned while benefitting the surrounding property; (ii) the term "spot zoning" refers to zoning of a parcel in a manner not consistent with the applicable comprehensive plan, but conditional rezoning does not have this effect; and (iii) since it is proper to change a zoning classification without imposing conditions, there is no reason why making a change subject to conditions would be illegal spot zoning. Conditional rezoning should be evaluated by the same standards as unconditional zoning.

    c)   Conditional rezoning is also criticized as a means of bargaining away the police power of the local government, but in reality this is an effective way to protect surrounding landowners. It does not limit the government's authority to reverse or alter its zoning decision.

    d)   Even though the legislature has not expressly authorized local governments to use conditional zoning, it has not prohibited the practice. The power to conditionally rezone may be implied because as a means of harmonizing competing interests the practice is within the spirit of the zoning legislation.

    e)   P claims that, although the condition does not so state, D cannot unreasonably withhold its consent. This approach is unacceptable because the courts cannot insert a missing term. The original parties could have easily inserted the language P desires had they so intended. P's alternative claim that D was required while exercising its zoning power to include such a clause could lead to the invalidation of the original rezoning, a result P does not want because it was more restrictive.

7. Discretionary Zoning (Non-Euclidean Zoning). The need for some discretion in zoning has become apparent in recent years. Hence, things that were formerly forbidden are now permitted. The following are examples:

    a.   **Cluster zoning.** Rather than having 100 families living on 10,000 square-foot lots, some developers wanted to cluster the houses by putting them on smaller lots, leaving the unused land for a park or recreation area. The overall density does not change, only the distribution of the population. This was once forbidden but now is common.

    b.   **Floating zoning.** A city, as an example, can create a new zone but not provide any geographic location for it. A developer can come along and apply to have the zoning for his tract of land changed to the "floating" zone. Once forbidden, this is now a common way of encouraging new types of developments.

    c.   **Planned unit developments.** This takes cluster zoning one step further and permits several different uses to be clustered on one tract of land. Thus, an apartment building may be next to a single-family home, which may be next to a park area.

C. NONTRADITIONAL ZONING OBJECTIVES

1. Aesthetic Legislation. The old rule was that cities could not use their police power to accomplish goals that were purely aesthetic. The modern trend is contra. In fact, zoning commissions may have architectural review boards composed of nonelected people who, based on aesthetics, approve or deny building permits.

a. **Architectural style--State *ex rel.* Stoyanoff v. Berkeley,** 458 S.W.2d 305 (Mo. 1970).

1) **Facts.** Action to compel issuance of a building permit. P applied for a permit to build on a lot he owned in a very exclusive town which is a suburb of St. Louis. Pursuant to city ordinance, the designs for P's house had to be approved by the city architectural board. The houses in the area of P's lot were of traditional architecture. P's planned house was ultramodern. The board found P's planned house to be grotesque and refused to approve the plans. P sued as noted above. City (D) proved that P's house would cause neighboring houses to decline in value. The trial court found for P and D appeals.

2) **Issue.** May a building permit be refused if a proposed house is found to be grotesque by the city architectural board?

3) **Held.** Yes. The lower court is reversed.

   a) The stabilizing of property values is one of the most cogent reasons behind zoning ordinances. It is well within the promotion of the general welfare as stated in the enabling act.

   b) Property which offends sensibilities and debases property values affects not only adjoining property owners but also the general welfare. Grotesque structures, detrimental to the value and welfare of surrounding property and to the general welfare and happiness of the community, are to be avoided.

   c) Aesthetic considerations are a matter of general welfare.

   d) The fact that the ordinance provides for an architectural board, composed of three architects (nonelected officials), is not an impermissible delegation of power. The general standards provided for in the statute are sufficiently specific to guide the board. This is adequate protection against the exercise of arbitrary and uncontrolled discretion of the city council. Further, after an adverse determination, a property owner may appeal to the city council.

b. **Aesthetic compatibility and harmony--Anderson v. City of Issaquah,** 70 Wash. App. 64, 851 P.2d 744 (1993).

1) **Facts.** Anderson (P) applied to the City (D) for land use certification to develop property zoned for commercial use. P submitted plans for a commercial building to D's various departments and confronted an obstacle only when he sought approval from the Development Commission, which administers and enforces the City's land use regulations. The Issaquah Municiple Code ("IMC") provides that buildings must be "compatible" with existing buildings; "harmony in texture, lines, and masses [is] encouraged;" "monotony" is to be avoided; the project should be "interesting." On the street where P proposed to build his retail warehouse there were several gas stations, a Victorian era house used as a visitors' center, a bank, an Elk's hall, an auto

repair shop and a veterinary clinic with a cyclone-fenced dog run. After three appearances before the Commission and repeated attempts to comply with the Commissioners' interpretation of the IMC, P's application was denied. P appealed to the City Council, which affirmed. P filed suit, alleging that IMC building design requirements are unconstitutionally vague. The trial court dismissed P's complaint. P appeals.

2) **Issue.** Are the IMC sections at issue here unconstitutionally vague on their face?

3) **Held.** Yes. Judgment reversed.

a) "The purpose of the void for vagueness doctrine is to limit arbitrary and discretionary enforcements of the law."

b) The language used in the IMC does not give effective or meaningful guidance to applicants or design professionals. No applicant can determine whether her project is going to be seen by the Commission as "monotonous" or "harmonious."

c) The Commissioners attempted to communicate to P their own individual, subjective feelings and to enforce their own arbitrary concept of IMC provisions. "The words employed are not technical words which are commonly understood within the professional building design industry. Neither do these words have a settled common law meaning."

d) Aesthetic standards are an appropriate component of land use governance when such standards give clear guidance to all parties concerned.

c. **Limitation on residential signage--City of Ladue v. Gilleo,** 512 U.S. 43 (1994).

1) **Facts.** Gilleo (P) placed a 2- by 3-foot sign on her front lawn printed with the words "Say No to War in the Persian Gulf, Call Congress Now." After the first sign was removed and a replacement knocked down, P went to the police, who informed P such signs were prohibited in Ladue (D). P filed suit alleging that D's ordinance violated her First Amendment right of free speech. The district court issued a preliminary injunction against the enforcement of D's ordinance. P placed an 8.5-by 11-inch sign in a second story window stating, "For Peace in the Gulf." D repealed the original ordinance and enacted a replacement which prohibited all signs except those that fall into one of 10 exemptions. The exemptions include for sale and other like signs; church, religious institution and school signs; commercial signs in commercial areas; and on-site advertising. Part of the new ordinance indicated D's concern in enacting the new ordinance: proliferation of signs in a residential area would cause clutter, cause a decline in property values and may cause safety and traffic hazards to motorists and pedestrians. P amended the complaint to address the new ordinance. The district court held the ordinance unconstitutional and the court of appeals affirmed, holding the ordinance invalid as a "content based" regulation since D treated commercial speech more favorably than noncommercial speech. D petitioned for certiorari.

2) Issue. Does D's ordinance violate P's First Amendment right to free speech?

3) Held. Yes. Judgment affirmed.

a) In *Linmark Associates, Inc. v. Willingboro*, 431 U.S. 85 (1977), we found unconstitutional an ordinance prohibiting homeowners from placing "For Sale" or "Sold" signs on their property in that it restrained the free flow of truthful information. *Linmark* is in some respects the mirror image of this case. In *Linmark*, the city's interest was in maintaining a stable, racially integrated neighborhood. D's interest here is minimizing visual clutter. D's interest is no more compelling than those at stake in *Linmark*. Also, Linmark's ordinance applied only to a form of commercial speech; D's ordinance covers "such absolutely pivitol speech as a sign protesting an imminent governmental decision to go to war." The impact of D's ordinance is greater than in *Linmark*. P and others are forbidden to display any sign on their property, foreclosing a complete medium and a unique and important means of communication. "Although prohibitions foreclosing entire media may be completely free of content or viewpoint discrimination, the danger they pose to freedom of speech is readily apparent—by eliminating a common means of speaking, such measures can suppress too much speech."

b) In *Metromedia, Inc. v. San Diego*, 453 U.S. 490 (1981), we held unconstitutional a San Diego ordinance imposing substantial prohibitions on outdoor advertising displays within the city in the interest of traffic safety and aesthetics. We found that the city treated commercial speech more favorably than noncommercial speech and in effect eliminated the billboard as an effective medium of communication for noncommercial messages.

c) Regulation of speech may be impermissibly underinclusive. An exemption may represent a government effort to give one side an advantage over another in expressing views in a debatable public issue. Alternatively, through the restriction of general speech and exemptions, the government may attempt to select suitable subjects for public debate, thereby attempting to control "the search for political truth." D claims that its ordinance is content neutral and triggers neither of these concerns. D argues that the mixture of prohibitions and exemptions in its ordinance "reflects legitimate differences among the side effects of various kinds of signs." The exemptions are not likely to contribute to clutter. Only a few residents at a time display "for sale" and like signs. D has only a few churches, schools and businesses.

d) However, D's exemptions demonstrate that D has determined that the interest in permitting some messages to be conveyed through residential signage outweighs D's aesthetic interest in eliminating outdoor signs.

e) D's ordinance is not a mere regulation of the time, place or manner of speech simply because P and others remain free to use other means of communication like hand-held signs, telephone calls, newspaper advertisements. We are not persuaded that what means of communications exist for P and others are adequate substitutes. Signs displayed at one's residence carry a unique message. They identify the speaker, an important component of efforts to persuade. They reach neighbors. They have played an important part in political campaigns. "A special respect for individual liberty in the home has long been part of our culture and our law; that principle has special resonance when the government seeks to constrain a person's ability to speak there."

2. Household Composition.

a. **Introduction.** Many efforts have been made to restrict land use based on the composition of the household. Usually this is intended to prevent boarding houses, fraternity houses, or overcrowded conditions. Such zoning ordinances do present significant constitutional issues, however.

b. **Exclusion of nonfamilies--Village of Belle Terre v. Boraas,** 416 U.S. 1 (1974).

Village of
Belle Terre
v. Boraas

1) **Facts.** The Village of Belle Terre (D) restricted land use to single-family dwellings, excluding lodging houses, boarding houses, frater-nity houses, or multiple-dwelling houses. "Family" was defined as one or more persons related by blood, adoption, or marriage, living and cooking together as a single housekeeping unit, exclusive of household servants, or not more than two persons living and cooking together as a single housekeeping unit who were not related by blood, adoption, or marriage. Boraas (P), the owner of a house in the village, and three of six tenants in the house who were unrelated by blood, adoption, or marriage, sought an injunction under 42 U.S.C. section 1983 declaring the village ordinance unconstitutional (after they were served with an order to remedy violations of the ordi-nance). Ps claim that the ordinance interferes with a person's right to travel, that it interferes with the right to migrate to and settle within a state, that it bars people who are uncongenial to the present residents of D, that the ordinance expresses the social preferences of the resi-dents for groups that will be congenial to them, that social hom-ogeneity is not a legitimate interest of government, that the restriction of those whom the neighbors do not like intrudes on the newcomer's rights of privacy, that it is of no rightful concern to villagers whether the residents are married or unmarried, and that the ordinance is antithetical to the nation's experience, ideology, and self-perception as an open, egalitarian, and integrated society. The district court held the ordinance unconstitutional and the court of appeals affirmed. D then appeals to the Supreme Court.

2) **Issue.** May a city use household composition as a basis for zoning?

3) **Held.** Yes. Judgment reversed.

   a) The ordinance is not aimed at transients, involves no procedural disparity inflicted on some but not on others, and involves no "fundamental" right guaranteed by the constitution (*e.g.*, voting, the right of association, the right of access to the courts, any rights of privacy, etc.).

   b) Police power is not confined to elimination of filth, stench, and unhealthy places, but may be used to lay out zones where "family values, youth values, and the blessings of quiet seclu-sion and clean air make the area a sanctuary for people." Thus, the ordinance is a reasonable, not arbitrary, exercise of discretion by D.

4) **Dissent.** The ordinance violates equal protection and unnecessarily burdens plaintiffs' First Amendment rights of freedom of association and their guaranteed rights of privacy. Further, the ordinance limits the density of occupancy of only those homes occupied by unrelated persons, thus reaching beyond control of the use of land or the density of population and instead undertaking to regulate the way people choose to associate with each other within the privacy of their own homes.

5) **Comment.** The California Supreme Court has held a similar ordinance to be unconstitutional. The Supreme Court itself held invalid a single-family zoning ordinance that defined "family" as no more than one set of grandchildren. [Moore v. City of East Cleveland, 431 U.S. 494 (1977)] The reason was that the intrusion into the family was too great; the Court could not defer to the legislative findings. *Belle Terre* was distinguished because it affected only unrelated individuals.

City of
Edmonds
v. Oxford
House, Inc.

c. **Family composition rule--City of Edmonds v. Oxford House, Inc.,** 514 U.S. 725 (1995).

1) **Facts.** The Fair Housing Act ("Act") prohibits housing discrimination against handicapped persons. Section 3607(b)(1) of the Act exempts reasonable governmental restrictions on the maximum number of occupants permitted to occupy a dwelling. Oxford House (D) opened a group home for 10-12 recovering alcoholics in Edmonds (P). P's zoning code prescribes that occupants of single-family dwellings must compose a "family." The code defines a family as "an individual or two or more persons related by genetics, adoption, or marriage, or a group of five or fewer persons who are not related by genetics, adoption or marriage." P issued a criminal citation to the owner and a resident of the group home. D asked P to make a reasonable accommodation pursuant to the FHA. P declined but passed an ordinance allowing group homes as permitted uses in multifamily and general commercial zones. P sued D in district court seeking a declaration that P's ordinance is exempt from the FHA provisions. D counterclaimed, charging that P failed to make a reasonable accommodation by permitting the home to remain. In response to cross motions for summary judgment, the trial court found for P. The court of appeals reversed. The Ninth Circuit's decision conflicts with an Eleventh Circuit decision; we granted certiorari to resolve the conflict.

2) **Issue.** Does P's family composition rule qualify as a restriction regarding the maximum number of occupants permitted to occupy a dwelling within the meaning of the FHA's absolute exemption?

3) **Held.** No. Judgment affirmed.

a) Reserving land for single-family homes maintains the character of neighborhoods, allowing "zones" where family values, youth values, quiet seclusion and wholesome air create a sanctuary. To limit land use to accommodate such a zone, a city must define the term "family." Thus, family composition rules are essential to maintain single-family use restrictions.

b) In contrast, maximum occupancy restrictions cap the number of individuals permitted per dwelling in relation to the available floor space or number and type of rooms. These restrictions are to maintain health and safety by preventing overcrowding.

c) While maximum occupancy rules clearly fall within the FHA's exemption, "rules designed to preserve the family character of a neighborhood, fastening on the composition of households rather than the total number of occupants living quarters can contain, do not."

d) P's contention that because its rule caps at five the number of unrelated persons permitted to occupy a single-family dwelling, it falls within the exemption is erroneous. P's rule does not indicate the maximum number of persons permitted to occupy a house. Unlimited siblings, their parents and grandparents could live in P's single-family zone without offending the rule.

e) We decide here only the threshold question. It remains for the lower court to determine whether P's actions against D violate the FHA's provisions against discrimination.

3. **Exclusionary Zoning.** By regulating various zoning requirements (density, minimum floor space, types of housing), a community can separate the rich, the poor, and the middle class. The old line of cases required that the zoning requirement or regulation bear a rational relationship to a permissible governmental purpose. One of these purposes was to prevent overcrowding.

a. **Exclusionary goal.** If the particular zoning ordinance bore no reasonable relationship and had an exclusionary purpose, it was struck down.

b. **Modern trend—the fair share test.** Some recent cases have held that any zoning ordinance with an exclusionary impact must be scrutinized in light of the needs of the region. The impact of this is that developing communities must have their share of low and moderate income housing.

c. **Application--Southern Burlington County NAACP v. Township of Mt. Laurel,** 336 A.2d 713 (N.J. 1975).

Southern Burlington County NAACP v. Township of Mt. Laurel

1) **Facts.** The Southern Burlington County NAACP (P) brought suit against the Township of Mt. Laurel (D), claiming that its zoning ordinance, which permitted only single-family detached dwellings, unlawfully excluded low and moderate income families from the town. The trial court declared the ordinance invalid and ordered D to present a plan of affirmative public action designed to enable and encourage the satisfaction of the indicated needs. D appeals; P, which contended that the relief was not broad enough (*i.e.*, that D should have considered the regional housing needs of low and moderate income families without limitation to those having past, present, and prospective connections with the town), also appeals.

2) **Issue.** May a developing municipality, by a system of land use regulation, make it physically and economically impossible to provide low and moderate income housing in the municipality for the various categories of persons who need and want it and thereby exclude such people from living within its confines because of the limited extent of their income and resources?

3) **Held.** No. Judgment affirmed.

   a) D's zoning ordinance is presumptively contrary to the general welfare and outside the intended scope of the zoning power. A facial showing of invalidity is thus established, shifting to the municipality the burden of establishing valid superseding reasons for its action and nonaction.

   b) Considering the basic importance of the opportunity for appropriate housing for all classes, no municipality may exclude or limit categories of housing solely for fiscal reasons.

   c) Every developing municipality must, by its land use regulations, presumptively make realistically possible an appropriate variety and choice of housing.

   d) When land use regulation has a substantial external impact, the welfare of the state's citizens beyond the borders of the municipality cannot be disregarded.

   e) When it is shown that a developing municipality has not made realistically possible a variety and choice of housing, a facial showing of violation of substantive due process or equal protection has been made out and the burden shifts to the municipality to establish a valid basis for its action.

   f) A developing municipality's obligation to afford the opportunity for decent and adequate low and moderate income housing extends at least to that municipality's fair share of the present and prospective regional need therefor.

   g) A municipality should first have full opportunity to itself act without judicial supervision. Therefore, a detailed court order should not be issued.

d. **Mount Laurel II.** Eight years after *Mt. Laurel, supra*, was decided, the case was consolidated for appeal with five others and came before the court because of noncompliance with the mandate of the original opinion. In *Southern Burlington County NAACP v. Township of Mt. Laurel (Mount Laurel II)*, 456 A.2d 390 (N.J. 1983), the New Jersey Supreme Court held that courts may take the lead in enforcing fair distribution of all income classes among residential areas. The court reasoned that the constitutional power to zone, as a portion of the police power, must be exercised for the general welfare. Thus, zoning regulations that do not provide the requisite opportunity for a fair share of the region's needs for low and moderate income housing are unconstitutional. To ensure compliance with this rule, the court held that every municipality must provide a realistic opportunity for decent housing for at least some part of its resident poor who now occupy dilapidated housing. Each municipality designated by the State Development Guide Plan ("SDGP") as a growth area must also provide opportunities for a fair share of the region's present and prospective low and moderate income housing needs. It was determined that only judges selected by the Chief Justice would hear all future *Mount Laurel* litigation to insure consistent development of judicial rules and all such litigation should be disposed of in a single trial with one appeal. The court further determined that the builder's remedy, which allows a builder who unsuccessfully proposes a lower income housing project to recover damages, should be granted in most cases unless there are overriding reasons for the denial of the project, and that SDGP designations should normally control the applicability of the *Mount Laurel* obligation to particular municipalities.

4. **Regulating Growth.** Local communities have become increasingly active in regulating their growth in order to foster a certain type of community ambiance. Sometimes this takes the form of trying to limit the growth of the community.

VIII. EMINENT DOMAIN

A. INTRODUCTION

1. **Defined.** Eminent domain is the power of the government to take privately owned land for public use. Under the Fifth Amendment of the United States Constitution, "just compensation" must be made for the taking.

2. **Government "Taking."** If the government uses its eminent domain powers and takes land, it must pay for the land. Whether particular government action constitutes a "taking" is a frequently litigated issue; a taking may be explicit or implicit. If the government takes the property outright, it follows a condemnation proceeding. In some areas, the government must first attempt to purchase from the landowners, but in most jurisdictions, the government petitions the court to condemn the land. Each person having an interest in the subject property is notified, and a trial is held. The government must prove its authority to condemn as well as the value to be paid for compensation. Implicit takings are more troublesome, because the parties may not even agree whether there has been a taking.

B. PUBLIC USE

1. **Introduction.** Condemnation of private property for a private use or purpose is forbidden; the power of eminent domain only extends to condemnation for a public use or purpose. Normally, this means that the government cannot take private property only to turn around and give or sell it to another private party. However, the meaning of the term "public use" depends on what the legislature declares to be the public interest. For the most part, the courts defer to legislative declarations of purpose.

Hawaii Housing Authority v. Midkiff

2. **Public Use that Benefits Individual Homeowners--Hawaii Housing Authority v. Midkiff,** 467 U.S. 229 (1984).

   a. **Facts.** In Hawaii, the state and federal governments owned 49% of the land and 72 private owners owned another 47%, leaving only 4% of the land for all other owners. The legislature of Hawaii was concerned that highly concentrated land ownership was responsible for skewing the state's residential fee simple market and inflating land prices, as well as injuring the public tranquility and welfare. In response, it enacted the Land Reform Act of 1976, which created a procedure for condemning residential tracts and transferring ownership to the existing lessees. To accomplish this purpose, the Hawaii Housing Authority (D) was established. D held hearings on the proposed acquisition of Midkiff's (P's) land, ordered P to negotiate with the lessees, and, failing negotiations, ordered P to submit to arbitration. P filed suit in United States District Court, seeking an order declaring the Act unconstitutional. The district court found the Act constitutional under the Public Use Clause as a valid exercise of the state police powers. The Ninth Circuit reversed, holding that the takings failed to constitute a public use because the state was not putting the land to public use, but was taking private property and transferring it to other private parties. D appeals.

b. **Issue.** Does the Public Use Clause of the Fifth Amendment to the United States Constitution, applicable to the states through the Fourteenth Amendment, prohibit the compensated taking of title in real estate and transfer to lessees?

c. **Held.** No. Judgment reversed.

1) In *Berman v. Parker*, 348 U.S. 26 (1954), the Court held that the power of eminent domain could be used to redevelop slum areas in the District of Columbia, even though this meant that the condemned property would be sold or leased to private interests. Once the public purpose is established, Congress was permitted to use the necessary means to accomplish it, even if the use of eminent domain had the effect of taking property from one businessman for the ultimate benefit of another.

2) Courts should defer to a legislative determination of a public use, so long as the use is not clearly without reasonable foundation. When the exercise of eminent domain power is rationally related to a conceivable public purpose, a compensated taking is not proscribed by the Public Use Clause. The fact that property taken by eminent domain may be transferred to private parties does not necessarily mean that the taking has only a private purpose.

3) Hawaii's attempt to reduce the perceived social and economic evils of a land oligopoly interfering with the normal functioning of the residential land market is a classic exercise of the state police power. The Act's approach to correcting the problem is not irrational. The federal courts may not second guess the wisdom of the approach taken by Hawaii, so long as the power is not used for a purely private taking.

3. **Commercial and Industrial Development.** As discussed in the *Midkiff* case, the Supreme Court upheld the use of eminent domain by Congress to redevelop a slum area in the District of Columbia. State legislatures have used the eminent domain power to assist in commercial and industrial development as well, finding the public use in the need to provide employment and tax bases for the localities involved. For example, in *Poletown Neighborhood Council v. City of Detroit*, 304 N.W.2d 455 (Mich. 1981), Detroit condemned a residential neighborhood to allow General Motors to construct an assembly plant. General Motors had threatened to move its manufacturing facilities to another state unless Detroit came up with a site for a new plant that met General Motors' requirements. The court determined that the power of eminent domain was properly used to accomplish the public purpose of reducing unemployment.

C. TYPES OF TAKING

1. **Physical Invasion.** Inverse takings were referred to above. If the government invades property substantially enough, it must pay for this de facto taking, even though it has not undertaken a condemnation proceeding. This principle is referred to as inverse condemnation. Physical invasion includes noise, vibration, odors, etc. In this respect it is somewhat similar to nuisance law.

2. Permanent Physical Occupation a Taking--Loretto v. Teleprompter Manhattan CATV Corp., 458 U.S. 419 (1982).

    a. Facts. Loretto (P) bought a New York City apartment building in 1971. The previous owner permitted Teleprompter (D) to install cable on the building and granted D the exclusive privilege of providing cable TV services to the building's tenants. Initially, D's cables did not service P's building but were part of a highway of "crossovers," meaning lines extending from one building to another. D connected a "noncrossover"—a line providing service to a building's own tenants—to P's building two years after she bought it. A 1973 state law prohibited landlords from interfering with the installation of cable TV facilities and from demanding payment from cable companies in excess of an amount deemed reasonable by the state. At that time, reasonable payment was set at $1.00. P sued D, alleging that D trespassed and that the statute allowed taking without just compensation. The trial court held for D and was affirmed on appeal. P appeals.

    b. Issue. Is a minor but permanent physical occupation authorized by government a "taking" of property for which just compensation is due?

    c. Held. Yes. Judgment reversed.

        1) There is no set formula to determine whether compensation is constitutionally due for a government restriction of property. The degree of interference and economic impact are significant considerations. But when the intrusion is a permanent physical occupation, a taking has occurred, regardless of whether the government's action serves important public interests or has only a slight economic impact on the owner. Moreover, constitutional protection of private property rights does not depend on the size of the area permanently occupied.

        2) Under this test, D's installation on P's building is a taking. The statute involved here is a valid regulation within the state's police powers. However, it frustrates P's property rights to the extent that compensation is due her.

    d. Dissent. The Court's application of a rigid, per se rule undercuts a carefully considered legislative judgment concerning landlord-tenant relationships. The statute here seeks to carefully balance the interests of all private parties.

3. Taking by Regulating. If the government regulates land to the point that it loses all of its value, the injured party can either sue to have the regulation invalidated or seek damages in an inverse condemnation suit. The difficult problems arise when not all the value is lost, but a significant part of the value is.

    a. Harm. Some courts hold that the test for determining whether the land has been regulated to the point it has been "taken" involves looking to see if the regulation has as its goal and effect protection of the public from harm. If this is the case, the regulation is a valid exercise of the police power.

b. **Loss of economic value.** Other courts look to see if the regulation deprives the affected land of any practical economic value. The land must have practically no economic value left to it. Sometimes even severe loss is not enough to constitute a taking. [*See* Euclid v. Ambler Realty, *supra*] In *Penn Central*, *infra*, the Supreme Court held that the landowner must be left with some reasonable economic value.

4. **The Harm Test--Hadacheck v. Sebastian,** 239 U.S. 394 (1915).

a. **Facts.** Hadacheck (P) was convicted of a misdemeanor for operating a brick kiln in violation of a city ordinance. Sebastian (D) was the chief of police. P operated a brickyard on a parcel of land which, due to the fine quality of its clay, was particularly well adapted to such an operation. Subsequently, the land was annexed by the city of Los Angeles. Later an ordinance was passed prohibiting the operation of brick kilns in the area of town in which P's kiln was located. P continued to run the kiln and was convicted of violating the misdemeanor ordinance and jailed. P sought habeas corpus relief. It was undisputed that on P's land was high quality clay and that the clay could not be transported to some other location. P contended that he was deprived of his property by the ordinance. The state supreme court denied the habeas corpus relief. The Supreme Court granted certiorari.

b. **Issue.** Does a city ordinance prohibiting the operation of a heretofore lawful enterprise amount to an implicit taking of the business's property?

c. **Held.** No. Judgment affirmed.

1) We are dealing with one of the most essential powers of government. To hold that a city cannot change its laws to prohibit existing activities such as P's would preclude development and fix a city forever in its primitive conditions.

2) There must be progress and vested private interests must yield to that. This is true even in cases like this where the newly prohibited business is not a nuisance per se. Police powers can be used to regulate a business which is not a nuisance per se.

3) Thus, the city can prohibit the operation of brick kilns such as P's. This does not mean, however, that the city can absolutely deprive P of his property. The city, for example, could not prohibit P's removal of clay from his land.

4) P contends that the Equal Protection Clause should apply to prevent the city from prohibiting his kiln operation since he has shown that other kilns are permitted in other parts of the city. We reject this contention. Even if brickyards in other localities within the city are not regulated or prohibited, it does not follow that they will not be.

5) Further, we reject P's contention that the ordinance fosters a monopoly and suppresses competition.

d.   **Comment.** The Court held that the city was justified in finding that brickyards, as a class, adversely impacted upon neighboring land. In sum, the Court looked upon the brickyard as a "harmful" or "noxious" use which, like a nuisance, could be abated.

Pennsylvania
Coal Co.
v. Mahon

5.   **Total Restriction of Use of Land--Pennsylvania Coal Co. v. Mahon,** 260 U.S. 393 (1922).

a.   **Facts.** The Mahons (Ps) purchased the surface rights to certain land from the Pennsylvania Coal Co. (D), which in the deed expressly reserved the right to mine underneath the surface. P built a house on the property. Several years later, Pennsylvania enacted the Kohler Act, which forbids mining of coal in such a way as to cause subsidence of human dwellings. Ps sought an injunction against D's mining of coal under their house. The state courts upheld the statute and D appeals.

b.   **Issue.** May a state regulate use of private property so as to prevent the property owner from using its property?

c.   **Held** (Holmes, J.). No. Judgment reversed.

1)   Exercise of the police power necessarily affects some property rights. Government could not act if it had to pay for every diminution of property values caused by the laws it enacts. However, the exercise of the police power is limited by due process.

2)   One consideration in determining the limits is the extent of the diminution. When it reaches a certain magnitude, there must be an exercise of eminent domain and compensation to sustain the state's action.

3)   In this case there is a single private house. The source of damage to such house is not a public nuisance; damage is not common or public. In dealing with Ps' position alone, it is clear that the statute does not disclose a public interest sufficient to warrant so extensive a destruction of D's constitutionally protected rights to mine its coal.

4)   A strong public desire to improve the public condition is not enough to warrant achieving the desire by a shorter route than the constitutional way of paying for the change. Whether compensation is required for taking is a matter of degree. Clearly, it is here so required. The statute is unconstitutional in providing for such a drastic taking without compensation. So far as private persons or communities have seen fit to take the risk of acquiring only surface rights, the fact that their risk has become a danger does not warrant giving to them greater rights than they bought.

d.   **Dissent** (Brandeis, J.). The right of an owner to use his land to mine coal is not absolute. He may not so use land as to create public nuisance; and uses, once harmless, may, owing to changed conditions, threaten the public welfare seriously. Whenever they do, the legislature has power to prohibit such uses without paying compensation; and power to prohibit extends alike to manner, character, and purpose of the use. A prohibition of mining which causes subsidence of structures is obviously enacted for a public purpose; and it is likewise clear that mere notice of intention to mine would not in this connection secure public safety. The majority's conclusion that the statute is unconstitutional seems to rest upon the assumption that in order to justify such an exercise of the police power there must be "an average reciprocity of advantage" as between the owner of the property restricted and the rest of the community, and that such reciprocity is lacking here. Reciprocity is an important consideration where a state's power is exercised for the purpose of conferring benefits upon property of a neighborhood, as in drainage projects; or upon adjoining owners, as by party wall provisions. But where police power is exercised, not to confer benefits upon property owners, but to protect the public from danger and detriment, there is no room for considering reciprocity of advantage. There was no reciprocal advantage to the owner prohibited from using his oil tanks, brickyard, billiard hall, oleomargarine factory, etc., unless it be the advantage of living and doing business in a civilized community. That reciprocal advantage is given to the coal operators by the Act.

e. **Comment.** There was no fact-finding as to the "commercial practicability" of mining after the state interference by the Kohler Act.

6. **Historical Landmarks--Penn Central Transportation Co. v. City of New York,** 439 U.S. 883 (1978).

Penn Central Transportation Co. v. City of New York

a. **Facts.** Grand Central Terminal in New York City (D) was designated an historical landmark in 1967 under New York City's Landmark Preservation Law. In 1968, Penn Central Transportation Co. (P), owner of Grand Central Terminal, entered into a renewable 50-year lease with UGP Properties, Inc., under which UGP was to construct a multistory office building above the terminal. A noted architect was hired to design the proposed structure and two different plans (one for construction of a 55-story building and the other for a 53-story building) were submitted to the Landmarks Preservation Commission for approval. Both proposals were rejected and P sued D, claiming that its property had been taken without just compensation. The trial court granted injunctive and declaratory relief to P but referred the question of damages to the appellate division. The appellate division held that the restrictions on development of the terminal were necessary to promote the legitimate public purpose of protecting landmarks, and reversed judgment. The New York Court of Appeals then affirmed and P appeals to the Supreme Court.

b. **Issue.** May a city restrict development of individual historic landmarks, beyond applicable zoning regulations, without a "taking" requiring payment of just compensation?

c. **Held.** Yes. Judgment affirmed.

1) The question here revolves around two basic considerations: (i) the nature and extent of the impact on P, and (ii) the character of the governmental action.

2) The "taking" may not be established by merely showing a government-imposed inability to further develop a property, nor is a diminution in property value determinative. Zoning laws have these effects

yet are constitutional because they are part of a comprehensive plan for achieving a significant public purpose, as is D's law.

3) P claims the law is discriminatory and arbitrary. Yet numerous other structures are likewise under the landmark regulations. Even if P does not receive benefits to completely offset its burdens, valid zoning laws may have a similar effect. If P finds application of the law to be arbitrary, it may obtain judicial review of any commission decision.

4) The government has not taken P's airspace for its own purpose, but for the benefit of the entire public. It has done so pursuant to a legitimate interest in preserving special buildings. The Landmark Preservation Law does not effect a taking of P's property.

5) Finally, the impact on P is mitigated by the existence of Transferable Development Rights ("TDRs"), which gives P the opportunity to enhance other properties. P has not been completely prohibited from making improvements. Only the two drastic proposals were rejected by D. Thus P may yet be permitted the use of at least some portion of its airspace.

d. **Dissent.** A literal interpretation of the Fifth Amendment would clearly favor P. Even the majority's more relaxed approach would result in a decision for P.

1) P's valuable property rights have been destroyed. Destruction of rights is a taking, except in two instances: (i) prohibition of nuisances and (ii) prohibitions covering broad areas that secure an average reciprocity of advantage, such as the zoning laws. Neither exception applies here.

2) The people generally, not P individually, ought to pay the cost of the recognized public benefit of having P's property preserved. D contends that the transfer development rights granted to P with respect to other properties was "just compensation" if in fact there was a taking. However, because the lower court found no "taking," the question of whether or not just compensation has already been awarded was never considered.

First English Evangelical Lutheran Church of Glendale v. County of Los Angeles

7. **Remedies--First English Evangelical Lutheran Church of Glendale v. County of Los Angeles,** 482 U.S. 304 (1987).

a. **Facts.** The First English Evangelical Lutheran Church of Glendale (P) owned a campground which contained several buildings. Following a forest fire, a flood destroyed P's buildings. Due to the flood hazard, the County of Los Angeles adopted an ordinance preventing the construction of any building within the flood protection area that included P's property. About a month later, P sued D, claiming damages for inverse condemnation and loss of use of its property. The appellate court upheld the trial court's dismissal of the complaint on the ground that P could not maintain an inverse condemnation suit based on a regulatory taking. P would first have to obtain a declaratory judgment or mandamus, and then seek compensation only if D chose not to exercise its power of eminent domain. P appeals.

b. Issue. May a landowner obtain damages for governmental taking of his property before it is finally determined that the regulation constitutes a taking of the property under the Fifth and Fourteenth Amendments?

c. Held. Yes. Judgment reversed.

1) The Fifth Amendment does not prohibit the taking of private property, but requires the government to pay compensation for such a taking. If government action works a taking, the government has a constitutional obligation to pay just compensation. The inverse condemnation action reflects the self-executing character of the Fifth Amendment.

2) It is also clear that although property use may be regulated, regulation that goes too far constitutes a taking. Inverse condemnation results from a regulatory taking not accomplished through the normal exercise of eminent domain through condemnation procedures.

3) The California Supreme Court in *Agins v. Tiburon*, 598 P.2d 25 (1979), *aff'd on other grounds*, 447 U.S. 255 (1980), disallowed damages occurring prior to the ultimate invalidation of a challenged regulation, believing that mandamus or declaratory relief, not inverse condemnation, is the appropriate relief at that stage. This holding does not comport with the Fifth Amendment because a temporary taking may also require payment of just compensation.

4) If the government takes land even for a limited period, it could cause a significant loss to the private owner. When such a temporary loss constitutes a taking, the Fifth Amendment requires the public burden to be borne by the public. This does not apply to mere fluctuations in value resulting from the process of governmental decisionmaking, which is an incident of ownership.

5) This rule that the government must compensate for temporary takings does not limit government flexibility. The government can still decide to terminate the taking regulation, or it can exercise its power of eminent domain. It just cannot avoid paying just compensation for property taken.

d. Dissent. A regulation that would constitute a taking if it became permanent might not constitute a taking if it is only temporary. The majority has improperly relied on cases involving physical takings. In regulatory cases, a taking only takes place if the regulation destroys a major portion of the property's value, but the majority has ignored this difference between physical and regulatory takings. California should be permitted to require a landowner to pursue an action to invalidate an ordinance before it can bring an action for just compensation.

8. **Access to Public Property--Nollan v. California Coastal Commission,** 483 U.S. 825 (1987).

    a. **Facts.** The Nollans (Ps) purchased a beachfront lot in southern California on the condition that they replace the existing structure with a new one. Ps applied to the California Coastal Commission (D) for permission to build a home like the others in the neighborhood, but D required Ps to grant a public easement across their property to the ocean. Ps sued and won a judgment. D appealed, but meanwhile Ps built the house. The state court of appeals reversed, and Ps appeal.

    b. **Issue.** If a state may not require uncompensated conveyance of an easement over private property, may it require the conveyance as a condition to its approval of a land use permit for the property?

    c. **Held.** No. Judgment reversed.

        1) It is clear that if D had simply required Ps to grant a public easement across their property, there would have been a taking. Such an easement constitutes a permanent physical occupation, and the right to exclude others is an essential stick in the bundle of rights that constitutes property.

        2) A land use regulation is permissible if it substantially advances legitimate state interests and does not deny an owner economically viable use of his land. If a condition is imposed short of an outright ban on construction, it must serve the same governmental purpose as the ban would. Otherwise, the condition is not a valid land use regulation but extortion. If the condition is unrelated to the purported purpose, the true purpose must be evaluated.

        3) In this case, D claims Ps' new house interferes with "visual access" to the beach, which in turn will cause a "psychological barrier" to the public's desire for access. D also claims Ps' house will increase the use of the public beaches. Each of these burdens on "access" would be alleviated by the easement over P's property. These arguments are nothing more than a play on words, however. The condition is not the exercise of the land use power for any of the state's purposes. It simply lacks any substantial advancing of a legitimate state interest.

        4) D's final justification is that the easement would serve the public interest, but a mere belief that the public interest would be served is insufficient. D must use its power of eminent domain to acquire the easement if it wants it.

9. **Rough Proportionality Standard--Dolan v. City of Tigard,** 512 U.S. 374 (1994).

    a. **Facts.** Pursuant to Oregon's land use management program, Tigard developed a Community Development Code ("CDC") that required property owners in the Central Business District to provide 15% open space and landscaping, limiting structures and paved parking areas to 85% of a parcel; required new development to dedicate land for a bicycle/ pedestrian pathway; and required other improvements in the Fanno Creek

Basin. Petitioner Dolan applied to the City for a permit to double the size of her plumbing and electrical supply store and pave the parking lot. The permit was granted, subject to conditions imposed by the CDC. Dolan was required to dedicate a part of her property lying within the 100-year floodplain for improvement of a storm drainage system along Fanno Creek, and to dedicate an additional 15-foot strip of land adjacent to the flood plain as a bicycle/pedestrian pathway. Dolan was unsuccessful in her request for a variance. The City reasoned that the dedicated pathway would be used by additional customers and provide an alternate means of transportation, offsetting traffic; it reasoned that the floodplain dedication was reasonably related to Dolan's request to intensify the use of the site thereby increasing storm water flow. Dolan appealed unsuccessfully to the Land Use Board of Appeals. The court of appeals affirmed, as did the Oregon Supreme Court. We granted certiorari.

b. **Issues.**

1) Does an essential nexus exist between the "legitimate state interest in land use regulation and the permit condition exacted by the City?"

2) Does the degree of exaction demanded by the City's permit conditions bear the required relationship to the projected impact of Dolan's proposed development?

c. **Held.** 1) Yes. 2) No. Judgment reversed and case remanded.

1) In *Nollan v. California Coastal Comm'n*, 483 U.S. 825 (1987), we held that the government authority to require a landowner to deed portions of her property to the City was prohibited by the Fifth and Fourteenth Amendments. "Under the well-settled doctrine of 'unconstitutional conditions,' the government may not require a person to give up a constitutional right—here the right to receive just compensation when property is taken for a public use—in exchange for a discretionary benefit conferred by the government where the benefit sought has little or no relationship to the property."

2) The City's interest in prevention of flooding along Fanno Creek and the reduction of traffic congestion are legitimate public purposes and a nexus exists between preventing flooding and limiting development within the Creek's 100-year floodplain. Similarly, a pathway for bicycles/pedestrians provides a useful alternative to reduce traffic congestion.

3) In *Nollan, supra*, we said, "[A] use restriction may constitute a taking if not reasonably necessary to the effectuation of a substantial government purpose."

4) Here, the City required Dolan dedicate to the City all of her property that fell within the floodplain and the property 15 feet above the floodplain boundary; it required that Dolan's store not intrude on the greenway area. The City relied on tentative findings that stormwater flow from Dolan's property "can only add to the public need to manage the [floodplain] for drainage purposes" to conclude that the required dedication was related to Dolan's development plan. In regard to the pathway, the City found it "*could* offset some of the traffic demand...." (Emphasis added.)

5) The standard required by the Fifth Amendment is "rough proportionality," "[n]o precise mathematical calculation . . . , but . . . some sort of individualized determination that the required dedication is related both in nature and extent to the impact of the proposed development."

6) Here, the City not only wanted Dolan not to build on the floodplain, but it demanded her property along the Creek. "The City has never said why a public greenway, as opposed to a private one, was required in the interest of flood control," or why a recreational easement was required for flood control.

7) For Dolan, it means loss of the ability to exclude others, one of the most essential property rights. Even though Dolan is enlarging a retail establishment to attract more customers, she also wants to control the time and manner in which they enter. With the permanent recreational easement the City plans, Dolan would lose these rights along with the right to exclude.

8) The findings on which the City relies do not show the required reasonable relationship between the flood plain easement and Dolan's new building.

Lucas v. South Carolina Coastal Council

10. **Property Value Extinguished--Lucas v. South Carolina Coastal Council,** 505 U.S. 1003 (1992).

a. **Facts.** Lucas (P) purchased two beachfront lots in 1986 on which he planned to build single-family homes. Subsequently, in 1988 the legislature enacted the Beachfront Management Act ("Act"), which barred construction of occupiable improvements in an area that included P's lots. P did not contest the validity of the Act as a lawful exercise of police power, but filed suit, contending that the Act's complete extinguishment of his property's value entitled him to compensation. The trial court found for P; among its factual determinations were that at the time P purchased the lots, they were zoned for single-family residential construction and there were no state or county restrictions imposed on such use of the property. The state supreme court reversed; because P had not contested the validity of the statute, the court felt it was bound to accept the legislature's finding that new construction threatened this public resource, that the statute was designed to prevent serious public harm, and no compensation was due P. P petitions for certiorari.

b. **Issue.** Does the Act's effect of rendering P's property valueless accomplish a taking of private property under the Fifth and Fourteenth Amendments requiring payment of just compensation?

c. **Held.** Yes. Judgment reversed and case remanded.

1) The state supreme court erred in applying the "harmful or noxious uses" principle to decide this case.

2)   Regulations that deny the property owner all "economically viable use of his land" constitute one of the discrete categories of regulatory deprivations that require compensation without the usual case-specific inquiry into the public interest advanced in support of the restraint. Although the Court has never set forth the justification for this categorical rule, the practical—and economic—equivalence of physically appropriating and eliminating all beneficial use of land counsels its preservation.

3)   A review of the relevant decisions demonstrates that the "harmful or noxious use" principle was merely this Court's early formulation of the police power justification necessary to sustain (without compensation) any regulatory diminution in value; that the distinction between regulation that "prevents harmful use" and that which "confers benefits" is difficult, if not impossible, to discern on an objective, value-free basis; and that, therefore, noxious-use logic cannot be the basis for departing from this Court's categorical rule that total regulatory takings must be compensated.

4)   Rather, the question must turn, in accord with this Court's "takings" jurisprudence, on citizens' historic understandings regarding the content of, and the state's power over, the "bundle of rights" that they acquire when they take title to property. Because it is not consistent with the historical compact embodied in the Takings Clause that title to real estate is held subject to the state's subsequent decision to eliminate all economically beneficial use, a regulation having that effect cannot be newly decreed, and sustained, without compensation being paid to the owner. However, no compensation is owed—in this setting as with all takings claims—if the state's affirmative decree simply makes explicit what already inheres in the title itself, in the restrictions that background principles of the state's law of property and nuisance already place upon land ownership.

5)   Although it seems unlikely that common law principles would have prevented the erection of any habitable or productive improvements on P's land, this state law question must be dealt with on remand. To win its case D cannot simply proffer the legislature's declaration that the uses P desires are inconsistent with the public interest, or the conclusory assertion that they violate a common law maxim such as *sic utere tuo ut alienum non laedas*, but must identify background principles of nuisance and property law that prohibit the uses P now intends in the property's present circumstances.

d.   **Concurrence** (Kennedy, J.). In my view, reasonable expectations must be understood in light of the whole of our legal tradition. The common law of nuisance is too narrow a confine for the exercise of regulatory power in a complex and interdependent society.

e.   **Dissent** (Blackmun, J.). I find no clear and accepted "historical compact" or "understanding of our citizens" justifying the Court's new taking doctrine. Instead, the court seems to treat history as a grab-bag of principles to be adopted where they support the court's theory, and ignored where they do not.

f.   **Dissent** (Stevens, J.). The test the Court announces is that the regulation must do no more than duplicate the result that could have been achieved under a state's nuisance law. Under this test the categorical rule will apply unless the regulation merely makes explicit what was otherwise an implicit limitation on the owner's property rights. The Court is doubly in error. The categorical rule the Court establishes is an unsound and unwise addition to the law and the Court's formulation of the exception to that rule is too rigid and too narrow.

TABLE OF CASES

Page number of briefed cases in bold

Agins v. Tiburon - 167
Albert M. Greenfield & Co. v. Kolea - **74**
Alexander v. Andrews - 107
Anderson v. City of Issaquah - **152**
Anderson v. Mauk - **95**
Armory v. Delamirie - **9**
Arnel Development Co. v. City of Costa
   Mesa - **149**

Baker v. Weedon - **26**
Barton v. Thaw - 38
Bean v. Walker - **98**
Belle Terre, Village of v. Boraas - **155**, 156
Berg v. Wiley - **66**
Berman v. Parker - 161
Board of Education of Minneapolis
   v. Hughes - **103**
Boomer v. Atlantic Cement Co. - 117, **118**
Bridges v. Hawkesworth - 10, 11, 12
Broadway National Bank v. Adams - **35**
Bronk v. Ineichen - **60**
Brown v. Independent Baptist Church of
   Woburn - **37**
Brown v. Lober - **90**
Brown v. Voss - **128**

Caullett v. Stanley Stilwell & Sons,
   Inc. - **135**
Central Delaware County Authority v.
   Greyhound Corp. - **38**
Cheney Bros. v. Doris Silk Corp. - **5**
Chicago Board of Realtors, Inc. v. City
   of Chicago - **76**
Collard v. Incorporated Village of Flower
   Hill - **150**
Commons v. Westwood Zoning Board of Ad-
   justments - **146**
Conklin v. Davi - **83**
Cope v. Inhabitants of the Town of
   Brunswick - **147**
Crechale & Polles, Inc. v. Smith - **57**

Daniels v. Anderson - **106**
Davis v. Ward - 107
Delfino v. Vealencis - **44**
Dolan v. City of Tigard - **168**

Eagle Enterprises, Inc. v. Gross - 135
Eastlake v. Forest City Enterprises, Inc. - 149

Edmonds, City of v. Oxford House, Inc.
   - **156**
Elkus v. Elkus - **52**
Ellis v. Morris - **87**
Elwes v. Brigg Gas Co. - 10
Ernst v. Conditt - **63**
Estancias Dallas Corp. v. Schultz - **117**
Euclid, Village of v. Ambler Realty
   Co. - **143**, 163

Fasano v. Board of County Commissioners
   of Washington County - **148**
First English Evangelical Lutheran Church of
   Glendale v. County of Los Angeles - **166**
Frimberger v. Anzellotti - **91**

Garner v. Gerrish - **56**
Ghen v. Rich - **3**
Graham, *In re* Marriage of - **51**
Gruen v. Gruen - **20**
Guillette v. Daly Dry Wall, Inc. - **104**

Hadacheck v. Sebastian - **163**
Hannah v. Peel - 9, **10**, 11, 12
Hannan v. Dusch - **62**
Harms v. Sprague - **43**
Harper v. Paradise - **108**
Harper v. Paradise - **108**
Hawaii Housing Authority v. Midkiff
   - **160**, 161
Heifner v. Bradford - **110**
Hickey v. Green - **80**
Hilder v. St. Peter - **71**
Hill v. Community of Damien of Molokai
   - **136**
Holbrook v. Taylor - **122**
Howard v. Kunto - **15**

Ink v. City of Canton - **30**
International News Service v. Associated
   Press - 5

Jee v. Audely - **39**
Johnson v. Davis - **86**
Johnson v. M'Intosh - **2**

Keeble v. Hickeringill - **4**
Kendall v. Ernest Pestana, Inc. - **64**

Ladue, City of v. Gilleo - **153**

Lempke v. Dagenais - **87**
Lewis v. Superior Court - **107**
Lick Mill Creek Apartments v. Chicago
  Title Insurance Co - **114**
Linmark Associates, Inc. v. Willingboro
  - 154
Lohmeyer v. Bower - **82**
Loretto v. Teleprompter Manhattan
  CATV Corp. - **162**
Lucas v. South Carolina Coastal Council
  - **170**
Luthi v. Evans - **99**

Mahrenholz v. County Board of School
  Trustees - **28**
Mannillo v. Gorski - **14**
Marvin v. Marvin - **53**
Matthews v. Bay Head Improvement
  Association - **126**
McAvoy v. Medina - **11**
Messersmith v. Smith - **102**
Metromedia, Inc. v. San Diego - 154
Miller v. Lutheran Conference & Camp
  Association - **127**
Morgan v. High Penn Oil Co. - **116**
Moore v. City of East Cleveland - 156
Moore v. Regents of the University of
  California - **6**
Morse v. Curtis - 106
Mountain Brow Lodge No. 82, Independent
  Order of Odd Fellows v. Toscano - **29**
Murphy v. Financial Development Corp.
  - **97**

Nahrstedt v. Lakeside Village Condominium
  Association, Inc. - **142**
Neponsit Property Owners' Association v.
  Emigrant Industrial Savings Bank - **133**
Newman v. Bost - **19**
Nollan v. California Coastal Commission -
  168, 169

O'Keeffe v. Snyder - **17**
Open Door Alcoholism Program, Inc. v.
  Board of Adjustment - 137
Orr v. Byers - **101**
Othen v. Rosier - 123, **124**

PA Northwestern Distributors, Inc. v. Zoning
  Hearing Board - **145**
Penn Central Transportation Co. v. City of
  New York - 163, **165**
Pennsylvania Coal Co. v. Mahon - **164**
Pierson v. Post - **3**

Pocono Springs Civic Association, Inc. v.
  MacKenzie - **141**
Poletown Neighborhood Council v.
  City of Detroit - 161
Presault v. United States - 127, **129**

Reste Realty Corp. v. Cooper - **69**
Rick v. West - **140**
Riddle v. Harmon - **42**
Riverview Realty Co. v. Perosio - 68
Rockafellor v. Gray - **92**
Rolling "R" Construction, Inc. v.
  Dodd - 106
Rosengrant v. Rosengrant - **95**

Sanborn v. McLean - **133**
Sawada v. Endo - **48**
Shelley v. Kraemer - **138**
Smith v. Chanel, Inc. - **5**
Sommer v. Kridel - **67**
Soules v. United States Department of
  Housing and Urban Development - **59**
South Staffordshire Water Co. v.
  Sharman - 10
Southern Burlington County NAACP v.
  Township of Mt. Laurel - **157**, 158, 159
Spiller v. Mackereth - **44**
Spur Industries, Inc. v. Del E. Webb
  Development Co. - **119**
Stambovsky v. Ackley - **84**
State v. Buyers Service Co. - **79**
State v. Shack - **8**
State ex rel. Stoyanoff v. Berkeley - **152**
Sullivan v. Zoning Board of Adjustment - 145
Swartzbaugh v. Sampson - **45**
Sweeney, Administratrix v. Sweeney - **94**

Tulk v. Moxhay - **132**

United States v. 1500 Lincoln Avenue
  - **49**

Van Sandt v. Royster - **123**
Van Valkenburg v. Lutz - **13**

Waldorff Insurance and Bonding, Inc. v.
  Eglin National Bank - **109**
Walker Rogge, Inc. v. Chelsea Title and
  Guaranty Co. - **112**
Western Land Co. v. Truskolaski - **139**
White v. Brown - **25**
Willard v. First Church of Christ,
  Scientist - **121**
Woods v. Garnett - 105

NOTES

NOTES

NOTES

NOTES